The Psychology
of Cognition

The Psychology of Cognition

GILLIAN COHEN

*Department of Experimental Psychology,
University of Oxford*

1977

ACADEMIC PRESS

London   New York   San Francisco

A Subsidiary of Harcourt Brace Jovanovich, Publishers

ACADEMIC PRESS INC. (LONDON) LTD.
24/28 Oval Road,
London NW1

United States Edition published by
ACADEMIC PRESS INC.
111 Fifth Avenue
New York, New York 10003

Copyright © 1977 by
ACADEMIC PRESS INC. (LONDON) LTD.

Library of Congress Catalog Card Number 77 81382
ISBN: 0 12 178750 8

Typeset by C. F. Hodgson & Son Ltd., London
Printed in Great Britain by J. W. Arrowsmith Ltd., Bristol

Preface

The Psychology of Cognition examines some central topics in the study of thinking, and tries to evaluate, and set in perspective, the developments of the last decade or so in these areas. The common theme is the role of concepts, words and images in thought. The aim has been to extricate the main issues and problems from the steadily accumulating mass of data; to reveal the shape of the wood, and not to leave the reader lost among the trees. The emphasis is on the overall patterns of evidence that are discernible when we try to correlate the results of different methods—experimental testing, computer simulation, clinical studies and observation of everyday behaviour. An attempt is made to assess the relative power and scope of different methods, to discuss their limitations, and to show how models of cognitive processes gain support when the evidence from different sources converges. The book is designed to provide an intelligible introduction to cognition for readers not familiar with the subject, and an overview for those who already know the ground.

I am indebted to colleagues and students of the Department of Experimental Psychology in the University of Oxford for many helpful discussions; to my husband, who eliminated much that was unclear and awkward in the writing of earlier drafts; and to Anne Bell, who typed the final draft.

October, 1977   G.M.C.

v

Contents

1

Semantic Memory and the Structure of Knowledge

Semantic memory is concerned with the structure of knowledge, with how knowledge is stored, cross-referenced and indexed: it is concerned with the organization of everyday world knowledge, and with the representation of meaning. Semantic memory is not just an internal dictionary in which linguistic terms are listed and defined. The elements are concepts, and although most concepts have lexical labels, not all concepts are verbal ones. Concepts are defined by their properties and by their relationships to other concepts. Facts or propositions are represented by concepts linked in particular relationships, and sets of propositions combine to form related areas of knowledge. Although there is a common core of culturally shared knowledge, semantic memory is personal because each individual's knowledge and experience differs. It is not just a static mental encyclopaedia, but a working system, in which new facts are constantly being incorporated, stored knowledge is being updated and re-classified, and particular items of information are being sought, located, assembled and retrieved. It represents one of the most important, interesting and difficult areas of study in cognitive psychology today. Semantic organization is especially important because it is one of the most powerful and pervasive determinants of performance in mental tasks. How knowledge is arranged determines how we speak and how we understand, how we solve problems and how we remember. It is worth analysing in some detail the reasons why semantic memory is especially intractable to study, because many of these problems are endemic in cognitive psychology generally, and because the limitations which are inherent in our methodology are quite strikingly illustrated in this area. Methodological problems will form a recurring theme throughout this book. The validity of theories of cognitive function depends on the power of the research methods, so that we cannot hope to assess the value of the evidence, nor the truth of the conclusions unless we scrutinize the methods, probing their weaknesses, and trying to evaluate the advantages and disadvantages of different approaches.

I. METHODOLOGICAL PROBLEMS

What conditions should a model or theory of semantic memory fulfil, and by what criteria should it be judged? There are three main ways to evaluate models in cognitive psychology. The empirical method includes experimental testing and observation. The rational method is often falsely equated with untutored guesswork based on vague subjective feelings, intuitions or hunches, but is more properly characterized as the application of logical principles and of prior knowledge which is relevant to the problem being studied. Computer simulation provides a method which combines both rational and empirical approaches. The choice of method seems often to reflect the personal preferences of the researcher, or the fashionable approach of the moment, and there has been little attempt to examine and systematically assess the relative power and scope of these methodologies.

Obviously a major difficulty for the experimental investigation of cognitive operations is the inaccessibility of the phenomena being studied. The workings of semantic memory occur on the innermost loop of a chain of processing of which only the two ends, the stimulus or input end, and the response or output end, are observable. In consequence, experimental conclusions are necessarily inferential and results of even the best designed experiments need to be interpreted. Studying semantic memory is rather like attempting to find out how the books are classified, arranged and catalogued in a large lending library without being allowed to go inside. Suppose that the researcher may only sit at the door asking borrowers what they are looking for as they go in, recording how long they spend inside, and noting the number and type of books they bring out. It is doubtful if the information available to him would be sufficient to give an accurate idea of the lay-out and system operating inside the library, although he might be able to make some educated guesses. In the study of semantic memory even the most rigorous and ingenious experimental techniques are similarly limited.

Another obvious, but insufficiently acknowledged, problem for the experimental method is the existence of wide-ranging individual differences in cognitive functioning. This factor has been much neglected by cognitive psychologists in traditional studies of learning and memory. Experimenters have been content to make comparisons between groups, and to ignore quite glaring differences between the performance of individual subjects. Indeed, it is common practice to select subjects of similar age and educational background in order to avoid too great a disparity in results. This policy can result in models of performance which reflect the average performance of deliberately homogenized groups, but do not characterize any single individual. Currently, there is a growing awareness of the inadequacy of an approach which fails to take account of the rich variety of intellectual strategies and cognitive styles (Hunt et al., 1973; Hunt et al., 1975) that are exemplified in the performance of individuals. Semantic memory is, to a considerable extent, personal and idiosyncratic. Because each individual's life experience is unique, the contents of his store of knowledge will be unique. We don't all know the same facts or relate them together in the same ways. Although education imposes some degree of uniformity, in some areas of knowledge, we can be thankfully confident that the semantic memories of individual humans must be very diverse. It is this diversity of the knowledge structure which makes experimental results variable, and renders attempts to construct general models peculiarly problematic.

A valuable distinction between competence and performance was emphasized by Chomsky (1967) in the context of his syntactic theory, to explain the way in which the language user's speech and comprehension may deviate from the predictions of the model. "Competence" describes the structural model and the rules whereby it functions in a pure and ideal form. "Performance" refers to the way it actually functions in practice, when it is contaminated by many other factors which are extraneous to the competence model. Competence represents an underlying abstract system which is general and invariant, but this system is only very indirectly reflected in performance, which is individual and variable. The psychologist is faced with the double task of characterizing the underlying competence, and also identifying the factors that cause actual performance to deviate from the ideal standardized form which would be predicted on the basis of competence alone. The distinction is relevant in many aspects of cognitive functioning. A person's mathematical competence may be obscured by errors, lapses of memory or by the adoption of different strategies when he comes to carry out a particular calculation. In semantic memory, for example, a competence model may postulate a structure in which the word "log" is filed under two headings "fuel" and "mathematics". In practice, a particular person on a particular occasion would access one of these entries more rapidly and readily than the other, depending on such factors as his level of education, on whether he is a school teacher or a timber merchant, and on the context in which the word occurs. Performance data does not reflect the structure and processes of semantic memory at all purely. Many other variables including familiarity, context, errors, ignorance and the preoccupations and emotions of the individual intrude and influence the pattern of responses on which the experimenter tries to build a theory. It is his formidable task to parcel out these extraneous factors and isolate the underlying structure and mechanism.

Empirical methods include both experimental testing and also observations made in less structured situations. Clinical observations of the way in which a damaged mechanism breaks down can also provide useful information. A competence model gains corroboration when it predicts the empirical findings, but is not necessarily invalidated when the results fail to conform to the model, since the discrepancy may always be due to performance factors. While positive results can lend support to a competence model, negative results provide no reliable evidence for or against, so the competence-performance distinction is both a stumbling-block and a safety-net for the experimenter.

Quite a varied battery of experimental methods are available for studying semantic memory. We can present subjects with word lists, sentences or passages or text, and ask them to comprehend, to recognize or to recall. We can require them to answer questions; to judge propositions true or false; to scale pairs of words as semantically similar or different; to produce associates of designated words; and to classify sentences as nonsensical, ambiguous or metaphorical. Performance in all these kinds of task can be measured in terms of speed and accuracy. When the results of different experimental paradigms converge, and the same sort of patterns appear in the data from different tasks, then we can be more confident that they are a valid reflection of the cognitive structures and operations we are studying.

Rational criteria as well as experimental evidence may be invoked to assess the validity of models of cognitive functions. The growth of linguistics in recent years has invested rationalism with a new respectability. Linguists sometimes refer their theories to the intuitions of the native speaker. In cognitive psychology we could profit from a greater willingness to consider the intuitions of the native thinker.

Rational or *a priori* criteria include a mixture of logic, intuition, common sense and background knowledge. Background knowledge may include a wide spectrum of established fact from any related area. There are some general criteria which can be applied to any theoretical model, while other criteria are specific to the particular problem being studied. Some of the general criteria which are usually proposed for the evaluation of models are economy or parsimony, universality, completeness and precision or rigorousness. The usefulness of these criteria has too often been accepted as a matter of faith, but their relevance for psychological models is sometimes questionable. For example, it is not enough to say that a mechanism should be economical without specifying whether this constraint applies to storage space, to durability or to power consumption. Lacking this information, we cannot construct an ideal model of memory any more than an engineer could plan a heating scheme. A memory which stores multiple copies is wasteful of storage space, but more resistant to damage and decay. We need to know which is the more important consideration. Similarly, a mechanism which consumes more time and effort may achieve greater accuracy, but reduce the organism's capacity to carry out other ongoing functions.

The requirement of universality implies that, although the content of the system might vary, the semantic memories of all individuals should have the same basic structure, and function according to the same general principles. But strict adherence to this criterion can end in triviality. When we have stripped our model of memory clean of all the differences that exist between members of different cultures, between infancy and old age, between the stupid and the intelligent, the ignorant and the well informed, and abstracted what is common to them all, we are liable to end up almost empty-handed. A universal model of library systems may tell us only that the books are arranged on shelves, and the strictest adherence to the principle of universality in linguistic theory ends by telling us only that all languages have a subject–predicate construction.

The criterion of completeness is much more acceptable as a guiding principle in psychological research. The model which fits more of the data is a better model. A model is more complete, and therefore more valid, if it fits not only with the available experimental results, but also with clinical and physiological findings, and with our logical and common-sense intuitions as well. Evidential support for a theory is greater when it comes from several converging sources, since, although one alone might be flawed, they are unlikely to share the same biases. A model which is more rigorously and precisely specified is preferable to a model which is only formulated in vague general terms, since it will generate more specific testable predictions which can be confirmed or falsified, and the model can then be retained, modified or discarded accordingly.

For any model there are some quite specific *a priori* criteria which ought to be satisfied. Many of these arise out of common-sense considerations about what properties the system must have if it is to do its job. In semantic memory, for example, a model should include a storage lay-out, and also mechanisms for the acquisition of new knowledge and for the retrieval of old knowledge. It is also important that it should be able to erase, correct or modify stored knowledge in the light of new information. In order to do this a semantic memory needs to have some kind of a perceptual interface so that sensory inputs and stored knowledge can connect. A semantic theory should also provide some means of distinguishing between two kinds of knowledge. Psychologists like Tulving (1972) have recently adopted a distinction between semantic and episodic knowledge. These two kinds of knowledge have been variously characterized as type and token, lexical and topical, permanent and temporal–contextual, or necessary and accidental. The precise nature of the distinction being made varies somewhat with the terminology. The term semantic memory is used to refer to a store of more or less permanent knowledge, of facts that are true independently of context, such as that cats are animals, that leopards have spots, that roses are red, and that two and two make four. Episodic memory refers to a store of personal experiences, and knowledge that is relative to a given context, such as what X had for breakfast today, and that Y's shirt is blue. The models of organization in memory discussed in this chapter are concerned with semantic memory. Episodic memory has received less attention although it must obviously play a large part in everyday cognitive functioning. In practice there is no sharp dividing line between semantic memory and episodic memory. Any model which proposes to make a distinction of this kind must also supply an interface between the two kinds of knowledge, and must tell us something about how items of information are classified and allocated to one or other of the two knowledge systems. How many leopards do we have to see before we know that spots are a defining characteristic, and not an accidental, episodic feature? How does information get transferred from a lexical definition to an episodic store when we find out that not all roses are red? It is clear, *a priori*, that a semantic memory system must be dynamic. It must be capable of constant modification as new information is acquired, and we do not need to set foot in the laboratory to know that a static model cannot be correct.

It is also evident *a priori* that a major problem for any semantic theory will be the choice of a basic unit. A familiar problem in the psychology of perception, it is equally crucial in cognition and linguistics. Many semantic models propose that the basic units or elements are defined by labelled relationships to other units (Quillian, 1968; Schank, 1972; Rumelhart *et al.*, 1972). The problem is that semantic relations hold over different sizes of unit. Individual words like "black" and "white" may be linked by the relation of opposition. A causal relation may hold between whole conceptual clusters such as "food" and "growth". Presuppositions and implications commonly apply to whole propositions. In "He succeeded in starting the car" it is the whole proposition that implies "the car was mechanically unreliable". Contextual effects may operate over even larger spans, so that the title of a chapter may affect the interpretation of a sentence in it, or the setting of a conversation govern the meaning of a remark. To accommodate these facts, a semantic memory system must permit relations between whole configurations of units, as well as between individual units.

It is also clear that semantic memory should not be confined to purely verbal units of whatever size. Knowledge is not only stored as lexical items, but as sensory images. The concept of "bird" includes visual, auditory and tactile imagery as well as a lexical definition. In attempting to cope with this problem, theorists have proposed a conceptual base which is abstract and non-linguistic in character (Schank, 1972) or consists of semantic primitives (Anderson and Bower, 1973). While this formulation avoids equating knowledge with language, it leaves the exact nature of the conceptual base rather ill-defined and unclear.

These are all *a priori* conditions which a semantic theory should satisfy. Yet the empirical tradition has had a strangle-hold on psychology for so long, that thinking out the *a priori* conditions for a theory is still liable to be dismissed as armchair speculation, and "intuition" is often used in a pejorative sense. But the exercise of logical reasoning and common-sense insight before beginning an experimental investigation can save a great deal of time. Similarly, rational considerations are needed in order to work out the implications and evaluate the usefulness of one experiment, before rushing forward to the next. Most psychological experiments need careful *post hoc* interpretation. Used in conjunction, the rational and empirical methods have a powerfulness which neither has alone.

A detailed discussion of the use of computer simulation, its achievements and its limitations appears in Chapter 7. We might note here, however, how well computer simulation illustrates the falseness of the opposition between the rationalist and the empiricist approaches. A programmer uses both logical principles and empirical data to construct his simulation, which is itself an experimental procedure. Simulation has the great merit of refining and disciplining the intuitions of the native thinker; of forcing them to be detailed, rigorous, highly specific and internally consistent. It has the disadvantage of operating within the technical limitations of the computer, so that the model necessarily reflects properties of the machine which may or may not be analogous to the human mind. Just as performance factors intrude in human experimental studies, so different kinds of performance factors are present in the output of a computer simulation. Capacity limitations typically restrict the simulation to a small part of the memory system (Frijda, 1972). Suppose our observer, who sat outside the lending-library door trying to infer how it worked, went away and designed his own miniature library system. To be practicable he might have to restrict his mini-library to only two dozen books, and to omit those parts of the system concerned with acquiring new books and with discarding or replacing old ones. Because his version is so small-scale, and so incomplete, he cannot know whether it is a replica of the real library, or only an alternative way of doing the same job. This is a recurrent dilemma for computer simulation. Compared with experimental studies using human subjects, it is easier to control, but the results are just as hard, or harder, to interpret.

II. EXPERIMENTAL FINDINGS

Recall and recognition experiments have provided some valuable clues to the working of semantic memory, and only a selection of those which seem to highlight the most important features of the memory system are discussed here. Many studies using different paradigms have shown that people have strong spontaneous tendencies to organize items into categories and sub-categories, and to use imposed groupings of this kind to aid recall (Mandler, 1967). When subjects have learned lists of words, category clusters can be observed in the ordering of their responses, with, for example, food words and animal words grouped together. If the material to be learned lends itself to hierarchical grouping into categories and sub-categories, then recall is greatly improved. For example, a list which can be organized into categories of food and tools, and then sub-divided into sub-categories such as vegetables and meat, and gardening tools and carpentry tools, is much easier to learn than a list of unrelated items.

Similar clusterings occur in free association experiments (Deese, 1962). In these experiments the subject is presented with a single stimulus word and asked to respond by producing associated words. The nature and grouping of the elicited response words can reveal the underlying semantic organization. Typically, subjects respond with batches of words from the same category, and then pause before beginning to search another related category. Miller (1971) asked subjects to sort words into categories, and found that hierarchical structures emerged. The use of cueing techniques also reveals categorical organization in memory. Tulving and Pearlstone (1966) showed that forgotten items can often be recalled by category cues. A subject may remember that "kite" was on a list when he is given the cue "toy". Wickens (1970) showed that in learning successive lists of words there is less interference from prior lists when a new list is of a different class. If all the lists consist of similar items, recall of later list items is impaired by proactive interference or inhibition, the earlier lists inhibiting the recall of items in the later list. However, if the earlier lists consist of one semantic category (such as names of towns), and a later list is composed of a different category (such as animals), the phenomenon Wickens (1970) calls "release from proactive inhibition" occurs. The switch to a new category reduces interference, indicating that the different categories are functionally separated in memory. There is also evidence that category clustering is not just an experimentally induced phenomenon, not just a strategy adopted in the artificial situation of laboratory testing. Morton and Byrne (1975) recorded housewives' responses when they were asked to list the items required to equip a house, and found their responses were systematically grouped either by category (furniture, linen, china etc.) or by place (bedroom, kitchen etc.). When they were asked to recall ingredients for recipes these were clustered according to the temporal order of handling. For any material, more than one classification scheme is usually possible. If we consider how words can be elicited by crossword clues of very varied kinds, it is obvious that memory organization is a very complex cross-referencing system. Anderson and Ortony (1975) comment:

> The *a priori* arguments for a dynamic knowledge structure are also, we believe, compelling. Consider, for example, the case of "piano" in the two sentences "Pianos can be pleasing to listen to" and "Pianos can be difficult

to move". ...In one context "piano" is a member of the same category as "harmonica" ... in the latter case "sofa" would be a cohyponym. ...There are so many ways in which every object can be classified ... there are cases in which only the context will help us to determine how to classify an object.

The experiments reported by Anderson and Ortony, and by Morton and Byrne (1975) confirm that the adoption of one classification rather than another can be manipulated by context.

Besides providing evidence for the organization of items into labelled clusters, experiments also show extensive restructuring of sentences and passages of text in memory. Bartlett (1932) and later Sachs (1967) have shown that memory for the gist of a passage is quite accurate and durable, while memory for the verbatim wording is much more ephemeral. Kolers (1966) made the same point in an experiment testing the recall of lists of words by bilingual subjects (1966). Recall was facilitated by repetition of the same word in the second language as well as by repetition in the same language. These experiments suggest that items are stored as non-verbal concepts, and are independent of the original wording, or the original language.

Another group of experiments has demonstrated that subjects not only re-structure the text, but that they also make inferences from it and store this derived information additionally. Bransford *et al.* (1972) and Bransford and Johnson (1973) have extensively used a false recognition paradigm to reveal the constructive and elaborative processes that occur when mental representations of sentences are stored. Subjects who have heard the sentence "Three turtles rested on a floating log and a fish swam beneath them" tend to falsely recognize the sentence "Three turtles rested on a floating log and a fish swam beneath it" because they have derived this inference from the original. Similarly, subjects who are presented with the anomalous sentence "The floor was dirty because Sally used the mop" may make an anomaly-reducing assumption like "The mop was dirty". Frederiksen (1975a) has found that repeated presentations of input sentences increases the amount of derived or inferred information, so that this process of inferring and elaborating appears to take place at the input stage rather than at the stage of recall. The nature of this interpretive elaboration can be controlled by the context. Anderson and Ortony (1975) manipulated intra-sentence context, and showed that while "fist" might serve as an effective cue for the recall of the sentence "The accountant pounded the desk", the cue "hammer" would be more effective as a cue for recalling "The accountant pounded the stake". Different assumptions about the instrument used in the pounding have been made in each case. These experimental results have important consequences for model-building. The mechanism of semantic memory must be active and dynamic; it must construct, not merely record; it must be flexibly responsive to context, and be capable of adopting different strategies and goals.

III. MODELS OF SEMANTIC MEMORY

Some examples of four different kinds of semantic model have been selected for discussion, namely, the space model, the dictionary model, the network model and the set-theoretic model. Although it is possible to point out some of the merits and failings of each, it is scarcely possible to evaluate them comparatively because they are not always very clearly distinct from each other, and because some are more detailed and specific than others.

A. Space Models

Space models apply a procedure known as componential analysis in order to find the key attributes or dimensions in terms of which items within a given semantic area are represented and related to each other. Subjects are asked to group items such as kinship terms (Romney and D'Andrade, 1964) or colour terms (Fillenbaum and Rappoport, 1971) and to rate them for similarity. From this data, kin terms appear to be grouped according to sex, generation and lineality, and each can be located on a three-dimensional space. Colour terms cluster mainly by hue, with the dimensions of brightness and saturation being less salient (Fig. 1). This method is more

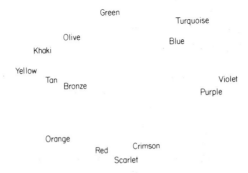

Fig. 1. A two-dimensional space representation of colour terms (adapted from Fillenbaum and Rappoport, 1971).

difficult to apply when the terms being studied are not defined by the presence or absence of a limited set of discrete properties. Many semantic attributes like age, strength, size and I.Q. are continuously graded rather than discrete, and common objects like dogs and chairs are defined by a variable collection of not very specific attributes. While it is fairly easy to decide that red and orange are more similar than red and blue, it is more difficult to decide whether a bench is more like a stool or more like a sofa. As Fillenbaum and Rappoport found, although inter-subject agreement is quite good for grouping colour and kinship terms, individuals differ in their judgements about other kinds of words. Osgood *et al.* (1957) used scaling judgements. They asked subjects to rate test words along various scales, and detected a three-dimensional space in which items were placed with reference to three main polar axes: good–bad, strong–weak and active–passive. These kind of analyses tend to confound the response biases of the experimenter with those of his subjects. His selection of the test words for the experiment affects which dimensions emerge. These models are concerned only with the meaning of words, not of propositions or larger units. They are purely storage models, mapping a tiny fragment of the mental lexicon, and lacking the dynamic, context-sensitive character revealed by the experiments on memory and comprehension.

B. Dictionary Models

Katz and Fodor (1963) proposed a semantic theory incorporating a dictionary in which words are defined by lists of semantic features or markers (like animate/inanimate; male/female). The system also contains projection rules, so that some senses of a word are ruled out by other words with which it is combined in a sentence. For example, words with the marker "inanimate" cannot be the subject of verbs with the marker "animate", so that, in this system, the mountains cannot skip like rams, nor the little hills like young sheep. In fact, many of the objections made to the space models apply equally to this one. To define even simple words would require immensely long lists of features and projection rules. Because it is static and inflexible, the model is too restrictive. It rules out metaphors, puns, jokes and new usages, and takes no account of the linguistic setting or the situational context. It does not explain how a linguistically anomalous sentence like "Getting blood from a stone" can be a perfectly intelligible way to describe asking a mean man for money. It is the interaction of language and sense experience which validates usages like "the biting wind", "his steely eyes" and "a stormy meeting", and a semantic model must permit word meanings to shift or expand, and show how a novel or metaphorical use may be assimilated into the standard meaning of the word (Chafe, 1970). In Section E a more elaborate version of a dictionary model is outlined, which overcomes some of these difficulties, but all dictionary-type models are limited by being restricted to linguistic meanings and divorced from the world of perceptual experience.

C. Network Models

Network models of memory consist of nodes and links. The nodes are atomic units representing concepts and the links represent labelled relations between concepts. The network may be arranged in an hierarchical tree structure of sets and super-sets (see Fig. 2), the organization being similar to that revealed by the recall experiments which showed category clustering. In the Collins and Quillian model (Quillian, 1968; Collins and Quillian, 1969) words are defined by class membership and a property list, and the storage system generates quite specific predictions about sentence comprehension. New input sentences are mapped on to the existing knowledge structure. The model assumes that in understanding sentences, or judging them to be true or false, the time taken is determined by the distance between the relevant nodes, so that it should be faster to verify the truth of a sentence like "A canary is a bird" in which only one link separates the nodes, than "A canary is an animal" in which two links must be traversed.

In this version of the model, properties specific to an exemplar are stored with that exemplar, and properties common to the class are stored only at the class node. This arrangement means that "A robin has a red breast" should be verified faster than "A robin can fly". The property of being red-breasted is stored at the "robin" node; but the class property of being able to fly is only stored at the "bird" node so that a rather cumbersome two-stage retrieval process is necessary. (You have to check that a robin is a bird, and that birds can fly in order to verify that robins can fly.) This makes the model

Fig. 2. An hierarchical network model (adapted from Collins and Quillian 1969).

economical in storage space, since class properties are only represented once, instead of redundantly with every class member. However, it is clearly uneconomical in retrieval time. While economy in storage may be the most important constraint in computer simulation, speed of access may be more important in humans. In subsequent versions of the theory (Collins and Loftus, 1975) it is conceded that class properties may often be stored with the specific exemplars. When, for instance, an individual learns that robins lay eggs before he learns that egg-laying is a general property of birds, then egg-laying will be initially stored at the robin node, and later re-duplicated at the bird node. It is not necessarily assumed that the earlier specific entry must be erased when the class entry is made later.

Collins and Quillian's model was designed for computer simulation, so that it is necessarily on a small scale, and incorporates only a small sub-set of possible relations. The major links consist of "isa" and "hasa" relations, as in "A robin *is a* bird" or "A robin *has a* red breast". Other links consist of conjunctive relations, disjunctive relations and a residual class of other relations which are not specified. Fillmore's (1968) theory of case grammar argued that many kinds of relations have linguistic and psychological reality. The hierarchical network works best for biological examples like the birds and the bees, but it is not clear if it could handle a sentence like "Unemployment in Britain in the 1930s was due to the slump in world trade more than the greed of the industrialists", which includes spatial, temporal, causal, possessive and comparative relations. It is easy, of course, to point out what is missing in small-scale models, but if the original model could be extended without radically changing its character, then incompleteness is not a serious defect. An hierarchical tree structure could be viewed as one part of a more complex multi-dimensional network. An extended version of the model could be devised to provide a mechanism for the acquisition of new knowledge, for the modification or correction of existing knowledge, and for more types of relations.

How well are these network models supported by experimental results? Collins and Quillian's prediction that reaction times to judge sentences true or false would be a function of semantic distance is usually borne out. Sentences like "A canary is a bird" can be judged true faster than sentences like "A canary is an animal", in which the terms span a greater semantic distance, but this result is also predicted by the conjoint frequency principle, which states that the more frequently we have experienced the two elements of the sentence occurring together, the faster we respond. If subjects are asked to rate sentences for conjoint frequency, these ratings will predict the obtained reaction times (Conrad, 1972; Wilkins, 1971). Usually frequency is confounded with semantic distance, but not always. By the semantic distance principle (see Fig. 2) "A dog is a mammal" should be faster than "A dog is an animal", but the frequency principle predicts the opposite, since we more often think of dogs as animals. The results favour the frequency principle. Rips *et al.* (1973) suggest that frequency ratings are measuring subjective semantic distance which, in some cases, differs from, and overrides the objective semantic distance represented in the model.

A further problem for the Collins and Quillian model is the typicality effect. It is difficult for them to account for observed differences in reaction times to judge sentences of the form "An S (subject) is a P (predicate)" for different instances of S when the objective semantic distance is equal. Why is it easier to agree that a robin is a bird, than that a flycatcher or an osprey is a bird? Unfamiliar or atypical examples are more difficult, so either the frequency principle or a typicality principle must be invoked to explain these findings; semantic distance on the network is not the only determinant of retrieval time, and some paths are stronger or faster than others. Originally the model made the assumption that the time to move between any two nodes should be equal, constant and additive, but a model in which the activation of associative paths is all-or-none is counter-intuitive. Later versions modified this assumption and allowed that links might have different strengths and different travel times. More frequently-used links would have faster travel times, so this amended version of the Collins and Quillian model is able to account for the effects of typicality and conjoint frequency. We commonly feel differing degrees of confidence in our responses, as if links are more or less strongly activated. Subjectively there is a continuous dimension of truth value rather than an absolute dichotomy between truth and falsity. The modification which allows links to have differential strengths solves the problem of typicality, and opens the way for intermediate truth values.

Collins and Quillian postulated a mechanism called intersection search, which provides a partial explanation of how words which have several meanings can be interpreted within a sentence. Such words would have different representations for each meaning, so that, for example, "plant" would appear both as a super-set of "flower", and a sub-set of "industrial buildings". An input sentence like "A daisy is a plant" would initiate activation spreading outwards from the "daisy" node and from both "plant" nodes, but the only intersection found would be daisy—flower—plant. According to the model, this interpretation of the sentence can be checked afterwards by reference to the contextual environment or syntactic rules. A mechanism is also proposed whereby particular paths can be primed, or preactivated by foregoing context or recent use. Experiments by Mackay (1973) have shown that alternative meanings of ambiguous words may not be consciously considered when the context indicates which is most probable. Reading a paragraph about factories, or standing on the site, we can understand a sentence like "The plant is near the road" without botanical speculation. The intersection search mechanism therefore has to include some device whereby the search is biased, and certain paths are pre-primed to activate more readily or strongly. It is still difficult to explain the very fast reaction times for the rejection of sentences like "A daisy is a fish" as false. Why does the intersection search terminate so rapidly? As Collins and Loftus (1975) have pointed out, the model needs to incorporate a decision mechanism so that the number and type of links activated during the intersection search can be evaluated as positive or negative evidence. Different links would then contribute different amounts of evidence. Once the links are allowed to have different evidence value as well as different strengths it is easier to account for the fast negative response times. A sentence like "A fire-engine is a cherry" can be rejected as false although both concepts are linked by the common property of redness, since the "redness" link is judged to contribute only a small amount of positive evidence. In this later version of the model, some links are labelled as mutually exclusive, so that "A duck is an eagle" is judged false in spite of both being linked to the superordinate "bird". The two routes to the super-ordinate are mutually exclusive. Yet another modification of the model is proposed by Collins and Loftus to account for the finding that the time taken by subjects to produce an instance when given a category (saying "apple" when given "fruit", for example) may differ from the time taken to produce the category when given an instance (saying "fruit" when given "apple"). This finding necessitates the further assumption that the strength of activation of a link may vary asymmetrically with the direction of search.

Model builders have tended to regard the role of linguistic and perceptual context, and the use of mnemonic strategies to re-organize inputs, as extraneous activities obscuring a more orderly underlying design, but experimental results highlight their importance.

Supporting evidence for an hierarchical organization of semantic memory comes from some clinical case studies reported by Warrington

(1975). Three patients with some cerebral atrophy showed selective impairment of semantic memory. Although they had no deficits of perception, short-term memory span, or intellectual function as measured by I.Q. tests, they had difficulty in recognizing the names or pictorial representations of objects. The most interesting feature of these cases was that the broadest superordinate categories were spared while subordinate category names, and lower order attributes were not available. Patients identified a hammer as "some kind of tool" but could not be more precise. Shown a picture of a duck, they could answer the question "Is it an animal?" but not "Is it a duck?" or "Is it dangerous?". They also showed some dissociation of pictorial and verbal information since they were not equally impaired in the recognition of words and pictures. These cases seem to exhibit a semantic memory organization similar to the Collins and Quillian model, but with only the higher nodes still intact. How much significance can be attached to so small a number of case studies is difficult to judge. More extensive investigation might throw up different patterns of selective impairment in semantic memory. As yet these findings are only straws in the wind. It is interesting to note the way in which the earlier and simpler version of the Collins and Quillian network model has been extended and amplified to accommodate experimental findings, and to counter the logical objections which exposed its inadequacy. The later version is much more complex, but has greater explanatory power and a wider scope of application. The original model was a competence model, but the modifications have incorporated performance factors.

D. Set-theoretic Models

Set-theoretic models of semantic representation are more similar to the space models discussed earlier, but whereas the space models were mainly concerned with mapping storage, the set–theoretic models (Meyer, 1970; Schaeffer and Wallace, 1970) have been designed to explain how we comprehend sentences expressing logical relations like "All robins are birds" (All S are P) and "Some birds are robins" (Some S are P). In these models, each concept is represented by a set of elements including its descriptive features and properties, and the names of its super-sets and sub-sets. Concepts which share any of these elements form intersecting sets, or one set may be included within another as in Venn diagrams (see Fig. 3). The model makes some of the same predictions as the Collins and Quillian hierarchical model, though for different reasons.

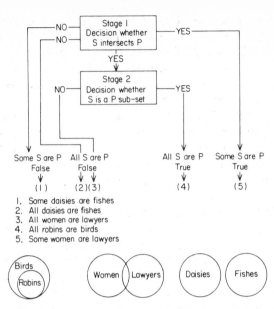

Fig. 3. Meyer's (1970) model for the retrieval of information about the relation of S and P (adapted). 1, 2 and 5 are judged faster than 3 and 4.

Verification of input sentences proceeds by searching throught sets, not traversing links, and differences in response time are attributed to category size, and not to semantic distance. It takes longer to verify that robins are animals than that robins are birds, because the animal category is larger and so takes longer to search through. In many examples the three factors of semantic distance, category size and conjoint frequency are all confounded; the higher the node, the larger the category, and the less familiar is the relationship, so the experimental results are mostly equivocal. Further experiments (Landauer and Meyer, 1972; Smith *et al.*, 1974) have confirmed that judgements do reflect a category-size effect, but this interacts with conjoint frequency, with degree of relatedness or similarity between the instance and the category, and with whether the proposition is true or false.

Meyer has proposed a two-stage process for retrieving information from a set-theoretic model (1970) to explain the differences in response time to judge true and false statements with different quantifiers (the All–Some difference). Figure 3 shows how Stage 1 consists of checking for an intersection between the sets, S and P. Stage 2 consists of searching through the intersection. False statements of both the All and the Some type (All daisies are fishes, Some daisies are fishes) can both be rejected equally fast at Stage 1 without needing to proceed to Stage 2 since there is no intersection. The model thus succeeds in explaining the fast negative responses which were difficult for the Collins and Quillian model to accommodate. Meyer's Predicate-Intersection Model (PIM) also explains why his subjects found it easier to judge true Some statements than true All statements (Some women are lawyers is easier than All robins are birds). Some S are P is confirmed at Stage 1 by the existence of an intersection, but the second stage, searching through the elements of the two overlapping sets, is necessary to establish whether All S are P. In fact, this finding may depend on the particular examples selected. Familiar generalizations, clichés and tautologies like "All ravens are black" or "All heroes are brave" may be accepted more readily than the less often asserted "Some ravens are black" and "Some heroes are brave". A serious problem for Meyer's Predicate-Intersection Model is his assumption that there are some completely non-intersecting sets. Are any pairs of sets totally unrelated? Daisies and fishes are both members of the class of living things, and may share some features (like being sometimes found in parks). The model does not tell us how distant the relationship must be to constitute a non-intersection, but the existence of non-intersecting sets is crucial to the hypothesized two-stage retrieval process.

With some further assumptions the model can handle the problem of typicality, and explain why it is faster to judge that robins and sparrows are birds than geese and penguins. The speed of response depends on the extent of the overlap between S and P and the salience or importance of the shared features. Smith *et al.* (1974) and Rips (1975) claim that their Feature Comparison Model (FCM) fits the obtained data better than Meyer's Predicate-Intersection Model. According to the FCM all features of S and P are compared first, and if a fixed criterion of similarity is exceeded, a fast positive response is made. In the FCM, response time is determined by two variables: semantic relatedness or typicality, and category size. When the S is an atypical member of the set, the similarity check falls short of the criterion, and a further stage of checking for the presence of critical defining features is necessary before the S can be accepted as a P (see Fig. 4). An atypical S therefore takes longer to verify than a highly representative S. The FCM predicts that the degree of semantic relatedness will affect response time for both true and false statements at Stage 1. It should take longer to reject "A daisy is a fish" than "A daisy is a stone" because daisies and fishes are more related categories by way of both being members of the set "living things". Meyer's PIM predicts no effect of relatedness on judgements

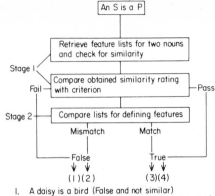

I. A daisy is a bird (False and not similar)
2. A duck–billed platypus is a bird (False but similar)
3. A penguin is a bird (True but atypical)
4. A robin is a bird (True and typical)

Fig. 4. A two-stage Feature Comparison Model (Smith *et al.*, 1974) for testing the relation of S and P. Typical instances are judged faster (4 is faster than 3), and dissimilar instances are judged faster (1 is faster than 2).

of false statements, since in his model the sets do not intersect and so their features are not compared. The degree of relatedness should only affect the time for true judgements. Experiments by Rips (1975) confirmed the FCM prediction that the degree of semantic relatedness affects both true and false judgements. The FCM also predicts that category size should influence judgement time, with the effect of category size being located at the second stage of checking the critical defining features. Since large categories logically have fewer defining features than small categories, it should take fewer comparisons and less time to decide if an instance is a member of a large category. A more general objection to the FCM is that it is hard to believe that feature comparisons are always and necessarily involved in accepting or rejecting all kinds of statement. Subjectively, we seem to know that dogs are animals, and that roses are flowers, and chairs are furniture without resort to comparison of features. On the other hand, the class membership of novel or atypical instances is something we often have to take on trust from our informants. I would agree that a cassowary is a bird because I have been told so, but I have never seen one and have only a hazy idea of its features. Indeed it is doubtful if defining feature lists can be supplied for many concepts. What are the defining features of a chair, for example? This problem is discussed in more detail in Chapter 6. The verification task used in experimental testing of these models is itself rather artificial, and Rips has noted that the relative speed of responses varies when All and Some statements are mixed (as opposed to being presented in blocks), and when Some is interpreted as meaning "some but not all", so that the results may well be reflecting particular strategies of knowledge retrieval, rather than the general structure of knowledge.

E. The Marker–Search Model

The marker–search model outlined by Glass and Holyoak (1975) is a network type of dictionary model, and is considered separately here because it was developed specifically to overcome some of the difficulties that confront the feature comparison, set–theoretic models. In the marker–search model, words are arranged in a network, and each word is associated with a defining marker, or markers, representing properties. Relations of entailment hold between the markers so that the defining marker for "bird" (avian) dominates or entails the markers (feathered) and (animate). Following the convention adopted by Glass and Holyoak the markers are represented in brackets. Relationships between markers may express a contradiction so that, although the markers (avian) and (canine) are both related to the common marker (animate), the intersection is labelled as a contradiction, to express the knowledge that a dog cannot be a bird and vice versa. Category relationships like All S are P, and Some S are P are defined by the marker relations. All statements are directly linked in an entailment relation. Some statements are only indirectly linked. So "All birds are animals" is true because the S marker (avian) directly entails the P marker (animate), and "Some animals are feathered" is true because the S marker (animate) and the P marker (feathered) are both indirectly linked by a common marker (avian). The marker–search model makes the useful distinction between two kinds of falsification—falsification by contradiction and falsification by counter-example. Both All and Some statements like "All/Some birds are dogs" may be falsified by contradiction, and in addition All statements like "All birds are canaries" may be falsified by a counter-example such as "robins".

The variability of response times is accounted for by the frequency principle. Search through the marker system does not necessarily proceed through logically ordered hierarchical levels as in Collins and Quillian's original model. The probability of accessing a given search path is determined by frequency, so response time does not depend on semantic distance. Search terminates as soon as an entailment relation, contradiction or counter-example is encountered, so response time does not depend on category size, since there is no need for exhaustive comparison of sets of defining features as in the FCM. The marker-search model can also handle the problem of typicality by invoking the frequency principle. "A robin is a bird" is verified faster than "A chicken is a bird" because the (robin) to (avian) link is a high-frequency path and would be accessed early in search. For the atypical instance "chicken", the (chicken) to (animate) path would more frequently be searched before the (chicken) to (avian) connection was found.

In evaluating the relative advantages and disadvantages of the marker-search model as compared with set-theoretic models, Glass and Holyoak point out that feature comparison models are more closely related to the world of perceptual experience, while the marker-search model is essentially a dictionary of linguistic meanings. However, any network model has the advantage that the links can represent a variety of relationships, so that network models can be extended. It is not easy to see how a set-theoretic model could represent any relationships besides class membership and properties. In Chapter 6 it is argued that many concepts cannot be defined adequately by a set of features, but depend on the relationships between the features. For example a botanical species may be defined by being smaller than another species, flowering later, and being found further south. The need to incorporate relations between features constitutes a serious limitation for set-theoretic models.

None of the models provides a fully comprehensive account of semantic structure and semantic processing. They suggest only ways in which limited parts of the system might handle a limited selection of types of material. Because they are essentially competence models, they cannot be falsified by negative experimental evidence. Discrepancies between the ideal predictions of the model and the actual performance of the human subject are to be expected. Nor is it easy to compare the weight of evidential support for different models, because the experimental results are often consistent with more than one hypothesized mechanism. There is no logical reason why all the processes of storage and retrieval of knowledge should conform to any single model. A composite or hybrid model comprising a combination of different mechanisms may be required to accommodate all the experimental data and observations. A theory of episodic memory need not necessarily conform to the same principles as semantic memory. It is clear that some factors which are powerful in affecting performance are lacking, or inadequately represented, in the models. Everyday knowledge is untidy, as well as amorphous, changeable, inaccessible, sketchy and idiosyncratic. Familiarity and frequency play a critical but ill-defined role in acquisition, storage and retrieval. Material may be classified in many different ways, depending on contextual cues which often cannot be clearly identified. Different strategies are employed in processing new knowledge depending on existing background knowledge, motivation, intentions and other factors which are difficult to specify and control. The comprehension of a single simple sentence involves the construction and storage of inferences and elaborated interpretations, and reshuffling or modification of information already in store. Permanent knowledge in the semantic memory store must interact with episodic knowledge. When we interpret the episodic sentence "The postman did not call today" we infer "There were no letters" by reference to our semantic knowledge that postmen call if and only if bringing letters. Frederiksen (1975b) has recently begun to study the much more complex logical and semantic structure of knowledge acquired from larger units of discourse, rather than single propositions, but the more we extend the scope of experimental investigations, the more difficult it becomes to construct a theory comprehensive enough to encompass all the findings.

REFERENCES

Anderson, J. R. and Bower, G. H. (1973). "Human Associative Memory". Winston-Wiley, Washington and New York.

Anderson, R. C. and Ortony, A. (1975). On putting apples into bottles—a problem of polysemy. *Cognitive Psychology* 7, 167-180.

Bartlett, F. C. (1932). "Remembering: A Study in Experimental and Social Psychology". Cambridge University Press, Cambridge.

Bransford, J. D. and Johnson, M. K. (1973). Considerations of some problems of comprehension. *In* "Visual Information Processing" (W. G. Chase, ed.). Academic Press, New York and London.

Bransford, J. D., Barclay, J. R. and Franks, J. H. (1972). Sentence memory: a construct versus interpretive approach. *Cognitive Psychology* 3, 193-209.

Chafe, W. (1970). "Meaning and the Structure of Language". University of Chicago Press, Illinois.

Chomsky, N. (1967). The formal nature of language. *In* "Biological Foundations of Language" (E. H. Lenneberg, ed.). John Wiley and Sons, New York.

Collins, A. M. and Loftus, E. F. (1975). A spreading activation theory of semantic processing. *Psychological Review* 82, 407-428.

Collins, A. M. and Quillian, M. R. (1969). Retrieval time from semantic memory. *Journal of Verbal Learning and Verbal Behaviour* 8, 240-247.

Conrad, C. (1972). Cognitive economy in semantic memory. *Journal of Experimental Psychology* 92, 149-154.

Deese, J. (1962). On the structure of associative meaning. *Psychological Review* 69, 161-175.

Fillenbaum, S. and Rappoport, A. (1971). "Studies in the Subjective Lexicon". Academic Press, New York and London.

Fillmore, C. (1968). The case for case. *In* "Universals of Linguistic Theory" (E. Bach and R. T. Harms, eds). Holt, Rinehart and Winston.

Frederiksen, C. H. (1975a). Effects of context induced processing operations on semantic information acquired from discourse. *Cognitive Psychology* 7, 139-166.

Frederiksen, C. H. (1975b). Representing logical and semantic structure of knowledge acquired from discourse. *Cognitive Psychology* 7, 371-458.

Frijda, N. H. (1972). Simulation of long term memory. *Psychological Bulletin* 77, 1-31.

Glass, A. L. and Holyoak, K. J. (1975). Alternative conceptions of semantic theory. *Cognition* 3, 313-339.

Hunt, E. G., Frost, N. and Lunneborg, C. L. (1973). Individual differences in cognition: a new approach to intelligence. *In* "Advances in Learning and Motivation" (G. Bower, ed.), Vol. 7. Academic Press, New York and London.

Hunt, E. G., Lunneborg, C. and Lewis, J. (1975). What does it mean to be a high verbal? *Cognitive Psychology* 7, 194-227.

Katz, J. J. and Fodor, J. A. (1963). The structure of a semantic theory. *Language* 39, 170-210.

Kolers, P. A. (1966). Interlingual facilitation of short term memory. *Journal of Verbal Learning and Verbal Memory* 5, 314-319.

Landauer, T. K. and Meyer, D. E. (1972). Category size and semantic memory retrieval. *Journal of Verbal Learning and Verbal Behaviour* 11, 539-549.

Mackay, D. G. (1973). Aspects of a theory of comprehension, memory and attention. *Quarterly Journal of Experimental Psychology* 25, 22-40.

Mandler, G. (1967). Organization and memory. *In* "The Psychology of Learning and Motivation" (K. W. Spence and J. T. Spence, eds), Vol. 1. Academic Press, New York and London.

Meyer, D. E. (1970). On the representation and retrieval of stored semantic information. *Cognitive Psychology* 1, 242-300.

Miller, G. A. (1971). Empirical methods in the study of semantics. *In* "Semantics: an Interdisciplinary Reader" (D. D. Steinberg and L. A. Jakobovits, eds). Cambridge University Press, Cambridge.

Morton, J. and Byrne, R. (1975). Organization in the kitchen. *In* "Attention and Performance" (P. M. A. Rabbitt and S. Dornics, eds), Vol. 5. Academic Press, London and New York.

Osgood, C. E., Suci, G. J. and Tannenbaum, P. H. (1957). "The Measurement of Meaning". Urbana, University of Illinois.

Quillian, M. R. (1968). Semantic memory. *In* "Semantic Information Processing" (M. Minsky, ed.). M.I.T. Press, Cambridge, Massachusetts.

Rips, L. J. (1975). Quantification and semantic memory. *Cognitive Psychology* 7, 307-340.

Rips, L. J., Shoben, E. J. and Smith, E. E. (1973). Semantic distance and the verification of semantic relations. *Journal of Verbal Learning and Verbal Behaviour* 12, 1-20.

Romney, A. K. and D'Andrade, R. G. (1964). Cognitive aspects of English kin terms. *In* "Transcultural Studies in Cognition" (A. K. Romney and R. G. D'Andrade, eds). *American Anthropologist* 66 (3), Part 2.

Rumelhart, D. E., Lindsay, P. H. and Norman, D. A. (1972). A process model for long term memory. *In* "Organization of Memory" (E. Tulving and W. Donaldson, eds). Academic Press, New York and London.

Sachs, J. S. (1967). Recognition memory for syntactic and semantic aspects of connected discourse. *Perception and Psychophysics* **2**, 437-442.

Schaeffer, B. and Wallace, R. (1970). The comparison of word meanings. *Journal of Experimental Psychology* **86**, 144-152.

Schank, R. C. (1972). Conceptual dependency: A theory of natural language understanding. *Cognitive Psychology* **3**, 552-631.

Smith, E. E., Shoben, E. J. and Rips, L. J. (1974). Structure and process in semantic memory: a featural model for semantic decisions. *Psychological Review* **81**, 214-241.

Tulving, E. (1972). Episodic and semantic memory. *In* "Organization of Memory" (E. Tulving and W. Donaldson, eds). Academic Press, New York and London.

Tulving, E. and Pearlstone, Z. (1966). Availability versus accessibility of information in memory for words. *Journal of Verbal Learning and Verbal Behaviour* **5**, 381-391.

Warrington, E. K. (1975). The selective impairment of semantic memory. *Quarterly Journal of Experimental Psychology* **27**, 635-657.

Wickens, D. D. (1970). Encoding categories of words; an empirical approach to meaning. *Psychological Review* **77**, 1-15.

Wilkins, A. T. (1971). Conjoint frequency, category size, and categorization time. *Journal of Verbal Learning and Verbal Behaviour* **10**, 382-385.

2

Visual Imagery in Thought

The status of visual imagery has fluctuated in importance at different stages in the history of psychology. Imagery aroused great interest among the pioneers such as Galton (1880) but the introspective methods of the day were inadequate to yield more than descriptive accounts of the nature of images, and some comments on individual differences in imaging ability (Betts, 1909). In the behaviourist era, imagery was not considered a respectable subject for study, and was severely censored. However, as Neisser (1972) has noted, the last decade has marked a revival of interest in cognitive processes, including imagery, together with the development of an experimental methodology much better equipped to investigate the role of images in thinking. At present, it is usual to find rationalist and empiricist traditions implicitly, if not explicitly, combined, and introspection is permitted to suggest experimental hypotheses, and is appealed to when different interpretations of results are possible.

Since imagery returned to fashion, interest has focused on its function: on what role, if any, it plays in thinking; and on whether it is a symbol system that can mediate thought as language does. Both introspective and experimental evidence seem to confirm that many operations of memory, planning and problem solving are accompanied by visual imagery which is helpful. The validity of these introspections, and the interpretation of the experiments are currently being questioned. Anderson and Bower (1973) have suggested that the pictorial images which we subjectively experience do not function in thinking, but are only a kind of mental embroidery, or epiphenomenon which illustrates, but does not mediate, the thought. According to this view, visual information is converted, and stored as abstract coded descriptions which are not accessible to consciousness, and it is these which function in memory and in thinking, rather than the pictorial images of which we are aware.

Whether images are pictures or descriptions, further subsidiary questions about the nature of images must also arise (Hebb, 1968). For example, do images actually possess sufficient clarity, stability, generality or specificity for the tasks in which they are supposed to be involved? Could a pictorial image be general enough to mediate abstract thinking? Or is imaging so closely related to perceiving that images are necessarily specific? The classical problems that puzzled Berkeley (1710) are still critically relevant today. For instance, if we can only form a specific image of a specific triangle this could hardly serve for thinking about the general properties of triangles. This problem can be overcome if an individual can store a set of specific images representing all possible forms of triangle: or, more economically, if his image of a triangle is a prototype or schema which represents the central tendencies of the set of all triangles. Work by Posner and Keele (1968) has shown that it is possible to abstract a prototype from a set of patterns which incorporates the common elements, and which can be used for recognition and classification of new instances (see Chapter 6, p. 150 for more details). The problem does not arise if abstract descriptions are substituted for pictorial images, since there is no difficulty in encoding general properties in a description. If imagery does seem to have a functional role, then it is also necessary to consider how far it is a separate symbol system independent of language, or whether it can only operate in conjunction with language.

I. THE FUNCTION OF IMAGERY

It is useful to review the experimental evidence concerned with the function of imagery in cognitive tasks first, and to postpone problems about its nature until later, since we are in a better position to make inferences about the characteristics of images if we can establish how they function.

A. Imagery in Recall

In recent years the role of imagery in recall has been intensively studied. Most researchers have not specified whether the images they are investigating are to be considered as mental pictures, or as more abstract symbolic descriptions. Many experiments of Paivio (1969) and others appear to show that imagery enhances recall, and this claim is based mainly on comparisons of the recall of material which is rated as having low image potential, and the recall of material which has high image potential. Lists of words like "truth, importance, democracy" are harder to recall than lists of words like "cake, giraffe, flag" and sentences such as "Punctuality is essential" are more difficult than sentences like "The cat wore roller skates". Numerous criticisms have been made of this type of experiment. The two kinds of material, do not differ only in image potential. Although experimenters usually try to control other factors known to affect recall, such as word frequency, syntactic class or structure, and word length, there are many other differences that might affect memorability. Words of low image potential are usually abstract rather than concrete. The abstract–concrete dimension, which is confounded with image potential in many studies, also affects recall (Richardson, 1975). Some abstract words are more lexically complex since they are often derived forms, and Kintsch (1972) has shown that these are harder to learn. Words like "freedom" and "owner" are examples of lexically complex abstract words derived from the simpler forms "free" and "own". While concrete, low imagery nouns are usually monomorphemic; some abstract words like "advantage" or "excuse" consists of more than one morpheme, and this may also make them harder to process and store. Abstract words are acquired at a later age, and it has been suggested (Carroll and White, 1973) that the earliest learned words are the easiest to retain. Abstract sentences may also be in some way less comprehensible, or more ambiguous, and comprehensibility is known to aid recall (Johnson et al., 1972). Because of these additional confounding factors it is not clear that the better recall of concrete material is due to imagery.

Similarly, giving subjects instructions to try to form images as they attempt to memorize will improve their subsequent recall, but this does not prove that the images produced the improvement. Instructions to generate related sentences or elaborated descriptions also result in improved recall, so that as Bower and Winzenz (1970) point out, it may be the effort to re-structure the material to be remembered which is crucial, rather than the images. A list of words like "cake, giraffe, flag" may be easier to learn because these items can all be represented in a compound image, or because they can be linked in a story framework. The same point can be made against the evidence from image-based mnemonics. One of the best known and most striking of these is the method of loci, or mental walk, said to have been used by Roman orators and recently revived for laboratory experiments. Recall of a list of items in the correct order is enormously enhanced if each item is mentally placed in a room of a well known house, or in a different building along a well known street. A mental walk retrieves the items. The mnemonist studied by Luria (1968) in the U.S.S.R. used this method with outstanding effectiveness. The pictorial nature of this device is apparent in the anecdote reporting that, on one of the rare occasions that the mnemonist forgot an item, it turned out that the item was a white egg which he had mentally placed in front of a white front door, and so failed to discern on his journey of recall. However, it can be argued that the crucial factor in this strategy is not the use of visual imagery, but the act of re-organizing the material to fit an already familiar scheme. Some non-visual mnemonics work in a similar fashion, as when we make up a sentence of words beginning with the initial letters of the colours of the spectrum or the parts of the alimentary canal. So, although subjectively and intuitively it seems quite convincing that visual imagery aids recall, the experimental evidence is not absolutely compelling.

B. Imagery in Problem Solving

When we come to consider the use of imagery in problem solving, the evidence is more anecdotal than experimental, but is impressive in quantity, if not rigour. According to Hayes (1974), most people report extensive use of imagery in mental arithmetic calculation, especially in holding sub-stage results, and calculating geniuses seem to rely on it more than usual. Many claim to need a blank space, free from visual distraction, on which to project their imagery. Highly skilled chess players report using visual imagery in considering projected moves. They perceive the positions of the pieces on the board in terms of the overall visual pattern, and appear to possess a sort of mental library of such patterns, associated with possible moves and likely outcomes, which they can consult (Chase and Simon, 1974). But although chess masters are much better at recalling authentic board positions than novice players, their visual memory for randomly placed pieces is not superior. This suggests that their mental representations of legitimate board positions are not just pictorial images, but rule-bound descriptions of the configurational relationships. Most people who are asked to work out Baylor's (1972) cube-dicing problems feel that they rely on imagery. Those problems concern a cube which is painted with red on the sides and blue on the top and bottom, and ask, for example, how many of the sections which result from the vertical and horizontal slicing of the cube into 27 mini-cubes, have both red and blue faces. Again, however, we cannot necessarily conclude that the subjectively experienced images mediate the solution to the problems. We cannot rule out the possibility that the cognitive processes involved in solving the problems employ structural descriptions rather than pictorial images. Recent work by Huttenlocher (1968) has suggested that visual imagery is used in the solution of logical problems such as linear syllogisms. Given premisses such as "A is bigger than B, C is smaller than B", it is thought that these are arranged mentally into an ordered spatial array, so that inferences can be made by simple inspection of the visual image. The answer to a question such as "Is B bigger than C?" can be read off the visual image (see Chapter 3 for further discussion of this theory). Some corroborative evidence for the view that imagery is involved in solving this kind of problem comes from a study of brain-damaged patients (Caramazza *et al.*, 1976). The patients had sustained damage to the right hemisphere resulting in the pattern of impairment typical of right-sided injuries. No disorder of language was observable, but there were deficits in visuo-spatial processing. These patients were tested on two kinds of problem: congruent problems in which the same terms were used in both premiss and question, such as "John is taller than Bill. Who is taller?" and incongruent problems in which the premiss and the question had different terms, such as "John is taller than Bill. Who is shorter?". They were able to solve the congruent problems, but failed with the incongruent problems. The authors suggest that the incongruent problems could not be solved by purely linguistic reasoning, and required a visual representation, which the damaged right hemisphere was incapable of constructing. Most of us rely on imagery in giving directions how to get from one part of town to another, planning how to seat the guests at a dinner party, or working out how to assemble a piece of machinery. The difficulty is that some few people claim to use little or no imagery at all, and yet are able to perform these tasks quite efficiently. If the problems can be solved just as well without imagery there are two possible conclusions. One is that some people do make use of imagery in thinking, but others can think equally well relying only on language, or on abstract representations. The second possiblity is that imagery is never the medium of thought, but that some people indulge in it as a kind of optional extra; their thinking is enlivened with illustrations that are not strictly necessary.

C. Imagery in Recognition

The importance of imagery in recognition is much better established. Firstly, there is evidence that visual patterns which seem too complex, or too amorphous, to label or verbalize, such as blobs, random scatters of dots, or snowflake patterns, can be recognized even after a delay. Experiments by Phillips and Baddeley (1971) showed that subjects could judge two dot patterns as same or different with delays of up to 9 s between the first and second pattern. This seems to show that recognition can be a process of matching a re-presented stimulus to a stored image, but Pylyshyn (1973) argues that the original patterns were stored as abstract descriptions, and that matching takes place at the level of these descriptions. Since subjects are not aware of forming and matching descriptions, these processes must be presumed to occur at an unconscious level. This argument is difficult to counter, but Standing's (1973) striking demonstrations of the almost unlimited capacity of recognition memory for pictures lend support to the view that visual memory exists, and functions as a system that is separate and distinct from verbal memory. After a series of several thousand pictures has been viewed only once, they can be recognized again, and distinguished from "new" pictures that have not been seen before with a high degree of accuracy. Recognition of verbal material is much inferior. Consequently, even if visual stimuli are stored in memory as abstract descriptions rather than as pictures, these abstract representations have special characteristics which are not shared by the memory representations derived from verbal inputs.

An ingenious series of reaction time studies by Posner *et al.* (1969) has also vindicated the role of visual imagery in recognition. In these experiments, subjects were asked to judge two letters "same" or "different". When two physically identical letters are presented simultaneously (e.g. AA) a fast visual match takes place. If the two letters are physically different, but have the same name (e.g. Aa) a verbal, name match takes place and the reaction time is reliably longer. When the two letters of a pair are presented successively, separated by a short interval, the first must be held in memory for matching against the second. The difference between the reaction times for fast visual matching of identical pairs, and slower matching of the same-name pairs is maintained. The first letter must have been stored as an image, else the fast visual match could no longer occur. Additional experiments have shown that if the first stimulus is not shown, but only named, it is possible to generate or construct an image of it to match against a second stimulus. A similar process may occur in everyday life when we search for a friend in a crowd. We construct an image of his face and figure, and look for a match.

A study of generated imagery by Tversky (1969) used successive presentation of schematic faces and their names. Subjects first learned to name the faces correctly, and were then asked to make same/different judgements on pairs which could be name–face, face–name, face–face, or name–name. Reaction times for the different-modality pairs could be as fast as for the same-modality pairs if, and only if, the subject could correctly anticipate the modality of the second stimulus. Thus, when the first stimulus was the name, and there was a high probability that the second stimulus would be a face, the subject generated an image of the expected face, and matching was as fast as for the face–face condition. Examination of the "different" responses confirmed that name–face pairs were matched in the visual "face" modality, because the time taken to judge such a pair "different" reflected the number of features by which the faces differed.

Shepard and his co-workers have carried out several ingenious series of experiments which demonstrate how mental imagery can be generated and manipulated. Shepard (1975) wrote

> there are significant senses in which it can be said that mental images do
> have a formal or structural relation to their corresponding external objects,
> and that mental images can be transformed in ways that are parallel or
> analogous to the kinds of transformations that occur in the corresponding
> external objects.

His experiments reveal an isomorphism, or functional equivalence, between mental images and perceptions of objects. For example, Shepard and Chipman (1970), using the shapes of the states of the U.S.A. as stimulus material, found that judgements of similarity made over the perceived shapes were highly correlated with judgements of similarity made when the shapes were imaged from memory. In a similar experiment, Shepard *et al.* (1975) asked subjects to rate the similarity of pairs of numbers presented, or imaged, in a variety of forms such as Arabic numerals, Roman numerals, dot patterns, written names etc. In some conditions, the numbers were presented in one form, but the subjects were asked to image them in a different form and rate their similarity in the imaged representation. The judgements of similarity were found to depend on the form in which the numbers were mentally represented, not the form in which they were perceived. If 3 and 8 were presented as Arabic numerals, and judged in that form, they were rated highly similar; but if they were mentally transformed to their dot pattern versions they were judged dissimilar.

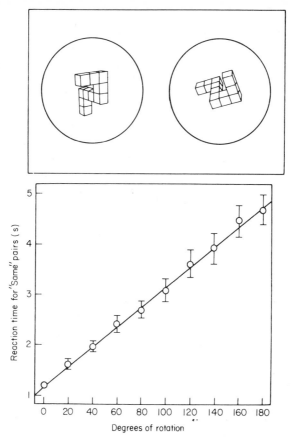

Fig. 1. Reaction times to judge whether two shapes presented at different orientations are identical. From Shepard and Metzler (1971).

Another series of experiments measured reaction times in matching tasks. Shepard and Metzler (1971) found that the time to judge whether two objects, seen at different orientations, were identical, was linearly related to the angular distance between them (see Fig. 1). It seems that one object has to be mentally rotated until it is in a corresponding orientation to the other. The operation of mental rotation appeared to take about one second for 50°. Cooper and Shepard (1973) studied mental rotation using alphanumeric characters which were either normal ("F"), or reversed, mirror-image forms ("ꟻ"). The characters were presented at various degrees of rotation, and the subject's task was to judge whether the character was "normal" or "reversed". Reaction times increased linearly with the

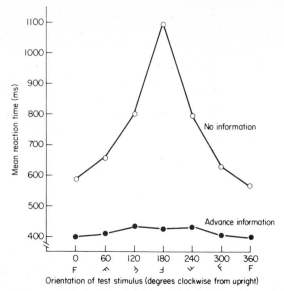

Orientation of test stimulus (degrees clockwise from upright)

Fig. 2. Reaction times to judge an alphanumeric character normal or reversed as a function of degrees of rotation. Redrawn from Cooper and Shepard (1973).

degree of rotation, being longest for the $180°$ inverted presentation, ("Ⅎ" or "Ǝ"). The reaction time reflects the time taken to rotate the character back to the upright before making the judgement. When subjects were given advance information, so that they knew beforehand which character would be presented, and at what degree of rotation, they were able to prepare a mental image of the expected character at the expected orientation, and make the normal/reversed judgement at a speed which was uniformly rapid, and did not vary with rotation (see Fig. 2). With no advance information an "F" at $180°$ has to be rotated back to the upright before it can be judged normal or reversed, and the time for rotation depends on the angular distance. When advance information is given, the subject can image a normal "F" at the $180°$ rotation before the stimulus appears, and then make a rapid, direct comparison between the image and the stimulus. In the no-information condition, the mental rotation has to be performed on the perceived stimulus, and inflates the reaction time; in the advance-information condition, the mental rotation is performed beforehand on the image and is not included in the reaction time.

The internal representations Shepard has studied are not just passively experienced. They are constructed, modified and manipulated to meet the demands of the task. The same kind of process occurs in everyday life when, searching for a mislaid book, we visualize it lying in various places and positions. But whether these internal representations should be classed as visual images is arguable. Shepard himself suggests that they may be abstract, schematic and amodal. His principle of isomorphism does not claim that internal representations are neural copies of external objects, but only that they have a second-order isomorphism, preserving the spatial relations of objects in a more abstract form, and that we operate on these mental constructs in ways that are analogous to the ways in which we operate on direct perceptions of external objects. Imaging and perceiving yield judgements which are qualitatively similar, and take the same amount of time.

II. THE NATURE OF IMAGERY

The importance of the recognition experiments is that they distinguish two kinds of visual image, both of which have a function in recognition. One is a direct memory image of a recently experienced *rather* stimulus; the other is an image generated or reconstructed after a lapse of time. It is also possible to distinguish another type of image which is completely novel and does not correspond to any previous experience, but is "imagined" and is perhaps built up from elements that have been experienced at different times. Novel images can be constructed from verbal descriptions. Much of the craft of the creative writer consists in his ability to use verbal descriptions so as to transfer to the mind of his reader the images he has constructed within his own mind. Types of imagery can be ordered along a kind of continuum according to whether they are more or less closely related to perception. After-images and eidetic imagery are like a prolongation of perception. Memory images may be of a recent perception that has never left consciousness, or may be reconstructed images of a long-past experience. The images of the artist may be created, not remembered, or may consist of a novel recombination of memory fragments. The hallucinatory images of mental illness or delirium are even further removed from the perceptions, past or present, of the individual. In discussing how far imagery functions in thinking, it is useful to bear in mind these distinctions between different kinds of imagery, and it seems obvious that they must vary greatly in utility. Similarly, in asking whether visual images are pictorial, or whether they are abstract descriptions, it is important to remember that these various kinds of image may be qualitatively different.

A. The Radical Image Theory

Those like Pylyshyn, and Anderson and Bower, who wish to deny a functional role to visual imagery, have been concerned to correct what they believe to be serious misconceptions of the nature of imagery. Choosing the easiest target, they have concentrated their attack on the so-called Naive Realist, or Radical Image school of thought. According to this view, images are mental pictures which are stored in memory in a raw, unanalysed and uncategorized form, and which can be retrieved and inspected when required. The inspection process is thought to resemble visual perception, and perhaps to involve the visual system. This characterization of imagery conforms to the usage of ordinary language, which commonly endows imagery with many perceptual qualities such as vividness, clarity or blurring. However, even if visual images are similar to visual perceptions it is misleading to describe them as unanalysed and uncategorized, since perception itself is the product of selective, organizational and analytic processes. Although neither the naive realists themselves, nor their antagonists, have made any such qualification, it could be argued that the term "mental picture" might be more appropriate for some types of image than for others. Eidetic images of the kind described by Stromeyer and Psotka (1970) are sometimes called photographic because of the detail and complexity they exhibit, but this kind of imagery is a rarity experienced by only a few individuals. It might also apply to images based on very recent perceptions, but not to reconstructed or novel images.

Evidence in support of pictorial images comes from studies (Kosslyn, 1973) showing that internal scan times are closely related to the properties of the original percept. Reaction times to verify properties of a remembered picture by consulting an image increase with the spatial distance between those properties in the original picture. Similarly, Moyer (1973) found reaction times to decide which of two named animals is bigger vary with the actual size difference. That is, it is quicker to decide that an elephant is bigger than a mouse, than to decide that an elephant is bigger than a horse. However, it is quite conceivable that this result could arise from consulting verbal or abstract descriptions instead of internal pictures, especially if the descriptions failed to include precise absolute values for animals' sizes.

Some attempts have been made to show that imaging competes with perception for the machinery of the visual system, so that the formation and retention of visual images is disrupted by a concurrent visual perception task (Atwood, 1971; den Heyer and Barrett, 1971;

Salthouse, 1974). The results of these experiments have been rather inconsistent. Atwood's study appeared to show a modality-specific interference effect, whereby recall of concrete, or easily imageable, phrases was impaired by a visual distractor task (responding to a visually presented digit), and recall of abstract phrases was vulnerable to auditory verbal distraction (responding to a spoken digit). Attempts to replicate Atwood's results have not been successful, and his experimental design has been criticized. In particular, some of his so-called abstract phrases which included items such as "Greed is the nature of pigs" and "Garden vegetables earn money" do not seem intuitively difficult to image. Moreover, the distractor tasks in this experiment were very undemanding, and were unlikely to cause much interference anyway. Den Heyer and Barrett (1971) presented subjects with letters arranged in a grid. Those subjects who performed an interpolated visual task requiring dot discrimination, could recall the identity of the letters but showed loss of the spatial-position information. Brooks (1968) asked his subjects to scan an image of the letter "F" in a designated direction, and to report whether each of the corners was external or internal. Responding visually, by pointing to the words "yes" or "no" interfered with the task more than responding "yes" or "no" vocally. More recently, attempts to replicate this result have shown that the interference arises because the direction of the internal scan is in conflict with the eye movements required by the visually directed pointing response. Experiments which aim to compare the effects of visual and non-visual distractor tasks need to equate the two distractor tasks for difficulty, and for compatibility with the primary task, before differential effects can be attributed solely to modality-specific interference. The hypothesis that seeing and imaging are necessarily imcompatible is not supported. It seems that visual imagery and visual perception may disrupt each other when image and percept are in conflict, but that interference does not arise when the image and percept are consonant.

The nature of this interference has been clarified in a series of experiments by Baddeley *et al.* (1975). They showed that the ability to visually track a moving light was impaired if Brooks' "F" test had to be performed concurrently, but was unaffected by a verbal concurrent task. Conversely, the tracking task interfered with memory for a spatial array, but did not affect memory for verbal nonsense material. Finally, Baddeley *et al.* combined the tracking task with a memory task involving either abstract noun–adjective pairs (like idea–original) or concrete pairs (like strawberry–ripe). If retention of concrete pairs is by imagery, these should be more impaired by the concurrent visual tracking task, but the results showed that both abstract and concrete material was equally affected by concurrent tracking. On the basis of these findings, Baddeley concludes that if imagery is an active manipulative process taking place in visual working memory then it is susceptible to disruption by concurrent visual perception, but that memory for concrete words or phrases does not necessarily involve images (see Section I(A)), and is not in conflict with visual perception.

In everyday life we may experience the imaging/perceiving conflict if we try to visualize a scene or a problem while driving a car. To some extent we do seem to need the mind's eye for seeing. Although the congenitally blind have no visual imagery, those who have lost their sight report that their imagery is undiminished. Prior visual experience is required for imaging, but not the peripheral mechanism of sight.

Those who are opposed to the radical image theory are convinced that a picture-like image would be unsuitable or inadequate for most cognitive tasks. Pylyshyn argues that we must posit "abstract mental structures to which we do not have conscious access and which are essentially conceptual and propositional rather than sensory and pictorial in nature". Such representations are more accurately referred to as symbolic descriptions than as images in the usual sense; and Anderson and Bower (1973) argue "that the representation of an image should be in terms of the abstract propositional system". One argument against pictorial images is that it would be uneconomical to store unanalysed visual perceptions, but appeals to economy cannot carry much weight as long as the limits of capacity are unknown. A more serious objection arises out of the problem of access. How can items be accessed and retrieved from memory if they are not labelled or classified? Sense data from other modalities like smell and taste are difficult to re-evoke at will if they cannot be named or described, so it seems likely that visual perceptions need to be labelled or classified if they are to be readily accessible. Indeed, Carmichael *et al.*, (1932) showed that ambiguous visual figures, for example, one that can be seen either as spectacles or as dumb-bells, are distorted when re-drawn from memory, so as to conform more closely to whichever label was adopted. Once images are labelled, then they are no longer identical with the original perceptions.

Neisser and Kerr (1973) noted that people appear to be able to extract information from images that could not easily be represented in a simple pictorial form, such as one item being concealed by, or hidden inside another. It is claimed that such information requires a three-dimensional mental representation, but it is perfectly possible that objects which conceal each other can be represented by a series of two-dimensional pictures giving different views of the objects. It is also claimed that pictorial representations could not encode information like "The lieutenant forged the cheque" as distinct from "The lieutenant signed the cheque", since the pictures would be identical. If we try to encode a sentence like "The boy throws the ball" in a pictorial image, how can we know, when we come to retrieve the image, whether the original sentence had been "The boy throws the ball", "The boy catches the ball" or "The boy plays with the ball"? Other conceptual distinctions such as time sequence, negation or absence, intentions and causality, are thought to be beyond the scope of mental pictures (J. R. Anderson, unpublished). These arguments provide compelling reasons for discarding the view that images are simple replicas of perceptions, but it does not necessarily follow that images must be symbolic descriptions or conceptual propositions instead. Any serious student of children's comic papers knows that there are effective conventions for express-ing causal and temporal relations, emotions and intentions within the pictorial mode. Many of the objections which apply to naive realist pictorial imagery do not apply to a more sophisticated, convention-alized pictorial imagery.

B. The Dual Coding Hypothesis

The dual coding hypothesis (Paivio, 1969) is a theory which leaves the exact nature of the image unspecified, but postulates two inter-connected memory systems, verbal and imaginal, operating in parallel. Clinical cases in which verbal memory and visual memory are damaged independently give empirical support to the theory. Patients who have sustained injuries localized to one side of the brain show this dissociation of the two memory systems. In Corsi's (1971) study, patients suffering from lesions of the left hemisphere were poor at recognizing recurring words in a series, but were able to recognize recurring abstract pictures. Patients with similar damage to the right side of the brain were impaired at picture recognition but performed normally with words. Even more strikingly, a Japanese patient with left hemisphere damage lost the ability to read Kana, the phonetic characters, but was still able to read Kanji, the ideographic characters (Sasanuma, 1974). These results indicate that verbal and visual recognition memory systems are functionally and topographically distinct, and that imagery is located primarily within the right hemisphere. The dual coding theory assumes that pictures, and concrete words that are easily imageable, may be represented in both verbal and visual memory, but abstract material is represented only in the verbal system. Chances of recall are thought to be improved by the availability of two alternative traces, so that easily imageable material is better remembered. However, it is by no means clear, as we have seen, that the superior recall of concrete material can be attributed to the use of imagery. Nor is it clear how a dual coding system would function for retrieval. While the clinical evidence shows that verbal and visual memory codes can operate independently in recognition, it is not evident quite how visual images could be accessed for retrieval independently of their verbal labels. If visual information can only be recalled via the verbal system then the advantages of a dual coding are lessened. Nevertheless, some kind of dual coding system does have the advantage of being able to represent some of the kinds of information that are difficult for pictorial images alone. Boys throwing balls, and lieutenants forging cheques present no problems if a combination of verbal and imaginal coding is employed.

C. The Conceptual–Propositional Hypothesis

Anderson and Bower (1973) claim that all knowledge is stored as abstract propositions. These are the outcome of processes of abstracting, summarizing and interpreting. Both verbal inputs and visual perceptions are transformed and stored as conceptual propositions. According to this theory, imageable material may be better remembered because it can be "unpacked" into a rich and detailed network of related propositions, whereas abstract verbal inputs cannot be so readily expanded in this way. Since images, like language, are simply a form of input which is transformed and stored as propositions, the only difference between the internal representations generated by a linguistic description of a traffic accident, and by the visual experience, would be in the amount of detail. Operations of memory and thinking occur within the conceptual propositional base. Anderson and Bower's conceptual propositions closely resemble the symbolic descriptions which, in Pylyshyn's view, provide a more adequate account of the mental representations conventionally known as "images". Subjectively experienced images are down-graded and classified as epiphenomena; their functional role is taken over by the conceptual propositions or symbolic descriptions, and these can be selective, general, proto-typical, abstract and unconscious. These assumptions are rather counter-intuitive in that they deny any significance to the subjective experience of consulting pictorial imagery in memory, and hence have difficulty in explaining the improvement in recognition which is obtained when images are subjectively prepared for matching or for search. Just as it seems intuitively obvious that no verbal description, however accurate and detailed, could capture all the richness of a visual scene, so it also seems unlikely that visual images could be very adequately represented in a propositional form. It is also difficult to reconcile the conceptual–propositional account with the results of the modality-specific interference experiments which suggested that images in working memory and visual perception are closely related.

D. Some Further Considerations

Those who wish to minimize or deny the function of imagery in thinking, should pause to consider the lavish use we make of visual aids in conveying information. We use pictures, diagrams, graphs and maps to present information in ways that are more readily grasped and more easily retained than verbal descriptions. We make rough jottings as we think or calculate. Visual information has one outstanding advantage over verbal information, in that many separate items or elements can be simultaneously presented to the mind. Verbal information is necessarily sequential, and items must be reviewed in succession. Because of this, some kinds of information, for example, instructions for assembling mechanical gadgets, may be quite easily expressed in diagrams, but may be almost impossible to convey by words alone. Visual aids are a kind of external imagery, just as written words are externalized verbal thoughts. The internal forms are less stable, and so less easily reconsidered and evaluated, than the external ones, but are fulfilling the same functions. When trying to assess the part played by visual imagery in thinking, it is important to remember that visual images are not just a kind of internal home movie. We can also construct and utilize second-order visual imagery: we can visualize graphs and lay-outs, maps, signs, symbols and written language, as well as scenery. Second-order visual imagery is not subject to the limitations that apply to first-order visual imagery, and can represent temporal, causal and class relationships by conventional symbolizations.

Because visual imagery has this special quality of allowing several elements to be contemplated simultaneously, of being easily manipulated, dismantled and reconstructed, it may be especially valuable in creative thinking. Although we are far from understanding the processes of creative thought, it seems to involve forming and evaluating novel combinations of elements. In the visual and decorative arts, in architecture and town-planning, sketches are tried out in the mind's eye before they emerge on to the drawing board.

Another way to evaluate the utility and efficacy of imagery in thought is to study the thought processes of those, like the deaf, who lack language, and whose thinking must be much more dependent on imagery; or those, like the blind, who lack visual imagery, and must rely on language and on tactile and kinaesthetic imagery. In practice, such studies are not very conclusive. It ought to be possible to classify those tasks at which the deaf succeed as tasks that can be performed without language, by means of imagery. However, even if we restrict ourselves to studying those who have been totally deaf from birth, and have not learned verbal language, it is still difficult to infer what form of symbolic representation they are using in thought. It is quite conceivable that they are using a second-order imagery based on their manual sign language. Similarly, it is not possible to conclude that the tasks at which the deaf fail, are tasks that are beyond the scope of an imaginal system. When the deaf fail, their failure may be due to many factors which are linked to deafness other than the inadequacy of their symbolic representation. The deaf have often had an extremely restricted life experience; their educational standard is not high, and they may be emotionally disturbed by testing, and not very highly motivated to succeed. In spite of these difficulties in interpreting the results, there is a reasonable consensus that the deaf can classify objects by physical characteristics, and make judgements of sameness and symmetry correctly. They do poorly at classifying by more abstract criteria, and at judgements of similarity, or of oppositions such as light–dark, large–small. There is also evidence that they have difficulty in remembering temporal sequences (Oleron, 1953; Furth, 1965). Imagery unsupported by language will serve for some, but not all, cognitive tasks (see Chapter 5).

In so far as the use of visual imagery is only an optional strategy in cognitive tasks, we would not expect to find the congenitally blind, who have no visual imagery, to be intellectually disadvantaged. It is likely that they would compensate for this lack by cultivating linguistic skill and haptic (touch and movement) imagery. But if there are any cognitive tasks for which visual imagery is the only, or the most effective form of representation, then differences in the performance of blind and sighted should be demonstrable. When sighted children learn a spatial lay-out by touch under blindfold conditions, they can visualize the lay-out, and can recall positions on it as well in the reverse as in the forward order. The blind children rely on haptic imagery which does not lend itself to reversal. While visual imagery allows multiple elements in a spatial array to be contemplated simultaneously, so that they can be read off in any order, haptic imagery seems to preserve a rigid sequential order (Millar, 1975). Sullivan and Turvey (1974) found that when normal sighted subjects try to remember the position and order of tactile stimuli delivered to one hand, their recall is impaired by visual distraction. It was inferred that tactile memory is supported by visuo-spatial coding. Although blind children are probably disadvantaged because their haptic imagery lacks the support of visuo-spatial recoding, blind adults compensate by using verbalization to support haptic imagery. While a verbal coding is still necessarily sequential, it seems to be easier to re-organize than a purely haptic coding. The blind are able to achieve high levels of skill in chess, logic and mathematics, so that, however useful visual imagery may be as an aid to thought, it is not a *sine qua non*. When haptic imagery is combined with verbal re-coding, no deficiency is apparent.

The evidence as a whole seems to call for compromise. Some images may be more like pictures and some more like abstract descriptions or propositions. Some kinds of information may be more suited to verbal coding, and some to visual coding. Some individuals may be more prone to rely on imagery in their thinking, while others, like the blind, develop alternative strategies and forms of representation. Comparison of the cognitive performance of the deaf and the blind gives some indication of the relative importance of language and visual imagery in thought. Since it is hard to detect any deficit in the performance of the blind, while the deaf exhibit quite marked difficulties, it is clear that the lack of language is by far the greater handicap. But to admit that thinking can be quite efficient in the absence of visual imagery is not to deny the usefulness of visual imagery to those who possess it; to admit that visual images are not suited for the representation of some more abstract relations should not obscure the fact that they are very well suited to represent other kinds of information, especially spatial relations. The attempts to deny images their role in thinking, runs counter to intuitive and experimental evidence, and impoverishes the nature of thought.

REFERENCES

Anderson, J. R. and Bower, G. H. (1973). "Human Associative Memory". Winston-Wiley, Washington and New York.

Atwood, G. (1971). An experimental study of visual imagination and memory. *Cognitive Psychology* 2, 290-299.

Baddeley, A., Grant, S., Wight, E. and Thomson, N. (1975). Imagery and visual working memory. *In* "Attention and Performance" (P. M. A. Rabbitt and S. Dornics, eds), Vol. 5. Academic Press, London and New York.

Baylor, G. W. (1972). A treatise on the mind's eye: an empirical investigation of visual mental imagery. Doctoral dissertation, Carnegie-Mellon University, Ann Arbor, Michigan.

Berkeley, G. (1710). "The Principles of Human Knowledge" (reprinted 1901). Clarendon Press, Oxford.

Betts, G. H. (1909). "The Distribution and Function of Mental Imagery". Teachers' College, Columbia University, New York.

Bower, G. H. and Winzenz, D. (1970). Comparison of associative learning strategies. *Psychonomic Science* 20, 119-120.

Brooks, L. R. (1968). Spatial and verbal components of the act of recall. *Canadian Journal of Psychology* 22, 349-368.

Carmichael, L., Hogan, H. P. and Walter, A. A. (1932). An experimental study of the effect of language on reproduction of visually perceived form. *Journal of Experimental Psychology* 15, 73-86.

Carramazza, A., Gordon, J., Zurif, E. B. and De Luca, D. (1976). Right hemispheric damage and verbal problem solving behaviour. *Brain and Language* 3, 41-46.

Carroll, J. B. and White, M. N. (1973). Word frequency and age of acquisition as determiners of picture naming latency. *Quarterly Journal of Experimental Psychology* 25, 85-95.

Chase, W. G. and Simon, H. A. (1974). The mind's eye in chess. *In* "Visual Information Processing" (W. G. Chase, ed.). Academic Press, London and New York.

Cooper, L. A. and Shepard, R. N. (1973). Chronometric studies of the rotation of mental images. *In* "Visual Information Processing" (W. G. Chase, ed.). Academic Press, London and New York.

Corsi, P. (1971). Cited by Milner, B., *in* Interhemispheric differences and psychological processes. *British Medical Bulletin Supp.* 27, 272-277.

Furth, H. R. (1965). "Thought without Language". Macmillan, London.

Galton, F. (1880). Psychometric experiments. *Brain* 2, 149-162.

Hayes, J. R. (1974). On the function of visual imagery in elementary mathematics. *In* "Visual Information Processing" (W. G. Chase, ed.), pp. 177-211. Academic Press, London and New York.

Hebb, D. O. (1968). Concerning imagery. *Psychological Review* 75, 466-477.

den Heyer, K. and Barrett, B. (1971). Selective loss of visual and verbal information in short-term memory by means of visual and verbal interpolated tasks. *Psychonomic Science* 25, 100-102.

Huttenlocher, J. (1968). Constructing spatial images: a strategy in reasoning. *Psychological Review* 75, 550-560.

Johnson, M. K., Bransford, J. D. and Nyberg, S. E. and Clearly, J. J. (1972). Comprehension factors in interpreting memory for concrete and abstract sentences. *Journal of Verbal Learning and Verbal Behaviour* 11, 451-454.

Kintsch, W. (1972). Abstract nouns; imagery versus lexical complexity. *Journal of Verbal Learning and Verbal Behaviour* 11, 59-65.

Kosslyn, S. M. (1973). Scanning visual images: some structural implications. *Perception and Psychophysics* 14, 90-94.

Luria, A. R. (1968). "The Mind of a Mnemonist". Basic Books, New York.

Millar, S. (1975). On the nature and functioning of spatial representations: Experiments with blind and sighted subjects. Paper presented at the International meeting of the Experimental Psychology Society, Cambridge, July, 1975.

Moyer, R. S. (1973). Comparing objects in memory: evidence suggesting an internal psychophysics. *Perception and Psychophysics* **13**, 180-184.

Neisser, U. (1972). A paradigm shift in psychology. *Science, N.Y.* **176**, 628-630.

Neisser, U. and Kerr, N. (1973). Spatial and mnemonic properties of visual images. *Cognitive Psychology* **5**, 138-150.

Oleron, P. (1953). Conceptual thinking in the deaf. *American Annals of the Deaf* **98**, 304-310.

Paivio, A. (1969). Mental imagery in associative learning and memory. *Psychological Review* **76**, 241-263.

Phillips, W. A. and Baddeley, A. D. (1971). Reaction time and short term visual memory. *Psychonomic Science* **22**, 73-74.

Posner, M. I. and Keele, S. W. (1968). On the genesis of abstract ideas. *Journal of Experimental Psychology* **77**, 353-363.

Posner, M. I., Boies, S. J., Eichelman, W. H. and Taylor, R. L. (1969). Retention of name and visual codes of single letters. *Journal of Experimental Psychology* **79**, Monogr. Supp. 1-16.

Pylyshyn, Z. W. (1973). What the mind's eye tells the mind's brain: a critique of mental imagery. *Psychological Bulletin* **80**, 1-24.

Richardson, J. T. E. (1975). Imagery, concreteness and lexical complexity. *Quarterly Journal of Experimental Psychology* **27**, 211-223.

Sasanuma, S. (1974). Kanji versus Kana processing alexia with transient agraphia. *Cortex* **X**, 89-97.

Salthouse, T. A. (1974). Using selective interference to investigate spatial memory representations. *Memory and Cognition* **2**, 749-757.

Shepard, R. N. (1975). Form, formation and transformation of internal representations. *In* "Information Processing and Cognition: The Loyola Symposium" (R. L. Solso, ed.). Laurence Erlbaum, Hillsdale, New Jersey.

Shepard, R. N. and Chipman, S. (1970). Second order isomorphism of internal representations: shapes of states. *Cognitive Psychology* **1**, 1-17.

Shepard, R. N. and Metzler, J. (1971). Mental rotation of three-dimensional objects. *Science, N.Y.* **171**, 701-703.

Shepard, R. N., Kilpatric, D. W. and Cunningham, J. P. (1975). The internal representation of numbers. *Cognitive Psychology* **7**, 82-138.

Standing, L. (1973). Learning 10,000 pictures. *Quarterly Journal of Experimental Psychology* **25**, 207-222.

Stromeyer, C. F. and Psotka, J. (1970). The detailed texture of eidetic images. *Nature, Lond.* **225**, 346-348.

Sullivan, E. V. and Turvey, M. T. (1974). On the short-term retention of serial, tactile stimuli. *Memory and Cognition* **2**, 600-606.

Tversky, B. (1969). Pictorial and verbal encoding in a short-term memory task. *Perception and Psychophysics* **6**, 225-233.

3

Problem Solving

Attempts to provide a general characterization of the process of problem solving have met, on the whole, with little success, being either too vague, or too incomplete, or both. This is hardly surprising, since the kinds of task which come under the heading of problem solving are extremely diverse. Problems which have been studied include such disparate tasks as solving anagrams (Ekstrand and Dominowski, 1965), syllogistic reasoning (Henle, 1962), laying out patterns of matches (Scheerer, 1963), getting hobbits and orcs across rivers (Thomas, 1971), constructing hat-racks (Maier, 1930) and measuring required quantities of water with pitchers of specified capacities (Luchins, 1942). To construct a theory of problem solving which will encompass all these is like trying to provide a theory of art broad enough to cover everything from pottery to electronic music, in that there is not a great deal of common ground.

There have been three major theoretical approaches to problem solving, and while none of them is sufficiently precise or comprehensive, each of them has yielded some interesting observations, which are briefly described below.

I. GENERAL THEORIES OF PROBLEM SOLVING

A. Information Processing Models

These are useful in providing a skeletal outline consisting of a set of labelled stages which serve as a basis for further analysis. However, the interesting issues turn out to arise at the point when we begin trying to unpack the boxes, and at this point we need to consider

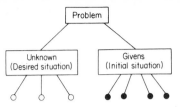

Fig. 1. Hypothetical representation of a problem in cognitive structure (from Greeno, 1973).

specific types of problem, not problems in general. This progression is illustrated in Greeno's (1973) discussion of problem solving. His general definition "the subject's task is to find a way of transforming the initial situation, or given variables, into the desired situation or unknown variables" (see Fig. 1) is expanded into a set of sub-processes (see Fig. 2). These stages are nested to emphasize that they might occur simultaneously, or in an overlapping sequence. Greeno's model becomes more interesting when he begins to unpack the "Retrieve relevant information" box, and distinguish between problems which require different kinds of retrieval. A problem like "How far is it from A to B?" may be solved by retrieving a complete operating rule which is already in store, like "Distance = speed × time". Problems like "Where have all the swallows gone?" can be solved by retrieving stored propositions, such as "Swallows are migratory birds" and "Migratory birds go south in winter". Other problems

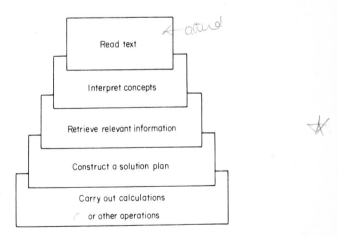

Fig. 2. Stages that probably are involved in solving a problem (Greeno, 1973).

require stored information to be restructured or transformed. If the problem demands an estimate of speed instead of distance, the operating rule must be transformed; or in some problems the elements of the problem may need to be re-classified instead. Transformation is required at the interpretation stage. In the classic "candle" problem, discussed by Glucksberg (1962), the subject is given a candle and a box of tacks, and told to fix the candle to the wall of the room. The box must be re-classified as a shelf, before a relevant operating rule can be retrieved, and the problem solved. The amount of re-structuring required at the interpretation or retrieval stages is an important aspect of problem difficulty, but when this factor is taken into account Greeno's analysis turns into a taxonomy of problems rather than a theory of problem solving.

Miller *et al.* (1960) proposed a general purpose means-end analysis program called TOTE (Test–Operate–Test–Exit) which could serve for solving problems (see Fig. 3). An initial test between the present state and the desired state is made; if these differ, an operation is selected, and carried out, followed by a further test; successive tests and operations continue until the goal state is achieved. One important feature of this model is that it shows how a problem may be divided into sub-goals, hierarchically arranged, and leading ultimately to the achievement of the overall goal state. Sets of TOTE units are linked to an overall TOTE. Another useful contribution is the emphasis placed by the model on a decision stage for determining when the desired goal has been achieved. However, the model does not go beyond stage labelling. It does not tell us how we characterize either the initial state, or the goal state of a problem; nor how we select which operations to perform; nor how we judge a solution to be adequate.

B. The Gestalt Approach

The main contribution of the Gestalt approach has been to emphasize

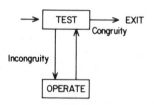

Fig. 3. The TOTE unit (Test–Operate–Test–Exit) of Miller *et al.* (1960).

the importance of perceptual set in problem solving. According to the Gestaltists, proper apprehension of the parts of the problem ensures that the "forces of organization" produce the solution. Exactly what these "forces of organization" are, and how they operate, is not specified. Most of their observations have been based on practical problems like the candle-box task discussed above. In another such example, the task is to fasten together two strings hanging from the ceiling, which are too far apart to be simultaneously grasped. The solution is to use another object present in the room (such as a pair of pliers) as a pendulum weight, and swing one string across to the other. The pliers must be perceived as a weight before the solution can be found, so perceptual re-organization must occur, and may be impeded by "functional fixedness"—a tendency to perceive objects as serving only their most common or most recent function. This observation has application in problem solving of many kinds. Failure is often due to the persistence of a rigid, inappropriate "set", which may have been established by earlier experience, or by the way in which the instructions are phrased. An inappropriate perceptual set may be dissipated by hints from the experimenter which serve to "re-centre", to direct attention to the salient aspects of the problem. In the above example, setting the strings in motion has been found to be effective in suggesting the pendulum solution.

Gestalt theorists like Duncker (1945) have also underlined the fact that possible solutions to a problem may vary in value. In his radiation problem, an inoperable stomach tumour is to be treated by radiation, but rays of sufficient intensity to destroy the tumour would be harmful to surrounding tissue. When subjects fail to hit on the correct solution, which is to focus intersecting weak rays on the tumour site, their proposals reveal the relative values they assign to eliminating the tumour, and to minimizing the damage to other areas. This is also a point with wide-ranging application, especially to problems occurring in everyday contexts, where any solution is prone to involve both advantages and disadvantages. Improving the economy requires a reduction in the rate of inflation, which may only be achieved by a concomitant rise in unemployment. Even if none of the possible solutions has attendant disadvantages, some may be more elegant, or more economical than others. Outside the laboratory, the schoolroom and the quiz programme, problems tend to have a range of possible solutions, and part of the task is to evaluate the values and costs of the alternatives. More recently, Decision Theory has provided a powerful tool for the analysis of the role of values and costs in problem solution.

C. The Stimulus–Response Theory

The focus of S–R theory has been on the mechanism of response selection in problem solving. In contrast to the Gestalt approach which has been mainly concerned with perceptual set, S–R theory provides an account of response set. According to this view, the problem constitutes a stimulus which is associated, with varying strength, to a set of responses and mediating responses. The strength of each response in the set is determined by the principles of conditioning; that is, responses most frequently reinforced are most strongly associated with the problem, and are therefore most likely to be elicited. This concept of a set of alternative responses ordered according to strength reappears in computer models as the Pushdown Stack (PDS), in which the most recent correct response is topmost, the next most recent second, and so on, on the principle of last in, first out. There is evidence to support the view that past

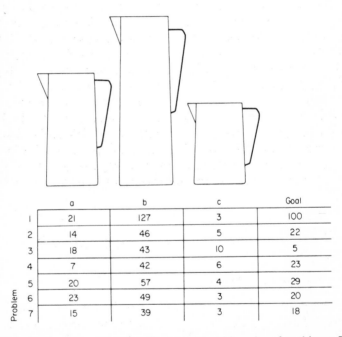

	a	b	c	Goal
1	21	127	3	100
2	14	46	5	22
3	18	43	10	5
4	7	42	6	23
5	20	57	4	29
6	23	49	3	20
7	15	39	3	18

Problem

Fig. 4. Fixation because of habit is illustrated by this series of problems. In each a quantity of water (the goal) must be measured out; there is an unlimited supply of water but the only tools available are three pitchers, a, b and c, the volumes of which are specified for each problem. Once the subject hits on a successful pattern of filling and pouring ($b-a-2c$) he tends to follow the pattern even when, in Problems 6 and 7, there is an easier solution.

experience does influence the choice of a response, or response strategy, as in Luchin's (1942) water-pitcher problem (see Fig. 4). In this task, subjects are asked to solve successive problems requiring given amounts of water to be measured using a set of pitchers of different capacities. They hit on a procedure of pouring from pitcher to pitcher which successfully solves the first few problems. Later problems in the series could be solved much more simply, but subjects tend to persist in using the cumbersome procedure adopted earlier. It is difficult to shift from the response strategy which has been reinforced by success on the earlier problems, but not all subjects show this inflexibility to the same extent. As a mechanism of problem solving, S-R associations do not explain the initial selection and characterization of the stimulus (the perception of the problem), nor the role of values and costs in choosing a response and evaluating a solution. It is also doubtful whether the theory can be applied to complex problems in which the "stimulus" consists of many elements in a complex relationship, and the "response" consists of many operations combined in a complex sequence. When the problem is a simple, well defined one such as "Solve the anagram ONLEF", the stimulus can be identified as the string of letters. But if the problem is something like "Invent a perpetual-motion machine" it becomes more difficult to discern what constitutes the stimulus.

If theories of problem solving are too sketchy, too incomplete, or too vague to be satisfactory, they have at least succeeded in drawing attention to the importance of a multiplicity of variables that affect performance. These fall into three major groups—those that originate in the nature of the problem, those that originate in the contextual setting of the problem, and those that originate in the problem solver himself.

II. VARIABLES IN PROBLEM SOLVING

A. The Nature of the Problem

Problems vary greatly in the extent to which they are well defined or ill defined. Lack of definition may characterize either the initial state (the problem elements), the goal state, or both. In a problem like "Find the square root of 169", both are well defined. In a problem like "Fix the electric light" or "Mend the car", the initial state is ill defined, but a problem like "Design a fine town centre" has an ill-defined goal state. Lack of definition is more characteristic of everyday problems than of those used in laboratory testing, and it is clear that the relative difficulty of the stages diagrammed in Fig. 2 must vary according to the state which is ill defined. In the car repair problem, the main difficulty is to analyse the initial state. In the town-centre example, the heart of the problem is to specify the exact nature of the goal state.

Problem solving is also greatly affected by the familiarity or unfamiliarity of the problem. Appropriate experience establishes perceptual or interpretive sets, and response or operator sets, which allow similar problems to be readily solved. Inappropriate experience may block the path to solution, and absence of experience may render the problem difficult or even insoluble. However, the fact that problem solvers display rigid sets, or fixedness, either in perceiving the problem, or in selecting responses, is not necessarily evidence of a faulty approach. In general, it is probably the most economical strategy to attack a new problem in terms of previous experience rather than tackling each one afresh. Unfamiliar problems which don't match previous experience will need restructuring if solution is to be attained. This act of restructuring or reformulation is commonly called "insight", and is contrasted with the more mechanical procedures applied when the initial problem is clearly formulated in such a way that the correct operations are self-evident. The process of "insight" or reformulation, often accompanied by an "Ah Ha" sensation, is itself difficult to describe. It seems to involve the recognition that classifying the problem elements in a different way, or selecting a different operation will "crack" the problem, and is mysterious because, introspectively, the solver is often confident that the new formulation will produce a successful solution *before* actually carrying out the processes.

Complexity is another obvious determinant of problem difficulty. The larger the number of elements in the initial state, and the more steps or operations required to reach solution, the harder the problem.

B. The Context of the Problem

The way in which a problem is presented may make it easier or harder to solve. In problems involving object manipulation, the physical location of the objects can affect performance. They may be positioned in such a way as to direct the subject's attention towards, or away from, the key elements. In the candle problem, if the tacks are not presented in the box, but separately, the box is less liable to be perceived as a container, and is more readily perceived as a possible shelf. In verbally presented problems, the phrasing can emphasize or obscure the salient elements of the problem. The instructions, and the way in which they are interpreted, exert a powerful influence on performance. In almost every kind of task, human performance reflects a speed–accuracy trade-off. A task can be carried out rapidly and carelessly, or slowly and carefully. The two criteria of success, speed and accuracy, tend to vary inversely, and the relative weight attached to each differs according to the task, the instructions received, how they are interpreted, and according to the personal cognitive style of the individual. This trade-off relation constitutes a serious difficulty for research on human performance. If an experimenter wishes to determine whether task A is more difficult than task B, he can only conclude that the tasks differ if one is performed both faster, and with fewer errors than the other. If the speed–accuracy trade-off differs for the two tasks, so that, for example, task A is carried out faster, but with more errors than task B, no conclusion can be reached. The experimenter may try to "fix" the speed–accuracy trade-off by giving instructions such as "Respond as fast as possible, but try not to make errors", but an instruction like this will not be interpreted uniformly by all subjects. If the experimenter decides to discard from the experiment those subjects who make more than a predetermined proportion of errors, or slow responses, he can ensure standardization of performance, but the results will only be representative of a selected sample of subjects.

In addition to the setting of the problem, and the instructions given, contextual factors in problem solving also include any preceding problems and the expectations engendered by them as in the Water Jug problems.

C. The Problem Solver

It is obvious *a priori* that performance in a problem solving task is determined by the characteristics of the individual problem solver as well as the problem itself. The general intelligence and the previous experience of the individual are perhaps the most powerful variables in determining the outcome in any task. In animal experiments researchers will carefully select "naive" animals, or those whose experience from birth onwards has been strictly controlled and matched. In human experiments the background knowledge and training of individual subjects varies greatly and usually only a very crude matching based on level education is attempted. Disparities between subjects may still be enormous. The star performer on an anagram problem may be a sparetime crossword freak, and the subject who can instantly solve the stomach tumour problem may have a sister who is a radiographer. Previous experience may have established highly relevant or wholly inappropriate sets before the subject comes into the experimental situation.

While the animal experimenter can exercise some control over motivation by, for example, a schedule of food deprivation, human subjects may be bored and sleepy, or alert and keen. Payment and bonuses may provide a considerable incentive for the impoverished, and none at all for the affluent. Subjects may want to impress the experimenter with their brilliance, or be quite indifferent to his opinion. Anxiety in the test situation may impair or improve performance according to the Yerkes Dodson law, which states that the optimum level of arousal varies with the difficulty of the task in such a way that high anxiety may be beneficial in simple tasks, but detrimental for very complex tasks. The level of anxiety induced by the testing situation is also liable to vary between subjects. Performance may also vary with age and sex. Older subjects tend to be more anxious than younger ones, and typically experience more difficulty with unfamiliar problems; problems which place a heavy load on memory; problems containing a high proportion of irrelevant information, and tasks which put a premium on speed.

Consideration of all these factors underlines the fact that the gap between competence and performance is likely to be very wide in problem solving, and that experimental results can, at best, provide only a rather distant and distorted reflection of the competence of the human problem solver. The experimenter may try to infer how the subject is solving a problem by systematically varying different aspects of the problem, and observing how these variations affect the subject's performance; or he may ask the subject to overtly verbalize his thought processes. These records, or protocols, cannot be taken as a completely accurate reflection of ongoing internal mental operations. Subjects usually report feeling that they are unable to verbalize rapidly enough to record all their thinking, and the instruction to "think aloud" may actually distort normal thought processes, inducing the subject to try to make his thinking more orderly and intelligible to the experimenter than it would otherwise be. Despite these drawbacks, protocols may yield useful insight into the processes that mediate problem solution. Another method of studying problem solving is to use computer simulation. A theory of problem solving can be tested by implementing the hypothesized processes in a computer program, and comparing the computer output with human performance. Some examples of this method are discussed in Chapter 7. These techniques allow the experimenter to identify some of the characteristics of human problem solving behaviour, but the large number of variables that can influence problem solving make it difficult to construct any general model.

The remainder of this chapter is concerned with logical reasoning problems. These have been selected for more detailed analysis because they illustrate many of the points made above; because the process of logical reasoning is a common factor in all kinds of problem solving; and because some interesting issues have arisen out of recent research in this area.

III. LOGICAL PROBLEMS

A. Processing Negative Information

It is generally, though not invariably, the case that negative propositions are harder to remember and take longer to judge true or false than affirmative propositions. This holds good whether the proposition has to be judged by reference to stored knowledge (as in "7 is not an even number"), or verified by matching against physical objects or pictures (as in "The green square is not on the left of the red circle"). A number of explanations have been advanced to account for this difficulty in handling negation, but none of them can accommodate all of the findings satisfactorily.

1. The Linguistic Explanation
The linguistic explanation assumes that negative propositions are harder to process because they require syntactic recoding. Working within the framework of generative grammar, Miller and McKean (1964) argued that negative sentences undergo syntactic transformation to the base affirmative form, and that the processing time for negatives reflects the extra time required for this transformation. In their experiment, reaction times did increase when subjects were induced to carry out the transformation, but there was no evidence that this stage necessarily occurs during the normal processing of natural language. A linguistic explanation fails to account for the fact that the difficulty with negatives diminishes or disappears entirely in some semantic contexts. There are some kinds of "natural" negatives which are handled as easily as affirmatives. An example of a natural negative is one which expresses exceptionality. Given an array of

eight circles, seven blue and one red, it is more natural, and more
rapid, to encode a description of the odd circle negatively as "Circle
3 is not blue", than to encode it affirmatively as "Circle 3 is red"
(Wason, 1965). Another kind of natural negative is one which denies
a previous assertion, or presupposition. In a pair of sentences like
"x exceeds y" and its denial, "x does not exceed y", the negative
does not cause difficulty, but if the negative is used "unnaturally" to
preserve or re-express the same meaning, instead of denying it, as in
the pair "x exceeds y" and "y does not exceed x" then the negative
is harder to process (Greene, 1970)*. Similarly, in everyday speech a
negative which denies a prior assertion (e.g. "The train is not late
today" following "The train is always late"), or negates a presupposition (e.g. "I don't want a drink") is not difficult to process.
These examples, which Wason calls "negatives in the context of
plausible denial", indicate the importance of contextual and semantic
factors, and show that an explanation of the negation effect in terms
of syntactic processing cannot apply to all classes of negatives. In a
recent study, Clark and Lucy (1975) found that sentences which are
negative in their literal, surface form, but positive in their conveyed
meaning, such as "Why not open the door?" yield verification times
consistent with an affirmative form, and sentences which are literally
affirmative but implicitly negative like "Must you open the door?"
produce response times more consistent with processing negatives.
This finding suggests that semantic factors are more powerful than
syntactic form in determining how a sentence is processed.

2. The Emotional Explanation

Eiferman (1961) has suggested that an emotional dislike of negatives
arises because they are associated with prohibition and frustration,
and so arouse anxiety and inhibit responses. This explanation is
consistent with theories of perceptual defence which give a similar
account of delayed recognition for words with unpleasant associations, but it cannot be an adequate account of the negation data,
since it must postulate that the emotional effect is strong enough to
carry over to non-prohibitive uses of the negative (as in "7 is not an
even number"), but somehow not strong enough to affect the natural
negatives. Since there is no obvious way to resolve this discrepancy,
the emotional explanation is unconvincing. The experimental results
on which Eiferman based this theory are, in any case, of doubtful
validity. Sentences containing prohibitive negatives took longer to
process than other sentences with non-prohibitive negatives, but the

---

* In fact, these examples of Green's are not well chosen because of course, "x
exceeds y" and "y does not exceed x" are not equivalent.

difference between the two groups of sentences persisted even when both were changed to an affirmative form. So the difference in difficulty of processing did not depend on the type of negative, but on other characteristics of the sentences.

3. The Ambiguity Explanation

A possible source of difficulty with some types of negative proposition is that the exact scope of the negative is not clear, and several interpretations are possible. In a sentence like "The dog did not chase the cat" it is not clear which element in the sentence is negated. This point is well illustrated in an experiment by Engelkampf and Hörmann (1974) which demonstrated difficulty in the recall of sentences like "The policeman did not stop the truck", but showed that the difficulty disappeared when the sentence was presented together with a disambiguating pictorial representation, e.g. "The *policeman* did not stop the truck" with a picture of a hitchhiker stopping the truck, while the policeman stands by; "The policeman did not *stop* the truck" with a picture of the policeman waving the truck along; or "The policeman did not stop the *truck*" with a picture of him stopping a car while the truck goes by. In everyday speech the scope of the negation is usually made clear by intonation, or, as in the natural negatives, by the context of the utterance, whereas experimental sentences are usually presented in written form, and without context. It seems likely, therefore, that some of the negation effect is due to the artificiality of the experimental task.

4. The Recoding Explanation

The negation effect is accounted for by the assumption that negative propositions are recoded to an affirmative form for comprehension and storage. This explanation is similar to the linguistic explanation, but the hypothesized recoding is semantic rather than syntactic. Sentences like "7 is not an even number" are translated to "7 is an odd number", and the extra step of recoding is reflected in longer verification times. Although the recoding operation would be quite simple for sentences in which the affirmative and negative forms are binary alternatives, it is less easy to apply to sentences like "The dog did not chase the cat", where the correct form of affirmative recoding is not clearly indicated. The ambiguity effects discussed above need to be incorporated into the recoding explanation. Attempts at affirmative recoding can sometimes be introspectively experienced, especially when processing sentences containing more than one negative. When applying for a British driving licence we are required to answer "yes" or "no" to the question "Are you without either hand or foot?", and a recent Italian referendum asked "Are you in favour of rescinding the law permitting divorce?". In examples like these people often find themselves trying to reformulate the question in a more positive version. However, in some cases recoding may remove the semantic implications which governed the choice of the negative form in the first place. If I say "It is not unlikely that X will get the job", I do not mean to assert "It is likely that X will get the job". I only intend to exclude one end of a scale that runs from certainty to impossibility.

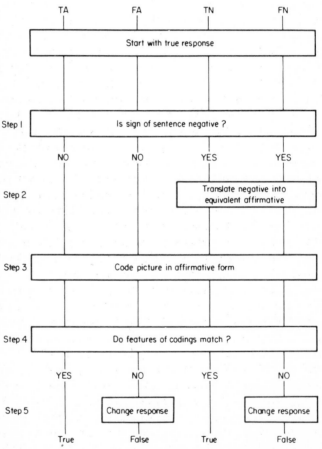

Fig. 5. A recoding model for processing negatives in binary situations (Trabasso *et al.*, 1971).

Experimental evidence of recoding comes from work investigating the latency of truth value decisions. Information processing models have been constructed by Trabasso *et al.* (1971) and by Clark and Chase (1972) to explain how positive and negative sentences are judged to be true or false descriptions of a pictorial representation. Trabasso's translation model is shown in Fig. 5. The model makes the assumption that subjects start with an initial bias to respond "true". In terms of the model, the response index is pre-set for "true". Consider a binary alternative situation in which the picture represents a circle which can be either blue or red. On a given trial the circle is blue. The True Affirmative (TA) sentence "The circle is blue" gives a direct match, and produces the response "true". The False Affirmative (FA) sentence "The circle is red" produces a mismatch at Step 4, and requires a shift in the response index to "false". The True Negative sentence (TN) "The circle is not red" requires recoding to an affirmative form at Step 2. The False Negative (FN) sentence "The circle is not blue" requires both the affirmative recoding, and the shift of the response index following a mismatch. The obtained order of latency for these four types of sentence is TA, FA, TN, FN. Responses of "false" are slower than "true", and negatives take longer than affirmatives. It is additionally assumed that the operation of recoding negatives to affirmatives takes longer than the mismatch detection and response shift (Step 2 takes longer than Step 5) to account for the finding that TN is slower than FA.

For non-binary situations, as when the circle could be any colour, Clark and Chase proposed a conversion model (Fig. 6), which can handle cases in which the negatives cannot be recoded as affirmatives because the correct affirmative form is not known. This model codes negatives by bracketing the proposition with a negative sign outside the bracket. Verification involves matching both the bracketed elements and the signs. Again suppose a picture showing a blue circle. The TA sentence "The circle is blue" is coded with a positive sign as [True (the circle is blue)]. The FA sentence "The circle is red" is also coded positively as [True (the circle is red)]. Negative sentences are coded with a negative sign, so that the TN "The circle is not red" produces [False (the circle is red)], and the FN "The circle is not blue" produces [False (the circle is blue)]. The picture is coded in Step 3 as [True (the circle is blue)]. At Step 4 the inner brackets are compared, and a mismatch shifts the response index to "false". At Step 6 the signs in the outer brackets are compared, and if these fail to match the response is changed to "true". This model fits the obtained order of response latencies, TA, FA, FN, TN. TN is

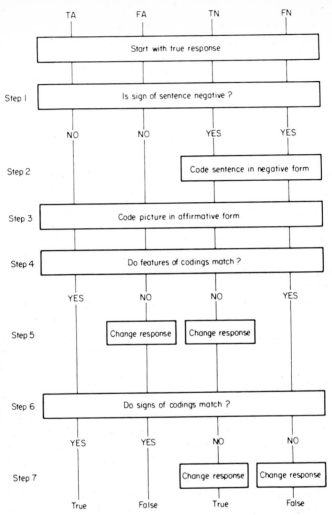

Fig. 6. A recoding model for processing negatives in non-binary situations (Clark and Chase, 1972).

slowest because it involves a double shift of the response index. FN needs only one shift because the outer signs mismatch. FA needs one shift because the inner bracket features mismatch, and TA needs no shift. To account for the finding that FN is slower than FA, the model makes the further assumption that a sign mismatch (the outer bracket) takes longer to process than a feature mismatch (the inner bracket). Figure 7 illustrates the processing of the TN sentence.

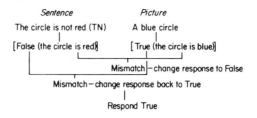

Fig. 7. Processing a True Negative sentence in a sentence-picture matching task.

It is important to remember that these models are based on the performance of highly practised subjects working as fast as possible on a task which excludes the contextual and semantic factors which influence the processing of negatives in everyday language, so that it is difficult to know whether these processing strategies would be employed in less artificial tasks. Also, since the recoding explanation of the negation effect rests on the assumption that there is an initial bias towards affirmative coding of information, it can be criticized as begging the question of why there should be such a bias. It is possible that affirmative coding is preferred because it conveys more precise information, or because it can be more easily represented in a visual image. In the sentence–picture matching task, when the verbal description is presented *before* the picture, subjects commonly report generating a visual image and matching the image to the picture, instead of converting the picture to a verbal coding and matching this to the sentence. Since images represent what is, rather than what is not, it is plausible that the preference for affirmative coding arises because it facilitates image-mediated matching. It is still not clear, however, why verbally based comparisons need to be carried out in the affirmative form. The bias toward an affirmative or positive coding may be a feature of human cognition with considerable generality, since it extends beyond the sentence processing tasks reviewed in this section. A similar phenomenon emerges in matching tasks when the subject is presented with two stimuli such as letters or shapes, and asked to judge them "same" or "different". It is usually (although not invariably) found that "same" judgements are faster than "different" judgements. A number of explanations have been advanced to account for the superiority of "same" judgements; for example, that subjects carry out a double check before deciding "different", or have a higher criterion, and require more evidence in order to make the "different" judgement. In effect, these explanations postulate a bias toward positive coding in the same way that the recoding models of negation assume an initial bias toward "true" responses and affirmative forms.

B. Processing Conditional Propositions

Wason and Johnson-Laird (1972) have reported results which appear to show that subjects have a built-in tendency to test the truth of conditional statements by seeking confirming instances, and fail to realize that a falsifying instance would be more conclusive. In one experiment, the subject is shown four cards displaying the symbols E K 4 7, and told that every card has a number on one side and a letter on the other. He is given the rule "if a card has a vowel on one side, then it has an even number on the other". His task is to name those cards, and only those cards, which need to be turned over to determine whether the rule is true or false. The great majority of subjects choose E and 4, when they should choose E and 7, since the rule would be proved false if 7 had a vowel on the other side. They neglect to look for falsifying evidence. Their choice of "4" is irrelevant because the rule does not necessarily imply its own converse; it is not the case that if there is an even number on one side then there must be a vowel on the other side. This failure persists through variations of the task using different symbols. When the array is a red triangle, a blue triangle, a red circle and a blue circle and the rule is "If there is a red triangle on one side there is a blue circle on the other", the subjects choose the red triangle and the blue circle, instead of the red triangle and the red circle. There are a number of possible explanations for this apparent failure to reason logically. It may reflect a bias towards seeking verification rather than falsification, as Wason suggests, but this offers us only a re-description of the subjects' behaviour, not an explanation of it. Alternatively, it could reflect a perceptual set, a bias of attention towards the items mentioned in the rule (Evans, 1972), but this perceptual matching hypothesis cannot explain why more concrete everyday versions of the rule tend to elicit correct solutions. When the cards showed a place on one side, and a means of transport on the other (Leeds, Manchester, train, car), and the rule was "If I go to Manchester, then I travel by train", a majority of the subjects reasoned correctly, and selected "Manchester" and "car". Their failure with the letter-digit and triangle-circle versions of the task must therefore be due to misinterpretation rather than to a general inability to reason logically. One possibility is that this misinterpretation originates from the difference between conditional abstract rules, and conditional everyday facts. An abstract, de-contextualized form of the problem, like the E K 4 7 example may be seen as an arbitrary rule rather like the rules of games or puzzles, which describe conventions rather than facts, like "If you throw a six, then you get two turns". Rules of this kind are prescriptive, but are neither true nor false. In everyday language, logical connectives have different connotations than they do in pure logic, and the "if . . . then" condition is commonly used to express temporal or causal connections as in "If I work too hard, then I feel tired". Whereas rules are more often bidirectional (if you throw a six, then you get two turns, and if you get two turns then you must have thrown a six), the causal types of connection expressed by the everyday conditional is more often unidirectional, so that while it may be true that working too hard results in tiredness, it is not the case that feeling tired necessarily implies having worked too hard. If a statement of the form "If P then Q" is bidirectional, then it follows that "If Q then P". The subjects who choose E and 4 in Wason's test misinterpret the rule as being bidirectional. In the Leeds, Manchester, car, train version they more readily perceive that it is unidirectional, and that even if going to Manchester implies travelling by train, travelling by train does not guarantee that the destination was Manchester.

In another of his experiments, which showed a similar reluctance to seek falsification, Wason (1960) presented subjects with the number series "2 4 6" and asked them to discover the rule governing the sequence. The subject could generate successive triplets, and the experimenter informed him whether each example did, or did not, conform to the rule. The subject was instructed to test his hypothesized rule until he was sure it was correct. In fact the rule was "Any numbers increasing in magnitude", but subjects were slow to discover it. Having formed an incorrect hypothesis, such as "Add two to each successive number" they continued to generate positive instance (10 12 14), instead of generating a negative instance which would have revealed that their hypothesis was incorrect. Even after receiving disconfirmation, subjects were reluctant to abandon their original hypotheses. Again it may be argued that this bias is acquired because it is appropriate in natural everyday situations. Everyday rules commonly have exceptions, so that negative instances may not convey much information. Generalizations like "Smokers get lung cancer" or "First-born children have greater academic success" are supported by an accumulation of positive instances, and are not invalidated by finding some instances of stupid first-born children or non-cancerous smokers. What the laboratory experiments have shown is not so much that people reason illogically, as that habits of reasoning acquired in everyday life are not appropriate in the decontextualized test situations. It is interesting to note that although the conditional problems seem to be easier when they are expressed in a concrete, rather than an abstract form, other problems, especially mathematical ones, may be easier when they are converted to abstract symbols. Abstraction seems to be helpful when the original problem contains irrelevant and distracting information, but can be solved by the application of fixed, well learned rules once it has been correctly formulated. Concretization may be more helpful as a checking device when it is not clear how the problem should be formulated. We can often decide whether an abstract problem has been correctly formulated by testing whether a concrete version gives a semantically acceptable answer.

C. Solving Three-term Series Problems

Three-term series problems, sometimes called linear syllogisms, or relational inferences, are problems in which inferences are drawn from premises stating a transitive relation such as "A is bigger than B, B is bigger than C". They have been quite intensively studied, and have produced considerable theoretical controversy. Some of the proposed models are outlined below.

1. The Operational Model
The operational model (Hunter, 1957) maintains that a unitary internal representation of the information in the premises is formed, so that the answer to a question such as "Which is biggest?" can be directly read off from the representation. For this to be possible, the terms must be arranged in a "natural" order. In the example above, A, B and C are arranged in order of size, and because the same relation "bigger than" is used in both premises, the internal representation is such that the terms are still correctly related even if the middle term is deleted $(A > B > C)$. This theory generates some predictions about the relative difficulty of various ways of presenting the premises. If the initial premises were "A is bigger than B, C is smaller than B" it would be harder to form the internal representation because both the relation and the order of the terms is different in the second premiss, so that it would be necessary to convert one of the relations and re-order the terms before a "natural" unitary representation could be formed.

2. The Spatial Imagery Theory
Huttenlocher's (1968) account of how three-term series problems are

handled extends the operational model and specifies the nature of the unitary representation which is created. This is characterized as a spatial image in which terms are placed along a vertical or horizontal axis, and read off from left to right, or from top to bottom. Problem difficulty is alleged to depend on two factors; the order of terms within each premiss, and the order of the premisses. The easiest form of the problem is one in which an end-item is the first term to be presented, and the order of presentation of the remaining items is such as to allow them to be consecutively entered into the imaged array working in a preferred direction (rightwards or downwards). Thus, $A > B$, followed by $B > C$ should be easier to process than $B > C$, followed by $B < A$. Evidence in support of this theory comes from the fact that the predicted order of difficulty is reflected in reaction times and errors in responding to questions. It has also been noted that, given a paper and pencil, subjects tend to jot down the terms along an axis in the way described, and that the same order of difficulty is found in a placement task requiring subjects to actually place coloured bricks in slots in a vertical array. It proves easier to place a blue brick following the instruction "The blue brick goes under the red brick" than the instruction "The red brick should be on top of the blue brick". Since this task involves a visually perceived array, and the results are similar to those obtained with the mental problem, it is argued that the mental representation in three-term series problems must be a visual image. However, these observations do not provide very strong grounds for inferring that the information is represented in a visual image since they are equally consistent with a verbal or conceptual re-organization of the information. The similarity between the block placement task, and the mental solution of three-term series problems could just as easily arise if the block task is verbally mediated instead of the verbal series being visually mediated.

3. The Linguistic Model

Clark (1969a, b) has proposed a linguistic model which is in conflict with both the Operational and the Spatial Imagery explanations. According to Clark's theory, the internal representation of the problem is not imaginal, and it is not unitary. His theory generates different predictions about problem difficulty. The linguistic model incorporates three principles. According to the first principle, a premiss such as "A is better than B" is transformed into two internal representations corresponding to "A is good" and "B is good".

Since the comparative relation is removed by this operation, it is necessary to assume some weighting of the terms so the relation can be retrieved later by a comparison of the weights. So the "A is good" representation has a greater weighting than the "B is good" representation. According to the second principle, an unmarked comparative adjective is more easily processed than a marked one. Unmarked adjectives such as good, tall, high, deep etc. are neutral, conveying only relative position on a scale. Marked forms like bad, short etc. convey absolute information as well. The unmarked form is often the name of the dimension (e.g. height). The unmarked question "How high is X?" carries no implication as to absolute height, whereas the marked question "How low is X?" implies that X is low. We use the unmarked form with quantitative units (e.g. 5-feet tall) not the marked form (5-feet short). However, experiments by Brewer and Lichtenstein (1974) failed to show any bias towards superior retention of unmarked forms in memory. In fact, the effect of marking is variable in concrete tasks, and depends on semantic context, implications and presuppositions. Banks *et al.* (1975) showed that subjects were faster at selecting the higher one of two pictured balloons which were up in the air (since these were both perceived as high), but faster at picking out the lower one of two yo-yos hanging down on strings (since these were both perceived as low). Clark's third principle concerns the congruence of the premisses and the question. Following "A is better than B, B is better than C", the congruent question "Who is best?" is easier to handle than the incongruent question "Who is worst?", which has to be converted. The linguistic model and the imagery model make different predictions about a class of premisses called negative equatives. Of the two premisses "B is not as good as A" and "A is not as bad as B", the imagery model predicts that the first should be harder because the image would have to be constructed in the non-preferred upward direction. The linguistic model predicts that the second should be harder because the adjective is marked. The results conform to the linguistic model, but it is quite possible that different strategies are employed in different circumstances. Wood (1969) claimed that subjects tended to shift from an image-based strategy to a verbal strategy with practice.

The image theory cannot account for the effect of congruence between question and premisses, because the same imaginal representation is constructed whatever the form of the original premisses. If the premisses "A is better than B, B is better than C" produce the imaged array

A
B
C

it should be just as easy to read off "Who is worst?" as "Who is best?". Many people are not aware of constructing imagery during this task, and even when imagery is reported, it is not clear whether it actually mediates the solution, or is simply a mnemonic aid. The linguistic theory accounts for the congruence effect, but as Potts and Scholz (1975) have pointed out, it cannot explain why the order of presentation of the premisses should influence problem difficulty when the model postulates separate representations for each premiss, not a unitary array. Potts and Scholz also showed that the congruence effect is only apparent when the premisses are immediately followed by the question, and not when the question is delayed. In everyday discourse, the question often precedes and elicits the relational information. If we ask "Who would be best for the job?" or "Do the Jones have a big house?" then answers like "Tom is better than Dick, but not as good as Harry" or "The Jones' house is bigger than the Smiths', but smaller than the Browns' " do not intuitively seem especially difficult to understand. Perhaps difficulties arising from the order of presentation are lessened when the context supplies a focus of attention. The models of reasoning derived from the abstract de-contextualized tests used in laboratory experiments seem very laborious and cumbersome. How far they have application to reasoning in natural context-bound situations is doubtful. Even in so far as the models are successful in representing the reasoning processes which are most typical of the subjects tested, there has been little attempt to explore individual differences in reasoning strategies.

One exception is a recent study by Shaver *et al.* (1975). They found evidence that spatial imagery is useful but not necessary for solving linear syllogisms. Problems involving those attributes for which different subjects consistently reported the same spatial arrangement were easier (above–below was easier than better-worse, and lighter-darker, which produced very inconsistent arrangements, was the hardest). Problems presented in writing were harder than when presented auditorily, perhaps because reading interferes with the construction of imagery, and subjects with higher scores for spatial ability performed better. The results suggested more use of imagery as the subjects became more practised, the opposite of Wood's finding. The authors concluded that imagery made it easier to hold the problem in short-term memory, but noted that subjects who did not give evidence of using imagery could still perform the task.

The variety of ways in which a problem can be organized and internally represented is illustrated in a deductive reasoning task described by Polich and Schwartz (1974). The problem is a whodunnit puzzle in which subjects are presented with varying amounts of information about a number of spies (their names, hair colour, locations and special expertise (see Fig. 8). Paper and pencil working provided direct evidence of the ways in which subjects arranged this information preparatory to deducing the identity of a particular spy from clues provided, and showed that a variety of different strategies were used. The alternative modes of representation were classified as matrix, network, grouping, re-writing in sentences and miscellaneous. The matrix mode generated more correct solutions, and was adopted more frequently as the amount of information supplied increased. This study suggests that Huttenlocher and Clark may both have overestimated the uniformity of the internal representations constructed by subjects in solving linear syllogisms.

In Chapter 1, the studies of semantic memory failed to produce compelling evidence that knowledge in the permanent memory store is uniquely represented in the structural form proposed by any one model. It also seems likely that the information supplied in problem solving tasks can be restructured in a variety of different ways. As so often in cognitive psychology, researchers have looked for structures and discovered strategies.

D. Making Predictions

Recent studies by Kahneman and Tversky (1973) showed that people tend to make predictions which are not in accordance with statistical probabilities. They ignore information about the prior probability of an event, and base their judgement primarily on two other factors which Kahneman and Tversky call representativeness and availability. For example, if asked to consider whether a certain person whose characteristics are described, is more likely to be a farmer or a scientist, people consider how far the individual possesses the characteristics they regard as typical of farmers or of scientists (representativeness), and may be influenced by how many instances of each profession are personally known to them (availability). They ignore information which is supplied by the experimenter about the relative numbers of farmers and scientists in the population, which

This is a problem about four different spies. Each of the spies has his contact located in a different location. Each spy also has a different spy speciality and a different colour of hair.

1. The spy with brown hair specializes in secret missile plans.
2. The spy whose contact is located in Peking specializes in germ warfare plans.
3. One of the spies has red hair.
4. The spy who specializes in electronic bugs has his contact located in Tokyo.
5. Paris is the contact location of one of the spies.
6. The spy who has black hair has his contact located in London.
7. The spy named Irving has grey hair.
8. One of the spies is named Boris.
9. The spy whose contact is located in London is named Edmond.
10. The spy named George specializes in germ warfare.
11. One of the spies specializes in scientific papers.

What is the name of the spy whose contact is in Tokyo?

Fig. 8. Example of deductive reasoning problem (four dimensions, four values). From Polich and Schwartz (1974).

determines the prior probability, and should be taken into account in making the judgement. If 50% of the population are farmers, and only 10% are scientists, then the probability of a given individual being a farmer is greater even if the individual is described as pale, intelligent and wearing spectacles. However, the way in which people operate in this kind of task is not so inept as it may appear. Statistical probabilities are more relevant to predictions about sets than to predictions about individuals. In everyday life, the prior probabilities may not be known, or they may be fairly similar for the alternative outcomes. When the prior probability has an extreme value, it may be given greater weight. If people were asked to rate the chance of a given individual being President of the United States, it seems intuitively obvious that they would pay more attention to prior probability, and place less weight on representativeness. Finally, although Kahneman and Tversky claim (1974) that people fail to combine information from prior probabilities with specific evidence, this may not be invariably so. In quoting terms for a life insurance policy, the insurance agent will take into account both the known probabilities of life expectation, and the specific age, health and way of life of the individual. In laying bets on a horse race, a serious betting man will take into account the number of runners (the prior probability) as well as the track records, breeding and fitness of the runners, and the weather conditions prevailing. In these examples, very strong specific evidence may outweigh prior probabilities.

These studies serve to demonstrate some of the limitations on the value of current models of problem solving. The models apply only to a restricted class of problems, and a restricted number of problem solvers. Experimenters have, on the whole, been too ready to conclude that, because performance is poor on certain experimental tasks, human reasoning processes are maladaptive. It would be necessary to broaden the scope of research, and to study a wider variety of logical reasoning problems in more natural contextual settings before any such conclusions could be warranted.

REFERENCES

Banks, W. P., Clark, H. H. and Lucy, P. (1975). The locus of the semantic congruity effect in comparative judgements. *Journal of Experimental Psychology, Human Perception and Performance*, **104** (1) 35-47.

Brewer, W. H. and Lichtenstein, E. H. (1974). Memory for marked semantic features versus memory for meaning. *Journal of Verbal Learning and Verbal Behaviour* **13**, 172-180.

Clark, H. H. (1969a). Linguistic processes in deductive reasoning. *Psychological Review* **76**, 387-404.

Clark, H. H. (1969b). The influence of language in solving three term series problems. *Journal of Experimental Psychology* **82**, 205-215.

Clark, H. H. and Chase, W. G. (1972). On the process of comparing sentences against pictures. *Cognitive Psychology* **3**, 472-517.

Clark, H. H. and Lucy, P. (1975). Understanding what is meant from what is said: a study in conversationally conveyed requests. *Journal of Verbal Learning and Verbal Behaviour* **14**, 56-72.

Duncker, K. (1945). On problem solving. *Psychological Monographs* **58**, 5, Whole No. 270.

Eifermann, R. R. (1961). Negation: a linguistic variable. *Acta Psychologica* **18**, 258-273.

Ekstrand, B. R. and Dominowski, R. L. (1965). Solving words as anagrams. *Psychonomic Science* **2**, 239-240.

Engelkampf, J. and Hörmann, H. (1974). The effect of non-verbal information on the recall of negation. *Quarterly Journal of Experimental Psychology* **26**, 98-105.

Evans, J. St. B. T. (1972). On problems of interpreting reasoning data. *Cognition*, 373-384.

Glucksberg, S. (1962). The influence of strength of drive on functional fixedness and perceptual recognition. *Journal of Experimental Psychology* **63**, 36-51.

Greene, J. (1970). The semantic function of negatives and passives. *British Journal of Psychology* **61**, 17-22.

Greeno, J. (1973). The structure of memory and the process of solving problems. *In* "Contemporary Issues in Cognitive Psychology" (R. L. Solso, ed.). The Loyola Symposium, Winston, Washington, D.C.

Henle, M. (1962). On the relation between logic and thinking. *Psychological Review* **69**, 366–378.

Hunter, I. M. L. (1957). The solving of three term series problems. *British Journal of Psychology* **48**, 286–298.

Huttenlocher, J. (1968). Constructing spatial images: a strategy in reasoning. *Psychological Review* **75**, 550–560.

Kahneman, D. and Tversky, A. (1973). On the psychology of prediction. *Psychological Review* **80**, 237–251.

Kahneman, D. and Tversky, A. (1974). Subjective probability: a judgement of representativeness. *In* "The Concept of Probability in Psychological Experiments" (C-A. S. Stael von Holstein, ed.). Academic Press, London and New York.

Luchins, A. S. (1942). Mechanization in problem solving: the effect of Einstellung. *Psychological Monographs* **54**, 6, Whole No. 248.

Maier, N. R. F. (1930). Reasoning in humans, I. On direction. *Journal of Comparative Psychology* **10**, 115–143.

Miller, G. A. and McKean, K. O. (1964). A chronometric study of some relations between sentences. *Quarterly Journal of Experimental Psychology* **16**, 297–308.

Miller, G. A., Galanter, E. and Pribram, K. H. (1960). "Plans and the Structure of Behaviour". Holt, New York.

Polich, J. M. and Schwartz, S. H. (1974). The effect of problem size on representation in deductive problem solving. *Memory and Cognition* **2**, 683–686.

Potts, G. R. and Scholz, K. W. (1975). The internal representation of a three term series problem. *Journal of Verbal Learning and Verbal Behaviour* **14**, 439–452.

Scheerer, M. (1963). Problem solving. *Scientific American* **208**, 118–128.

Shaver, P., Pierson, L. and Lang, S. (1975). Converging evidence for the functional significance of imagery in problem solving. *Cognition* **3/4**, 359–375.

Thomas, J. C. (1971). An analysis of behaviour in the hobbits-orcs problem. University of Michigan, Human Performance Center, Technical Report No. 31.

Trabasso, T., Rollins H. and Shaughnessy, E. (1971). Storage and verification stages in processing concepts. *Cognitive Psychology* **2**, 239–289.

Wason, P. C. (1960). On the failure to eliminate hypotheses in a conceptual task. *Quarterly Journal of Experimental Psychology* **12**, 129–140.

Wason, P. C. (1965). The contexts of plausible denial. *Journal of Verbal Learning and Verbal Behaviour* **4**, 7–11.

Wason, P. C. and Johnson-Laird, P. N. (1972). "The Psychology of Reasoning: Structure and Content". Batsford, London.

Wood, D. J. (1969). The nature and development of problem solving strategies. Unpublished D. Phil. thesis, University of Nottingham.

4

Language and Thought:
What is Language?

While it is not surprising that a relationship as complex as that between language and thought should have generated some controversial views, it is curious that they should have polarized to such an extent. According to one view, language is necessary for thought, and determines it; according to the opposite point of view, the development of thought is prior to, and necessary for, the development of language. A more intermediate position adopted by Vygotsky (1962), is that thought and language originate independently in the young child and combine in an interactive relationship at a later stage of development. Much of this disagreement arises because there has been little consensus as to what constitutes thinking, and what is to count as a language. Without some analysis of the nature of language, and of the nature of thought, we cannot decide what evidence is admissible to the argument. Trying to decide the direction of influence between language and thought is like asking whether the chicken or the egg came first, and one way to break out of this circle is to seek for limiting cases of eggs that exist without chickens, or chickens without eggs. In the case of language and thought, this means that instead of asking whether language determines thought or vice versa, we can also ask how complex and effective thought can be when language is absent, disordered, deviant or impoverished, or how well language can be mastered by the disabled thinker. By comparing the cognitive capacities of those who are normal language users with those who are a-linguistic, or language-handicapped, we can make some inferences about the role of language in thought. We should recognize that these inferences are, at best, quite crude and speculative because the comparisons are not clean. Differences between animals and humans, child and adult, the deaf and the hearing, and between members of one social or cultural group and another, are not confined to language use, and many other factors are reflected in the comparisons.

This chapter begins by considering some of the criteria for "language", and how far these are fulfilled by signalling systems other than ordinary human spoken language. The final section examines some of the differences between various human languages, and discusses how far these might reflect or produce cognitive differences.

I. THE NATURE OF LANGUAGE

Attempts to define the nature of language have characteristically displayed a marked degree of chauvinism. A typical procedure is to select what are thought to be the most important and fundamental attributes of human language, and to construct a list of these defining attributes. An example is Hockett's list of design features (Hockett, 1960) which are shown in Table I. It is apparent that all animal communication systems lack some of these features. However, to conclude that "no animal other than man communicates with language-like expressions" (Marshall, 1970) is trivially self-fulfilling if "language" is defined in terms of human language. From the fact that some features of human language are lacking, it does not necessarily follow that animal communications systems are "not language". Indeed, the stringent application of Hockett's criteria would rule out written human language (by 1, 2 and 3 in Table I); the speech of very young children (by 10 and 15); the sign language of the deaf, which is not wholly arbitrary; and the speech of aphasic and schizophrenic patients which might fail the semanticity requirement. Yet the status of these as "languages" is not usually questioned. Instead of listing defining features, and trying to determine a dividing line which separates "language" from "non-language", it is probably more interesting and fruitful to consider what are the similarities and dissimilarities of various systems of symbolization, and what are their advantages and disadvantages as media for communication, and media for thought.

The comparison of human language and animal signalling systems has been a crucial issue for nativist theories of language such as that of Chomsky (1965). For the nativist, language is both innate and species-specific to man, hence any similarities between human and

Table I. The comparison of vocal communication in animals and man. From W. H. Thorpe (1972).

Design Features (All of which are found in verbal human language)	1 Human paralinguistics	2 Crickets, grasshoppers	3 Honey bee dancing	4 Doves
1. Vocal–auditory channel	Yes (in part)	Auditory but non-vocal	No	Yes
2. Broadcast transmission and directional reception	Yes	Yes	Yes	Yes
3. Rapid fading	Yes	Yes	?	Yes
4. Interchangeability (adults can be both transmitters and receivers)	Largely yes	Partial	Partial	Yes
5. Complete feedback ("speaker" able to perceive everything relevant to his signal production)	Partial	Yes	No?	Yes
6. Specialization (energy unimportant, trigger effect important)	Yes?	Yes?	?	Yes
7. Semanticity (association ties between signals and features in the world)	Yes?	No?	Yes	Yes (in part)
8. Arbitrariness (symbols abstract)	In part	?	No	Yes
9. Discreteness (repertoire discrete not continuous)	Largely no	Yes	No	Yes
10. Displacement (can refer to things remote in time and space)	In part		Yes	No
11. Openness (new messages easily coined)	Yes	No	Yes	No
12. Tradition (conventions passed on by teaching and learning)	Yes	Yes?	No?	No
13. Duality of patterning (signal elements meaningless, pattern combinations meaningful)	No	?	No	No
14. Prevarication (ability to lie or talk nonsense)	Yes	No	No	No
15. Reflectiveness (ability to communicate about the system itself)	No	No	No	No
16. Learnability (speaker of one language learns another)	Yes	No(?)	No(?)	No

5 Buntings, finches, thrushes, crows etc.	6 Mynah	7 Colony nesting sea birds	8 Primates (vocal)	9 Canidae non-vocal communication	10 Primates—chimps, e.g. Washoe
Yes	Yes	Yes	Yes	No	No
Yes	Yes	Yes	Yes	Partly yes	Partly yes
Yes	Yes	Yes	Yes	No	No
Partial (Yes if same sex)	Yes	Partial	Yes	Yes	Yes
Yes	Yes	Yes	Yes	No	Yes
Yes	Yes	Yes	Yes	Yes	Yes
Yes	Yes	Yes	Yes	Yes	Yes
Yes	Yes	Yes	Yes	No	Yes
Yes	Yes	Yes	Partial	Partial	Partial
Time No Space Yes	Time No Space Yes	No	Yes	No	Yes
Yes	Yes	No?	Partial	No?	Yes?
Yes	Yes	In part?	No?	?	Yes
Yes	Yes	No?	Yes	Yes	Yes
No	No(?)	No	No	Yes	Yes
No	No	No	No	No	No
Yes (in part)	Yes	No	No?	No	Yes

animal languages are dismissed as coincidental and trivial. To the extent that animal languages are purposive, syntactic and propositional, so, Chomsky maintains, is an activity like walking (Chomsky, 1967). Because his interest in language is primarily structural, rather than functional, he finds the differences more striking than the similarities. But if we are asking how effective a language; of whatever kind, can be for thinking and communicating, then a functional analysis is more relevant than a formal one.

In the discussion which follows, the term "language" is used loosely to refer to various signalling and communicating systems, but its use is not intended to beg the question of their status. Nativists have denied that animal languages are evolutionarily more primitive stages of a development which culminates in human language, and Chomsky has dismissed any discussion of the evolution of language as "mere handwaving". Of course, it is true that the issue is extremely speculative, but it does serve to raise some interesting questions. Evolutionary theories of language are of two kinds (Sebeok, 1968). If language is considered as a unitary faculty then evolution would bring about quantitative changes, and species differences would be in degree of complexity. Alternatively, if language is considered to be a composite faculty arising from various independent roots such as the development of intelligence, memory, cerebral dominance and vocal mechanisms, which are acquired evolutionarily by a process of step-wise accretion, then qualitative differences of the kind represented in Table I might well occur. Mattingley (1972) has argued that human language originated in the co-development of two independent mechanisms, the intellect and the speech system. There is fossil evidence (Lieberman and Crelin, 1971) that Neanderthal man had a phonetic ability intermediate between non-human primates and modern man, but there is no reliable evidence for the evolution of intelligence in man. An increase of brain size is reported to have occurred about the time that man is thought to have become a social hunter (Campbell, 1971), but there is no reliable correlation of intelligence with cranial capacity, and no compelling reason to link the development of language with social organization, since animals such as wolves hunt socially, but have not developed a communication system of comparable complexity. Intellectual development does not necessarily promote linguistic development, and there is no sign that animal communication systems increase in complexity higher up the phylogenetic scale. Moreover, non-human primates are currently demonstrating that they have the cognitive capacity for complex linguistic skills which are not developed spontaneously in the wild (see pp. 80–87). Nevertheless there is some indication that communication systems are related to ecological pressures, since the bee's dance which conveys the location of the food source to other members of the hive, varies in complexity with the foraging range of the species (von Frisch, 1967). Since non-human primates clearly have the intellectual potential to learn more complex signalling systems than the calls, gestures and facial expressions that they spontaneously employ, and also have a social way of life which would be rendered more effective, as far as we can judge, by more complex exchange of information, other factors must be implicated in the acquisition of language. On the whole, the evidence for the evolution of language, either by continuous development, or by accretion of components, is too sparse to illuminate the relationship between human and animal languages.

Hockett's list of design features (Hockett, 1960) includes some which seem incidental and unimportant, and others which are more fundamental. We can select, on *a priori* grounds, those properties that seem to be most essential if a language is to function for thinking and for communicating.

A. Displacement

A language with displacement can symbolize objects and events not present in time and space. De Laguna (1927) remarked that "the evolution of language is characterized by a progressive freeing of speech from dependence on the perceived condition under which it is uttered and heard, and from the behaviour which accompanies it". For all kinds of thinking and communicating which involve planning for the future, hypothesizing, evaluating possible solutions, and drawing on past experience, it is necessary to symbolize states not currently being perceived by the thinker. Displacement makes education possible, and allows information to be transmitted from one generation to another, and from one individual to another, so that the accumulation of knowledge is no longer dependent on personal sense data, and the intellectual advance of the species can progress cumulatively. Natural animal languages do not appear to have this property. One exception is the language of the bees which can, as we have already noted, communicate food location within a limited range of spatial and temporal displacement. It is possible that a language can possess the property of displacement to varying degrees, and that it is not present or absent in an all-or-none fashion. The early speech of young children exhibits only minimal displacement as in comments on disappearance like "All gone", and requests for recurrence like "More". The ability to refer to objects more remote in space and time is quite slow to develop, but it is possible that this is a cognitive problem rather than a linguistic one, and the child has difficulty in conceptualizing larger distances in space and time.

B. Voluntary Control

This has been pinpointed as one of the most critical aspects of human language. Marshall (1970) distinguishes between informative and communicative signalling, and considers animal languages to be informative, but not communicative, because animal signalling is not "intentional". He claims that it is unintentional because it is not under voluntary control, and the signaller cannot choose to give or withhold the information. In response to external stimuli (such as food, or the presence of predators), or internal stimuli (such as fear, or sexual arousal) an animal behaves "in such a way as to" convey information to another animal. This is contrasted with intentional human signalling, in which one individual signals "in order to bring about a change" in another individual's behaviour. The operational criteria proposed for intentionality are that the signaller selects the appropriate signal from a range of alternatives, and continues to try variations until a goal is achieved. These criteria are not very satis-factory. Many animal signals such as threat gestures vary, at least in intensity, until they produce results, and not all human utterances are designed to change the hearer's behaviour. While intentionality is difficult to assess, it is obvious that a symbol system for thinking must be under voluntary control if thought is to be goal-oriented, rather than just random day-dreaming.

Prevarication is misleadingly listed by Hockett (1960) as a separate feature, but its importance does not lie simply in the ability to tell lies and jokes, but rather in the ability to symbolize what is not the case. In fact, therefore, it is an example of both displacement and voluntary control, and the same ability which allows us to deceive, and to fantasize, also allows us to think hypothetically.

C. Openness and Semanticity

If a language is to mediate intellectual progress, it must be capable of expressing new ideas and conveying new messages. To do this eco-nomically some structural rules of patterning are required whereby existing symbols can be recombined into novel meaningful patterns.

As with displacement, languages may possess this property in varying degrees, and Lyons (1972) has suggested that it is the greater complexity of the structural rules that distinguishes human language. Semanticity is commonly defined in terms of reference—the symbol system must be able to refer to objects and attributes in the real world; but this kind of reference is not enough to make a language functionally adequate. It must also be able to express relations of many kinds, and some of these were discussed in Chapter 2 when we noted that an image code might be deficient in this respect. For thinking complex thoughts and exchanging complex messages, naming is not enough; a language needs to be propositional.

D. Reflectiveness

Reflectiveness is what Hockett calls "ability to communicate about the system itself", or metalinguistic ability. This is an attribute of human language which is often cited, but rarely analysed sufficiently for us to assess its importance. It is not simply the ability to reflect about the language, or to discuss it, that is crucial; nor even the ability to understand the principle of symbolization, and the representational nature of signs. What is really essential is the ability to combine linguistic information and non-linguistic information, so that language can be interpreted on different levels, either literally, or with reference to the context and the pragmatic implications. It is this ability which allows us to interpret "It is eight o'clock" either literally as a clock reading, or pragmatically as "Hurry up, or you'll be late for work". The most sophisticated knowledge of the formal nature of language does not guarantee comprehension; we must also understand its function. We must be able to relate the purely linguistic properties of a message to our stored knowledge of the world, and our perception of the immediate situational context of the utterance.

What other characteristic does a language require if it is to serve for thinking? It is arguable whether the language needs to be internalizable. Should we deny that a man could think if he could only think out loud, or with a paper and pencil? It seems overrestrictive to insist that thinking be internal, yet subjects who are engaged in problem solving, and are asked to "think aloud" report that their overt verbalization cannot keep abreast of their inner thoughts, which are more rapid and less completely formulated. Rapidity and economy are among the advantages of internalized thought, but the thinker may also need to stabilize, manipulate, erase or modify the thinking symbols so that he can consider and evaluate a sequence, and discard, revise or accept a solution. For this kind of thinking, an externalized representation such as writing is clearly superior.

Recent attempts to teach artificial languages to chimpanzees have raised some fascinating issues, which are very relevant to the problem of the relationship of language and thought. Do the linguistic achievements of the chimpanzees reflect a cognitive capacity which existed previously independent of language? How far are the linguistic skills which they have acquired capable of mediating thought and communication? Do they resemble human language closely enough to counter the view that language is species-specific to man? The language learning of three chimpanzees, Washoe, Sarah and Lana are reviewed in some detail in the next section, so that we can attempt to answer these questions.

II. THE CHIMPANZEE LINGUISTS

A. Washoe

Gardner and Gardner (1969) have taught a chimpanzee called Washoe to use the American sign language for the deaf (Ameslan). The gestural signs are composed of 55 basic elements or cheremes (such as position in space, moving or stationary, one hand or two, type of movement, direction of movement, configuration of the hands etc.). Washoe has learned to produce 132 of these signs, and to comprehend rather more (Gardner and Gardner, 1975). Her vocabulary includes nouns, pronouns, verbs, adjectives, possessives, locatives, negatives and imperatives. She combines these in strings of up to five signs, and is able to recombine them to produce novel strings. Her language has semanticity in so far as she correctly names objects and events, and shows semantic generalization in her application of signs to novel examples. For instance, she learned the sign for "open" with reference to a door, and generalized this to boxes, cupboards, drawers and brief-cases. Her errors show an overgeneralization similar to that observed in the language of young children. Having learned the sign for "hurt" applied to a scratch, she applied it later to a tattoo mark, and to her trainer's navel: she generalized the sign for "flower" to "smell", and her errors are sometimes within-category substitution like "soap" for "toothbrush". Her communications are often requests for food, drink, cuddling and tickling. She comments on objects in the environment, and correctly answers *Wh* questions like "What is this? Where is the cup? Who is sleeping?" Interestingly, there are no reports of any ability to answer Why, How and When questions, so perhaps Washoe lacks concepts of causality and time, but children are also later in acquiring these. Her utterances are concrete, and of limited complexity.

Whether her language has syntactic structure is disputed. She uses some pronouns correctly, but no connectives. However, it is not clear how far her syntactic deficiencies reflect her own limitations, or the nature of the sign language itself, which is highly condensed, and omits articles, inflections, copulae and prepositions (Bellugi and Fischer, 1972). Washoe's utterances lack a stable ordering, so that subject and object are not distinguishable, and in this respect she is unlike young children, who use word order correctly and consistently. Whereas a child can reliably use the correct word order in a sentence asking an adult to tickle him (name of adult—tickle—name of self), Washoe's ordering is inconsistent and does not convey who is the intended agent, and who is the intended object of the action. However, Brown (1970) carried out a functional analysis of the speech of young children, and Table II shows that Washoe's utterances are functionally very similar, even if her syntax is inferior. In any case, comparisons with normal children are hardly fair to Washoe, since her language experience resembles that of a deaf child with deaf parents (Bronowski and Bellugi, 1970).

In studying Washoe and other animal linguists, the competence-performance problem arises in a special form. Whereas with adult humans it is assumed that competence exceeds performance, because much of Washoe's learning is imitative, and her use of language is context-dependent, her competence, or mental model of the language may actually be less adequate than appears from her performance. How far does Washoe's use of language reflect an internal understanding of her symbol system? No evidence is presented to show that Washoe can reject ill-formed sentences, so it is not clear that Washoe understands the rules governing sentence formation in Ameslan.

Displacement is minimal in Washoe's language, and as in early child speech, is confined to requests for recurrence ("More milk") and comments on disappearance ("Allgone cup"). Her use of language is closely tied to the immediate spatio-temporal context. Intentionality is clearly present in the utterances classified as Appeal–Action ("Please tickle") and Appeal–Object ("Gimme fruit"), since Washoe does persist with this kind of sign sequence until she gets what she is asking for. On one occasion she is reported

Table II. From R. Brown (1970).

Brown's (1970) scheme for children		The scheme for Washoe	
Types	Examples	Types	Examples
Attributive Ad + N	big train, red book	*Object–Attributable*	drink red, comb black
Possessive: N + N	Adam checker, mommy lunch	*Agent–Attribute*	Washoe sorry, Naomi good
		Agent–Object	clothes Mrs G., you hat
		Object–Attribute	baby mine, clothes yours
N + V	walk street, go store	*Action–Location*	go in, look out
		Action–Object	go flower, pants tickle
Locative N + N	sweater chair, book table	*Object–Location*	baby down, in hat
Agent–Action: N + V	Adam put, Eve read	*Agent–Action*	Roger tickle, you drink
Action–Object: V + N	put book, hit ball	*Action–Object*	tickle Washoe, open blanket
Agent–Object: N + N	mommy sock, mommy lunch	*Appeal–Action*	please tickle, hug hurry
		Appeal–Object	gimme flower, more fruit

to have forgotten the sign for "bib", and after some hesitation, invented a new one by drawing a bib shape on herself, so she fulfils Marshall's operational criteria for intentionality, persistence and variation of signal until the goal is achieved. Indeed, it is impossible to watch Washoe's language behaviour without being convinced that she not only intends, but is positively determined, to communicate.

Perhaps the most striking deficit is her failure to ask questions. In this she is quite unlike the young child whose conversation turns to an onslaught of *Wh* questions once the child catches on to the linguistic game of interrogation. Does Washoe use her language for thinking? She does not talk to herself as much as young children do, and it is only on a few occasions that she has been observed to use an isolated sign while alone. Of course, it is possible that she can internalize her signs, but there is no evidence that she does so. How far her cognitive development has been enhanced by having language does not seem to have been systematically explored. It would be interesting if it could be shown that her performance on problem solving and memory tasks had improved as a result of having a linguistic code. Currently, the Gardners have begun to train some more chimpanzees, beginning the training programme soon after birth, and they are confident that Washoe's achievements will be surpassed, and that the upper limits of chimpanzees' linguistic skills have not yet been revealed.

B. Sarah

Another chimpanzee, Sarah, has been taught an artifical language which is very different from Washoe's, and is in some ways more impressive. Premack (1970) deliberately set out to teach Sarah a language system, which, while being adapted to suit her capacities, would still be adequate to fulfil the more important criteria of "language", and thus convincingly demonstrate the chimpanzee's ability as a bona fide language user. On Premack's view, while phonology and the particular syntactic structure of human language are unique to man, the logical and semantic structure of language are not.

Sarah uses plastic chips of varying colour, size, shape and texture, each representing a word, which are arranged on a magnetic board in a vertical array to form sentences. This system relieves Sarah of the short-term memory load imposed by sequencing in a fade-out system, and there is no time pressure on comprehension since she can study an array as long as she likes. The vocabulary consists of items like the names of fruits; the names of her trainers, who figure in sentences as donors and recipients of objects; verbs like giving, cutting, inserting; and attributes like colours and shapes. Teaching is by operant conditioning. Correct responses are elicited and rewarded. The difficulty of a task can be controlled by varying the number and type of chips available to Sarah when she is constructing her sentences. Only a sub-set of the total vocabulary is available at any one time. Sarah has learned to understand and respond appropriately to sentences presented to her, and to construct her own sentences. Some of the aspects of sentence structure which Premack claims that Sarah has mastered are discussed below.

Sarah appears to understand the significance of word order in simple two-term relations like "Green on Red", as opposed to "Red on Green", when these are used to describe the relative positions of coloured cards. Sarah can correctly construct a sentence to describe how the cards are placed, or arrange the cards to correspond to a sentence. Even so, her ability to represent a spatial ordering correctly is not comparable with the ability to use ordering of symbols to represent more abstract relations like Agent–Action–Object, and it is doubtful whether Sarah's ordering is more than a kind of cross-modal matching.

Sarah has also learned to handle compound sentences like "Sarah insert (banana pail) (apple dish)", but as Fodor *et al.* (1974) point out, this does not prove that she understands the constituent structure of such a sentence. She could assign fruit to container correctly on the basis of the proximity of the symbols in the sentence. It seems unfair, however, to complain that Sarah lacks the sophisticated understanding of structural relationships within sentences possessed by professors of linguistics, and it would be more relevant to have some child–chimpanzee comparisons for this type of sentence.

Sarah responds correctly to both affirmative and negative interrogatives. The training technique utilized the animal's natural ability to distinguish between identical and non-identical pairs of objects. Presented with sentences of the form "A same as A?" Sarah replaces the question mark with the symbol for "Yes"; or, given "A same as B?" she responds "No". Similarly she responds "No" to the negative form "A not same as A?", and in "A is ? to B", she replaces the question symbol with the "not same as" symbol. As in other tasks, having learned the form with one set of vocabulary items, she transfers with about 80% success to sentences of the same form but with different lexical items.

Another set of tasks was designed to test Sarah's understanding of what Premack calls metalinguistics which corresponds to what, earlier in this chapter, we called reflectiveness or understanding of the principle of symbolizing. When she is shown a pairing of a plastic symbol, and its referent object, Sarah can affix the symbol for "is the name of" between them; or if the plastic chip is paired with a non-referent, she supplies "is not the name of". Asked what is the name of an object, she supplies the correct chip, and responds "Yes" or "No" correctly to questions like "A is the name of apple?". More impressively, when asked to assign attributes to the blue chip, which is the symbol for an apple, she assigns "red" and "round", the same attributes she assigns to the fruit itself. These achievements demonstrate that Sarah has some understanding of the relationship between the symbols she uses, and the objects they represent, but this is only a small part of metalinguistic ability (see Section I D).

Other achievements are pluralization, and the use of quantifiers like "All", "None", "One" and "Several" to describe sets of objects. Sarah correctly formulates sentences like "All the crackers are round" or "None of the crackers is round" to describe sets of crackers. She also appears to understand the sub-set/super-set relation in classifying colours, shapes, fruits etc.

Perhaps the most complex of Sarah's achievements is her mastery of conditional sentences of the If...then form. Given an apple and a banana within reach, Sarah learned to respond to sentences such as "If Sarah take apple then Mary give chocolate", or "If Sarah take apple then Mary not give chocolate". Again she was able to transfer successfully to novel versions of this form such as "If green is on red then Sarah take banana".

Sarah's language is more complex and abstract than Washoe's, but less spontaneous. Fodor *et al.* (1974) have remarked that, unlike the young child, she lacks genuinely productive syntax, and never acquires a new syntactic form without special training. Her language does not have that element of invention that is characteristic of child language. Although she has clearly mastered some of the rules which underlie linguistic skill, the overall impression produced by the reports of her performance is that she is playing a complicated kind of board game, rather than using language to communicate. It is difficult, though, to justify this view by stating precisely what are the missing elements. This same difficulty is highlighted by a recent study (Hughes, 1975) of severely aphasic children who were taught "Premackese". Although the non-verbal intelligence of these children was normal, their spoken language at 8–13 years old had not advanced beyond a 2-year-old level. Nevertheless, using the plastic symbol system, they were able to master several sentence forms, the use of negation, class concepts and some kinds of questions. Hughes concludes that there is a gulf between an artifical language like Premackese and normal human language, but cannot specify the nature of the difference.

C. Lana

A third chimpanzee, Lana, has been trained on a language system called "Yerkish" (Rumbaugh *et al.*, 1974) which is quite similar to Premackese. Lana has access to a console with a bank of 75 key words, which they call lexigrams, each differentiated by a geometric symbol. Lana selects and presses the keys to construct sentences, and the result is transcribed on to a screen so that she can read what she has "written". The position of the keys is varied, so that her selection is not spatially determined, and she must recognize the geometric patterns. Lana can name objects or request food, drink, tickling, grooming etc. She can complete valid sentence beginnings, and can erase invalid ones, and she also deletes or erases her own errors, which indicates considerable understanding of the structural rules of the language. This is particularly impressive since children are not able or willing to make judgements about the correctness of sentences until about 7 years old (Gleitman *et al.*, 1972). Lana sometimes asks the name of a novel object, and then uses the name to request the object, and she also invents novel sentences. Her syntax is less complex than Sarah's, but her use of language is more productive, communicative and conversational. She exhibits some degree of displacement, in that she can request a trainer who is out of sight to come into her room and tickle her. She also seems to have surpassed Washoe in her understanding of the use of word order to signify agent and object in tickling and grooming activities. Both Lana and Sarah probably benefit from having their sequences "written" so that the elements can be simultaneously perceived, whereas in Washoe's system the sequential order of the signs must be retained in memory.

Studies of language learning by chimpanzees have shown that the full potential of non-human primates has not been realized by the demands of their natural environment, and it seems likely that further improvements in training techniques will extend their linguistic skills still further. It is difficult to reconcile the results of these studies with a unitary view of human language, since the chimpanzees give evidence of possessing specific components of language, and lacking others, rather than just operating on a more primitive level. The language systems they have learned do serve for simple communication, but there is no indication that they have yet made the giant intellectual stride of using these symbols systems for thinking. Vygotsky (1962) wrote:

> In their ontogenetic development thought and speech have different roots. In the speech development of the child we can with certainty establish a pre-intellectual stage, and in his thought development, a prelinguistic stage. Up to a certain point in time the two follow different lines independently of each other. At a certain point these lines meet, whereupon thought becomes verbal and speech rational.

On his view, this meeting-point marks the origin of true language. It is not yet apparent that the lines have met for any of the chimpanzee language students.

III. THE SIGN LANGUAGE OF THE DEAF

Since it has been suggested that some of Washoe's shortcomings are imposed by the limitations of sign language, it is worth considering the nature of sign language in a little more detail. How adequately do sign languages, as used by deaf and dumb humans rather than chimpanzees, satisfy the criteria for language, and how well can sign language serve as a medium for thinking? Bellugi and Fischer (1972) noted that in speech, words can be produced at rates twice as fast as in signs. The rate of articulation of signs is much more sharply limited, but the rate of producing propositions is the same in signs as in spoken language, because the sign language is more condensed, and omits many of the functors such as articles, copulas and prepositions. This results in a telegrammatic style of communication similar to the speech of young children who show a similar kind of reduction in reproducing adult utterances. For the child, reduction serves to bring a sentence within his memory span. In sign language, the reduction is more likely to be a device to speed up transmission rather than being due to limitations of either the language itself, or of the language user. Some sign languages such as the Paget-Gorman system are much less condensed and include inflections. Schlesinger (1971) found evidence of some rules of ordering to distinguish subject and object in the uninflected Israeli sign language system, although typically these were not observed when contextual cues would serve to make the distinction. He noted also the spontaneous development of signing without specific training in deaf and dumb communities, and that these signs were generally intelligible to members of other communities. Sign production seems to show a certain flexibility, being more slurred, telegrammatic and unordered when there is a clear contextual background, and more careful and rule-bound when contextual cues are absent.

A recent study by Bellugi *et al.* (1975) suggests that signs are internalized, and function as a coding system in memory. They found a memory span of 4–9 signs, consistent with a rate of implicit signing roughly equivalent to the rate of overt signing. In a recall test, interesting differences were observed in the intrusion errors of deaf and hearing subjects. While the hearing tended to substitute acoustically confusable items (*House* for *Horse*), the deaf substituted items represented by similar signs (*Uncle* for *Horse*). Table III shows how the errors preserve the basic hand arrangement of the original sign. These errors provide strong evidence that signs function as an internal symbol system in memory, but do not indicate whether they are represented as visual or as kinaesthetic images, since both aspects are confounded. However, the fact that lists of items are remembered as signs in short-term memory tasks, does not necessarily indicate that conceptual thinking and problem solving are carried on using internalized signs, although it certainly suggests the possibility.

A case study reported by Newcombe (1975) suggests that the relationship between signing and thought is a complex one. Newcombe's patient was a deaf and dumb child, Adam, who was a-linguistic when he was referred to her at about 7 years old. The child was taught sign language, and learned to communicate effectively to the extent of being able to relate vivid imaginative stories to his teacher. The fascinating aspect of these stories is that they incorporate autobiographical elements and past events experienced before the child had acquired any form of language. Clearly, these experiences must have been represented in memory in a non-linguistic form, and were translated into the newly learned sign language at a later date. The fact that the thoughts ante-dated the linguistic realization indicates a clear dissociation of thought and language.

IV. LINGUISTIC RELATIVITY

When we come to make comparisons within the family of human languages, three questions arise:

1. Are there significant differences between languages?

Table III. From Bellugi *et al.* (1975).

Pairs differing only in movement

Sign Error Sign Error

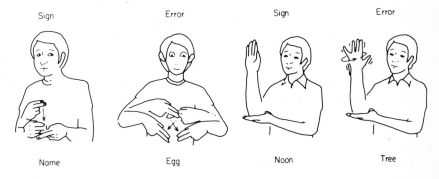

Name Egg Noon Tree

Pairs differing only in orientation

Sign Error

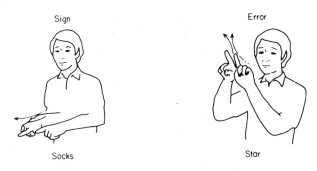

Socks Star

Pairs differing only in place of articulation

Sign Error Sign Error

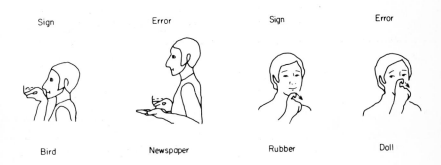

Bird Newspaper Rubber Doll

2. Are there differences in thinking between members of different language communities?

3. Are the differences in thinking and in language causally related? For the relativist, the differences between languages are more important than the similarities. The universalist believes that the underlying structure of all languages is essentially the same. The relativist view has been expressed by Whorf (1941) following in the steps of Humboldt and Sapir. He wrote "the forms of a person's thoughts are controlled by inexorable laws of pattern of which he is unconscious. These laws are the unperceived intricate systematizations of his own language". In its strong form the Whorfian hypothesis asserts that the particular language we speak determines the way that we think. In a weaker form, the hypothesis asserts that language influences, directs or biases our thinking rather than determining it. Even in the reformulated version, the terms of this argument are too imprecise for us to be able to assess its validity. What aspects of language are supposed to influence thought? We can distinguish several possibilities here—the richness of the vocabulary, the presence or absence of particular lexical items in the language; and the structural characteristics, or the particular syntactic forms, of the language. What aspects of thought are supposed to be influenced? Most of the cross-cultural studies have sought to relate linguistic differences to differences in perception and memory, and have not attempted to examine any possible differences in more complex mental processes, such as problem solving. Whatever aspect of thinking is being investigated, we need to ask whether language affects *what* is thought, or only *how* it is thought. Finally, it is not clear what is meant by "influence". Influence is a relative term. If language is only one of several "influences" on thinking, we need to know how strong it is compared with cultural, educational and socio-economic influences.

Chomskyan model. Chomsky distinguishes between the surface structure of language, and the underlying deep structure. In the early versions, Chomsky's theory implies that, although different languages may exhibit dissimilarities of surface structure, an underlying uniformity exists at the deep structure level. In 1965 Chomsky wrote "The existence of deep-seated formal universals...implies that all languages are cut to the same pattern, but does not imply that there is any point to point correspondence between particular languages." Since the semantic component is assumed to operate on the deep structure, rather than on the surface, semantic representations would have the inter-lingual universality claimed for deep structure, and this theory is therefore in conflict with Whorf's hypothesis that the diverse surface characteristics of language reflect diversities at the semantic or conceptual level. Other linguists have maintained instead that the semantic component maps directly on to the surface structure, and this view is compatible with the claim that surface differences correspond to semantic differences.

There are serious difficulties in finding unambiguous experimental evidence for linguistic relativity whether it is expressed in the stronger or the weaker form. If we find cognitive differences between speakers of different languages, we cannot attribute these to the linguistic factor unless we can eliminate, or parcel out other influences on cognition. Cognitive differences between ape and man, between younger and older children, between deaf and hearing, the urban and the rural population, the professor and the miner, cannot be set down to differences in language ability when other factors such as intelligence, education, training and experience may all be confounded with linguistic skill. If we find languages which lack particular lexical items, or grammatical forms, we are not entitled to infer that users of such languages necessarily lack the related mental concepts. Nor does the presence of a particular verbal label in the vocabulary of a language user guarantee that the underlying concept is fully understood. The literature of psychology contains many examples, such as "mind", "image" or "concept" itself, which do not have precisely specified and agreed meanings. Even when there appears to be co-existent linguistic features and forms of cognition, there is usually no clear evidence to establish a causal link between them, let alone to show the direction of causation. Furthermore, any causal links that do exist between language and thought are unlikely to be simple and unidirectional ones. New lexical items may develop to express new cognitive trends, and the new term may then influence our thinking, as the new term "Ms" developed out of the need to describe a female person irrespective of marital status, and its use is supposed to change some of the ways people think about women. Here the relationship of language and thought is bidirectional.

These problems are illustrated in many of the studies which have been designed to demonstrate linguistic relativity. At the lexical level, one of the ways in which languages vary is the richness of the labelling system used to mark within-category distinctions. Does this entail that the kind of semantic networks described in Chapter 1 must vary between languages? It has been noted that the Hopi Indians have a single term for flying objects encompassing insects,

aeroplanes and pilots; the Eskimos have many words for different
kinds of snow, and the Arabs many names for different kinds of
camel. What can be concluded from these observations? There are
two conditions in which a single lexical label will serve for different
items. One is when the context will usually make the distinction
clear; the other is when we do not need to make the distinction. In
English, we have only one word "bank" for the edge of a river, and a
financial institution, yet nobody would argue that we cannot distinguish between them. We do not need different words because context would almost always serve to indicate the reference. On the
other hand, although a teacher confronted with a new class is quite
capable of distinguishing the individual members before he or she has
learned their names, knowing their names does make it easier to
remember and refer to individuals. A single label of "child" would
not suffice because the individuals are all encountered in the same
contextual setting. Within our own speech-community the horti-
culturalist and the geologist can name sub-species of flower, and
kinds of rock, which the rest of us do not need to distinguish,
although we could learn to do so if we chose. The absence of lexical
labels does not imply that conceptual distinctions cannot be made.

There is experimental evidence to show that stimuli which have
unambiguous and economical verbal labels are more easily
remembered. "Codability" improves recognition of nonsense shapes
(Clark, 1965) and of colour chips (Brown and Lenneberg, 1954).
In a study of Wolof children, Greenfield *et al.* (1966) showed that
the acquisition of superordinate words like "colour" and "shape",
which are lacking in the Wolof language, but are learned in French at
school, improved the children's ability to group objects according to
these attributes. However, language learning was confounded with
general education and with city-dwelling, both of which could
contribute to cognitive changes. Carroll and Casagrande (1958)
investigated object grouping in Navaho children. In Navaho, verbs of
handling have different stems depending on the shape of the object
being handled, and Navaho-speaking children appeared to be more
sensitive to shape properties at an earlier age than the average English-
speaking child, whose perceptual grouping is dominated by colour.
However children with early experience of constructional toys performed like the Navahos, showing that shape awareness could be
either language-induced or culture-induced. The most reasonable conclusion is that verbal labels come into existence in response to the
needs of a particular way of life, and act to draw attention to significant perceptual distinctions and groupings, and to maintain them in
memory.

In studying linguistic relativity it seems particularly easy to fall into the "Can/Do" confusion which is prevalent in much of cognitive psychology. It may seem unnecessary to stress the obvious fact that while "do" implies "can do", and "can't" implies "don't", the reverse does not hold. "Can do" does not imply "do", and "don't" does not imply "can't". In many areas of research psychologists fail to make clear whether they are investigating norms or limits, habits or capacities. Because users of a particular language "don't" habitually express certain ideas, it does not follow that they "can't". Whorf produces no real evidence to support his contention that the Hopi Indians lack an objective sense of time because they express time in terms of subjective duration. In English we can conceptualize 3 weeks as well as a fortnight, and we can think of an event recurring every 6 years as easily as one recurring quinquennially. The absence of a term does not preclude the concept. When Whorf writes:

> Hopi 'preparing' activities again show a result of their linguistic thought background in an emphasis on persistence and constant insistent repetition. A sense of the cumulative value of innumerable small momenta is dulled by an objectified spatialized view of time like ours, enhanced by a way of thinking close to the subjective awareness of duration of the ceaseless 'latering' of events (Whorf, 1941).

This is a splendid imaginative piece of writing, but it is not psychology.

An experimental investigation by Ervin-Tripp (1964) of Japanese-American bilinguals provides more convincing evidence of the influence of language on the content of thought. She found that when a Japanese-American bilingual performed word-association or sentence-completion tests in Japanese, the responses were typical of Japanese monolinguals; when the same speaker performed the tests in English, the responses were typical of American monolinguals. For example, when asked to say what qualities they looked for in a husband, a female subject, when speaking Japanese, would stipulate that he should be pleasing to her family; and when speaking English, that she should be in love with him. The language being used clearly influenced the nature of the thought processes being tapped. Even so, the nationality of the *listener*, and the topic being discussed were also found to influence the kind of ideas expressed in conversation, independently of the language being used.

When lexical terms are not present in a language, but are needed to express new ideas, they are invented or borrowed from another language. Revived languages such as Modern Hebrew or Welsh have updated their vocabularies to meet the cognitive demands of the twentieth century in this way. Young children commonly invent words, and there are instances of similar productive inventions in the sign language of both chimpanzee and the deaf and dumb. Washoe combined the signs for "water-fruit" to refer to a melon, and in Newcombe's case-study, the child used the signs "sleep-think" to refer to a dream. In Chinese there are no words for "and" and "or", but conjunction and disjunction can be adequately expressed by other means. "A and B" is rendered as "There is A, there is B"; "A or B" as "If not A, then B". There is little reason to suppose that language acts as a cognitive strait-jacket. To the extent that languages are inter-translatable, the ideas that are expressed in one language can still be rendered, however clumsily, in other languages that lack the appropriate terms or structures.

The evidence for linguistic relativity is largely anecdotal and speculative. Where experiments have been carried out, it has not proved possible to disentangle the language component from other influences on cognition. Such as it is, the evidence suggests that a given language can influence habits of thought, semantic organization, and the ease and economy with which ideas can be expressed, but does not impose stringent limitations on cognitive functioning. In Chapter 5, when we come to examine the language—thought relationship by comparing thinking in animals, young children or those with language impairment, and normal language users, we should expect to find greater cognitive differences than when we make comparisons across different languages. We must also expect to find that such comparisons are even more contaminated by the other variables which affect cognition, and that the influence of the language factor is consequently even harder to assess.

REFERENCES

Bellugi, U. and Fischer, S. (1972). A comparison of sign language and spoken language. *Cognition* 1, 173-200.

Bellugi, U., Klima, E. S. and Siple, P. (1974-1975). Remembering in signs. *Cognition* 3, 93-125.

Bronowski, J. and Bellugi, U. (1970). Language, name and concept. *Science, N.Y.* 168, 669-673.

Brown, R. (1970). "Psycholinguistics". The Free Press, New York.

Brown, R. W. and Lenneberg, E. H. (1954). A study in language and cognition. *Journal of Abnormal and Social Psychology* 49, 454-462.

Campbell, B. (1971). The roots of language. *In* "Biological and Social Factors in Psycholinguistics" (J. Morton, ed.). Logos Press, in association with Elek Books, London.

Carroll, J. B. and Casagrande, J. B. (1958). The function of language classification. *In* "Readings in Social Psychology" (E. E. Maccoby, T. M. Newcomb and E. L. Hartley, eds). Holt, Rinehart and Winston, New York.

Chomsky, N. (1965). "Aspects of the Theory of Syntax". M.I.T. Press, Cambridge, Massachussetts.

Chomsky, N. (1967). The general properties of language. *In* "Brain Mechanisms underlying Speech and Language" (C. H. Millikan and F. L. Darley, eds). Grune and Stratton, New York and London.

Clark, H. J. (1965). Recognition memory for random shapes as a function of complexity, association value and delay. *Journal of Experimental Psychology* 69, 590-595.

De Laguna, G. (1927). "Speech: its Function and Development". Yale University Press.

Ervin-Tripp, S. (1964). An analysis of the interaction of language, topic and listener. *American Anthropologist* 66, 94-100.

Fodor, J. A., Bever, T. G. and Garrett, M. F. (1974). "The Psychology of Language: An Introduction to Psycholinguistic and Generative Grammar". McGraw-Hill, New York.

Frisch, K. von (1967). "The Dance Language and Orientation of the Bees". Harvard University Press, Cambridge, Massachusetts.

Gardner, R. A. and Gardner, B. T. (1969). Teaching sign language to a chimpanzee. *Science, N.Y.* 165, 664-672.

Gardner, B. T. and Gardner, R. A. (1975). Evidence for sentence constituents in the early utterances of child and chimpanzee. *Journal of Experimental Psychology: General* 104, 244-267.

Gleitman, L. R., Gleitman, H. and Shipley, E. (1972). The emergence of the child as a grammarian. *Cognition* 1, 137-164.

Greenfield, P., Reich, L. and Olver, R. (1966). On culture and equivalence, 2. *In* "Studies in Cognitive Growth" (P. Greenfield, L. Reich and R. Olver, eds). Wiley, New York.

Hockett, C. F. (1960). The origin of speech. *Scientific American* 203, 89-96.

Hughes, J. (1975). Acquisition of a non-vocal 'language' by aphasic children. *Cognition* 3, 41-55.

Lieberman, P. and Crelin, E. S. (1971). On the speech of Neanderthal man. *Linguistic Inquiry* 2, 203-222.

Lyons, J. (1972). Human Language. *In* "Non-verbal communication" (R. A. Hinde, ed.). Cambridge University Press, Cambridge.

Marshall, J. C. (1970). The Biology of communication in man and animals. *In* "New Horizons in Linguistics" (J. Lyons, ed.). Penguin Books, Middlesex.

Mattingley, I. G. (1972). Speech cues and sign stimuli. *American Scientist* 60, 327-337.

Newcombe, F. (1975). From a paper presented at a conference in the Department of Educational Studies, University of Oxford.

Premack, D. A. (1970). A functional analysis of language. *Journal of Experimental Analysis of Behaviour* 14, 107-125.

Rumbaugh, D. M., von Glaserfeld, E., Warner, H., Pisani, P. and Gill, T. V. (1974). Lana (chimpanzee) learning language: a progress report. *Brain and Language* 1, 205-212.

Schlesinger, I. M. (1971). The grammar of sign language and the problems of language universals. *In* "Biological and Social Factors in Psycholinguistics" (J. Morton, ed.). Logos Press, in association with Elek Books, London.

Sebeok, T. (1968). "Animal Communication: Techniques and Study of the Results of Research". Indiana University Press, Bloomington and London.

Thorpe, W. H. (1972). The comparison of vocal communication in animals and man. *In* "Non-verbal Communication" (R. A. Hinde, ed.). Cambridge University Press, Cambridge.

Vygotsky, L. S. (1962). "Thought and Language". M.I.T. Press, Cambridge, Massachusetts.

Whorf, B. (1941). The relation of habitual thought and behaviour to language. *In* "Language, Culture and Personality: Essays in Memory of Edward Sapir" (L. Spier, ed.). University of Utah Press.

5

Language and Thought: What is Thinking?

I. THE NATURE OF THOUGHT

Compared with the rich and detailed analyses of thinking presented by philosophers such as Gilbert Ryle in *The Concept of Mind* (1949), psychologists have tended to adopt a narrower interpretation. If thinking is to be amenable to experimental investigation, thought processes must start from a situation which is observable, specifiable and controllable, and must issue in some behavioural response which is also observable and measurable. This means that, for the psychologist, studies of thinking tend to be restricted to goal-directed reasoning, problem solving and categorization processes, and many kinds of mental activity which take place without identifiable input and output, such as believing, reflecting, considering, musing and imagining, are excluded.

Writing about the essential nature of thought, Craik (1943) asserted that "one of the most fundamental properties of thought is its power of predicting events". He considered that the function of thought is to create a model of reality by means of internal symbolism, and he isolated three essential stages in this process: the translation of external objects or events into symbols; the production of further symbols by inferential reasoning, hypothesizing or calculation; and the re-translation of these new symbols into external processes. How well does this definition capture the essence of thought? It is worth considering, by contrast, what kinds of processing are usually classified as "unthinking". A task may sometimes be accomplished successfully without involving thought if it is carried out automatically, and without conscious monitoring.

This kind of processing can be identified operationally, as well as introspectively, since it is typically faster than conscious processing, and can be more easily combined with a secondary concurrent task (Posner, 1973). Automaticity is achieved when tasks are highly practised and stereotyped. The skilled typist or car driver can perform automatically and without conscious awareness because their tasks are so highly practised that they do not require Craik's middle stage of inference making. By Craik's definition these operations are not thinking. Unconscious mental operations may be included within the definition of thinking if they are not of the automatic kind, but involve the production of novel inferences without the conscious application of logical rules. A task which is performed unsuccessfully is not necessarily unthinking. We consider that it involves thinking if a consistent pattern of errors reveals that the subject is forming hypotheses, although these are incorrect. We consider it unthinking if the errors are random, and show no consistent pattern, and no orderly links between input and output. Again, the middle stage, the formation of hypotheses or the application of rules, is being omitted.

There are a number of different kinds of thinking which psychologists customarily distinguish. These distinctions are vaguely formulated, and poorly understood, although they might be important if only they could be formulated more precisely. Creative thinking is generally considered to be qualitatively different from non-creative thinking, but there is little agreement as to the exact nature of creative thought. Creative thought is usually characterized as intuitive, original and productive. The criterion of relevance is added to exclude responses which are random or goal-less. To some extent the distinction between creative and non-creative thought overlaps with the distinction between divergent and convergent thinking, and is often treated as synonymous with it. According to Butcher (1968) "convergent thinking is the kind required to solve a problem which has one definite right answer, whereas divergent thinking is more open-ended, less analytical, the kind of thinking needed to tackle a problem where there may be any number of more or less right answers, or no right answer at all". This definition is unsatisfactory in that it distinguishes types of problem rather than types of thought process, and the type of problem does not necessarily constrain the type of thinking. Convergent thinking is sometimes described as rational, logical thought which follows an orderly sequence, but clearly this kind of thinking could produce one of the possible solutions in an open-ended divergent-type problem, and the solution so produced might be judged highly creative. A scientific break-through, or a technical innovation is quite likely to be of this kind. While it is hardly possible to be original or creative in solving a problem that has only one right answer, such as a crossword puzzle clue, the correct solution may be obtained by an intuitive hunch, without step-by-step logical reasoning. In this case, what Butcher would call a convergent problem can be solved by divergent-type thinking. In fact we are dealing with three different variables: creativity, which is a judgement made about the type of solution; open-endedness, which is a characteristic of the problem; and convergence/divergence, which is a description of the type of thinking involved in solving the problem. These three factors may be combined in various ways.

The prevailing conceptual confusion is mirrored in the experi-mental tests, and attempts to measure creativity have produced results which bear little relation to everyday usage of the term. Getzels and Jackson (1962) measured the ability to produce numerous and novel word associations, to think up bizarre uses for a paper-clip, to detect simple geometric shapes embedded in complex figures, and to invent endings for stories. These kinds of test are open to two major criticisms. Firstly, individuals who are generally agreed to be "creative", in the ordinary language sense of the term, like scientists, architects and composers, do not score especially well (Vernon, 1970). Secondly, although the novelty of responses to word associa-tion or story completion tests is easy enough to measure, the relevance, meaningfulness or appropriateness of these responses is not at all easy to judge objectively. Without some agreed criterion for relevance, there is no border-line between the originality of the genius and of the madman. The criteria we tend to apply are socially and culturally determined, and the controversial status of much of modern art attests to the changeable and subjective nature of our judgement. Work on creativity is a good illustration of one of the cardinal rules of cognitive psychology—that no experiments, however well designed and rigorously carried out, will clarify a confused and ill-defined concept.

Attempts to define intuitive or divergent thinking are also not very illuminating. Bruner (1960) writes "Intuitive thinking characteristi-cally does not advance in careful well-planned steps ... the thinker arrives at an answer, which may be right or wrong, with little, if any, awareness of the process by which he reached it". The product is a guess, a hunch, a flash of insight; the process is not conscious, not available to introspection, and not under voluntary control. We use some rather quaint analogies in trying to describe intuition, of which one of the most popular is the chicken farm analogy. Following a period of preparation (or egg collection?), a period of incubation is assumed to occur, after which ideas hatch out. Alternatively, intuition involves "mulling" ideas like claret. Both analogies suggest a spontaneous change occurring passively over time. This incubating or mulling stage is usually envisaged as being sandwiched between preparatory and judgemental stages which are rational and conscious. There does not, however, seem to be any compelling reason to suppose that intuitive thinking and rational, conscious thinking must be separate stages of a sequential process. Neisser (1963) suggests that the two kinds of thinking co-occur simultaneously:

> human thinking is a multiple activity ... a number of more or less independent trains of thought usually co-exist. Obviously, however, there is a 'main sequence' in progress dealing with some particular material in a step-by-step fashion. The main sequence corresponds to the ordinary course of consciousness. It may or may not be directly influenced by the other processes going on simultaneously. The concurrent operations are not conscious, because consciousness is intrinsically single.

If Neisser's view is correct, then attempts to characterize the thinking involved in a particular task as convergent or divergent, logical or intuitive, are misconceived, since a combination of both may be operating simultaneously.

On the whole our efforts to classify and define different kinds of thinking have not been very successful. The haziness which attends the concept of intuitive thought is made particularly obvious in the field of computer simulation (Chapter 7) where it becomes apparent that we cannot simulate intuitive thought processes because they are insufficiently understood. In Chapter 8 a similar obscurity surrounds the intuitive thought processes which are supposed to be a speciality of the right cerebral hemisphere.

The remainder of this chapter examines the cognitive capacities and limitations of thinkers who lack normal verbal language, and the kinds of thinking that can be carried on without verbalization.

II. THINKING WITHOUT LANGUAGE; THINKING WITH LANGUAGE DISORDERS

A. The Deaf

Some of the factors which make it difficult to evaluate the cognitive abilities of the deaf were noted in Chapter 2. The cognitive limitations of the deaf ought, in theory, to define a border-line between alingustic thought, and thinking that can only be accomplished by means of verbal language, but many factors prevent such a neat demarcation from emerging. As we noted, the deaf are not a very homogeneous group, because they have differing degrees of hearing loss, incurred at different ages, and have been exposed to different methods of education designed to inculcate some facility in oral language, or in manual language, with variable success. Because it is difficult to judge how far the deaf lack language, it is not possible to conclude that tasks which can be performed successfully by the deaf are tasks that do not require the use of language. Where cognitive limitations are apparent, they cannot necessarily be attributed to language handicap. By comparison with normals, deaf subjects may be less well educated, more emotionally disturbed, poorly motivated in test situations, distractable, and unable to understand the test requirements. All these factors, in addition to language deficiencies, may depress cognitive performance. Further problems arise in selecting suitable control groups with which to compare deaf subjects. If deaf children are matched with normal controls on chronological age, the deaf almost inevitably are disadvantaged by their educational retardation. If, instead, the deaf subjects are equated with normals on selected intelligence tests, this procedure may have the effect of ironing-out real differences between the deaf and hearing populations.

Oléron (1953) accepts the view that the deaf are "inferior to those with normal hearing, particularly in the domain of abstract mental activities". The findings he cites in support of this statement are mainly drawn from the results of sorting tasks. Although there is surprisingly widespread acceptance of performance on sorting tasks as a reflection of conceptual thinking, and an index of intellectual ability and capacity for abstract thought, some doubts may be felt about the validity of this test, and the criteria for "abstraction" are confused. When a subject is asked to arrange a set of objects into groups, groupings may reflect preferences, rather than the presence or absence of concepts. We cannot always infer what categories are being used in group formation, so that a given group may reflect either several small categories (e.g. toys and utensils) or a single large category (e.g. inanimate objects). The criteria for "abstraction" as used by different researchers may include any of the following.

1. The extraction of salient features (e.g. shape).
2. The use of superordinate classes (e.g. animals).

3. The use of classes which do not have common perceptual features (e.g. tools).
4. The ability to re-classify items into different groupings by new criteria.
5. The ability to explain the principles of classification that were used.

Oléron reports that the deaf have difficulty in shifting from one sorting principle to another, although they are able to make the shift if given hints from the experimenter. He also noted that when required to explain their sorting principles in writing, they used specific, concrete labels (like "blue") rather than conceptual class labels (like "colour"), and he regards this as a failure of abstraction. It seems doubtful, though, whether Oléron is justified in regarding the explanatory powers of his deaf subjects as evidence of conceptual limitations, rather than as linguistic limitations. It is difficult to interpret his results, since his deaf subjects must have had some linguistic proficiency if they were able to supply written explanations of their responses. The conclusion that their abstract thinking is defective does not, in any case, seem compelling.

Furth (1966) has maintained that the intellectual functioning of the deaf is only inferior in certain specific tasks, which are normally mediated by language, but that basic intellectual capacities such as conceptual thinking, abstraction and generalization do not depend on language, and so are not impaired by deafness. He goes so far as to assert "logical intelligent thinking does not need the support of a symbol system". This assertion is surprising in view of the facts that his deaf subjects do fail some logical tests, and that they are not wholly without a symbolic system. The poor performances of deaf subjects on a "Pick the opposite" task, and the difficulty they experience in remembering temporal sequences are ascribed to lack of language, since Furth considers that these tasks require verbal mediation. The failure of deaf children to understand the conservation of quantity and liquids until about 5 years later than normal children is attributed to intellectual retardation and cultural deprivation, rather than to language handicap, since the older deaf children perform correctly without any appreciable improvement in linguistic skill. In fact, Furth's claim that the deaf are not intellectually handicapped becomes virtually self-validating if any observed deficits can be attributed either to lack of verbal mediation, or to cognitive retardation. Furth's interpretation of the results of tests of logical reasoning is also questionable. His tests explored the ability to understand and use logical symbols. One of these tests is strikingly similar

Operation	Symbol	Instance	Response
Negation	$\bar{O}$	■●	−
Conjunction	O·△	▲	−
Simplification	△	■▲	+
Disjunction "Simple"	O/△	▲	+
Disjunction "Exclusive"	O/△	▲●	−
Disjunction "Addition"	O/△	▲■	+
Conjunction (1 negation)	$\bar{O}$·△	▲	+
Conjunction (2 negations)	$\bar{\triangle}$·$\bar{O}$	●	−
Negated conjunction	$\overline{\triangle·O}$	▲	+
Negated disjunction	$O\overline{/\triangle}$	■	+

Fig. 1. Sample of symbol, instance and response for ten types of logical operation.

to the task carried out by Premack's chimpanzee, Sarah, described in Chapter 4. Symbols for conjunction, disjunction and negation are combined with the symbols "B" for blue, and "R" for red, and applied appropriately to presentations of blue and red cards. (For example, B . R symbolizes "the blue card and the red card". B . R̄ symbolizes "the blue card and not the red card"). After learning these combinations, a transfer task was introduced, in which the logical connectives were combined with the symbols "C" (circular) and "D" (dark). On this transfer task only 11% of normal young children, and 64% of normal older children performed above chance level. All the deaf children failed. Clearly, the logical rule had nct been understood, since it could not be applied to a new situation. This result is especially odd in view of Sarah's record of 80% success on similar transfer tests. However, Furth tested a group of adult deaf subjects on the task shown in Fig. 1 and they learned to respond correctly, but the ability of the subjects to transfer these rules to novel stimuli was apparently not tested. Furth considers that this success is more significant than the failure of the deaf children on the transfer task, and still claims that no purely intellectual impairment is associated with deafness. His argument that logical thinking is independent of symbolization can hardly rest on these results, since the task did employ symbols. Perhaps Furth meant that logical reasoning can be mediated by visual symbols and does not depend on verbal ones. Even so, his deaf subjects do seem to have experienced more difficulty than normals, and to gloss over this difference is a doctrinaire rather than a genuinely scientific reaction.

The gap between the performance of deaf and normal subjects tends to widen as tasks increase in difficulty. It is still not easy to judge whether the deaf suffer from a general cognitive deficit, or whether it is their lack of language which penalizes the harder tasks more severely. The fact that the performance of the deaf continues to improve into adulthood, and responds to training, without a corresponding improvement in language, suggests that cognitive development is delayed, rather than blocked by deafness and is not wholly dependent on linguistic skills.

B. Aphasia and Schizophrenia

Groups such as aphasics, schizophrenics and sub-normals provide some further evidence for a partial independence of language and thinking. Lenneberg (1967) recorded that sub-normals may have I.Q.s as low as 30, and yet have adequate language. On the other hand, aphasics can perform at an average level on non-verbal visuo-spatial tests when their speech is grossly disordered, which suggests that cognitive functions are intact, and deficits are confined to tasks requiring verbal mediation. When Hughlings Jackson (1880) described an aphasic as "lame in thinking", he did not mean to imply that the intellect itself was impaired, but that its operation was hampered by the linguistic disorder, the absence of verbal crutches. Not all clinicians have agreed. Goldstein (1948) observed that aphasic patients showed the same kind of deviant performance on sorting tasks as the deaf. A similar difficulty in abstraction was revealed, according to Goldstein's criteria, by failure to shift to new principles of sorting, by rigid adherence to grouping by physical cues like colour and size, and by inability to classify objects by non-physical concepts such as function. Zangwill (1964) elects to discount Goldstein's findings, but allows that the performance of aphasic patients on non-verbal tests is probably well below their own pre-aphasic level, and that improvement in performance and language recovery frequently go hand in hand. The difficulty of devising a completely non-verbal task of sufficient complexity to be a really powerful test makes it hard to isolate a purely intellectual impairment in aphasics. Most high-level intellectual skills like playing chess, and solving mathematical problems normally involve verbal mediation, and, predictably, the performance of aphasics in these activities is depressed. The relationship of language and thought is obscured by the fact that we cannot estimate the degree of intellectual deterioration with any precision, nor specify the full extent of the language disturbance. Aphasics, like the deaf, are a mixed group, with varying degrees of impairment in comprehension and in speech (either or both), often associated with deficits in motor responses and in perception. When overt speech is disordered, it is not necessarily the case that inner speech is similarly disordered. The clinician observes malfunction in linguistic performance, but cannot guess how far linguistic competence is intact. And the psychologist cannot tell him whether the links between language and cognition exist at the level of performance, or at the level of competence.

Schizophrenic patients frequently have marked language abnormalities. Their speech has been described as "word salads". Even if syntactic structure is preserved, semantic constraints are commonly abandoned; seemingly unrelated words are juxtaposed; neologisms abound; and speech loses its communicative function, and becomes purely expressive (Stengel, 1964) and without relation to the context of utterance. In tests of comprehension, schizophrenics typically fail to make use of contextual constraints (Pavy, 1968). Although a low I.Q., declining with prolongation of the illness, is associated with schizophrenia, there is no abnormal divergence of verbal I.Q. and performance (non-verbal) I.Q., suggesting that intellectual and linguistic deterioration proceed concurrently (Payne, 1973). On memory-span tests, schizophrenics do not do well, and this may be due to a failure to recode single items into larger meaningful units. In a test of free recall, successive lists of words were presented, one word at a time. The words within each new list were increasingly related to each other, so that the amount of contextual constraint increased until the final list, in which the words formed a complete sentence. Whereas in normal subjects recall improved as the constraint increased, schizophrenic patients showed no improvement, and treated all the lists as if they were composed of unrelated words, instead of recoding into larger units. In sorting tasks, schizophrenic performance also seemed to reflect a memory deficit. They could sort items correctly according to one dimension (e.g. colour), but not when a second dimension (e.g. colour and size) had to be taken into account as well. They did better when they could see a "cue card", reminding them of the relevant dimensions. These memory defects could arise as a secondary consequence of failure to use verbal coding effectively. Another characteristic feature of schizophrenic thinking is over-inclusiveness. Category boundaries seem to be wider and less precise than in normals, so that, in object sorting, fewer and larger groups emerge; in word association tests, associates are distant and bizarre. We can surmise that in schizophrenia the kind of conceptual network described in Chapter 1 has loosened, and concepts are no longer tightly organized and strongly linked. Whether this breakdown is basically a linguistic one, which spills over to any tasks which are verbally mediated, or whether the breakdown is at a deeper conceptual level, which affects both verbal and non-verbal thinking, is not clear. It must also be remembered that these findings represent fairly crude generalizations made over various types of schizophrenia, and patients varying in pre-morbid I.Q., length of hospitalization and medication; and that general defects of attention and motivation present in schizophrenia are also reflected in the observed cognitive abnormalities.

C. Sociolinguistic Differences

A less extreme case of language handicap with cognitive conse-quences is alleged to exist in lower social classes (Bernstein, 1971). He noted that the verbal I.Q. of working-class boys was markedly depressed in relation to high non-verbal I.Q. scores, and distinguished between what he calls the "restricted code", predominant in the speech of the working class, and the "elaborated code", typical of the middle class. The restricted speech code is characterized by short sentences, little use of subordinate clauses, frequent shifts of topic and requests for reinforcement (You know?, You see?, O.K.?). The restricted code is very context-bound, draws on a limited number of alternatives, and is highly predictable. The elaborated code is much less predictable. The speaker selects from an extensive range of possible structures, the sentence structure is syntactically more complex, and speech is context-independent, so that informa-tion can successfully be communicated to others who do not share the knowledge and immediate percepts of the speaker. Bernstein considers that restricted-code users are severely handicapped educationally, because formal schooling requires the use of an elaborated code. The restricted code is unsuited for the exchange of information, and for the expression of abstract ideas, and results in a kind of learning which, according to Bernstein (1972), "never really gets inside to become integrated into pre-existing schemata", and "orients its speakers to a less complex conceptual hierarchy, and so to a low order of causality". These views have been strongly criticized by other linguists, who believe it is easy to underestimate the richness and versatility of working-class language, especially when data samples are collected by researchers who are not themselves members of the speech community being studied (Labov, 1966). Even if we accept that linguistic skill is impoverished in the lower social class, the educational consequences cited by Bernstein are entirely hypothetical. There is no empirical evidence that working-class boys are oriented to a low order of causality, whatever that may mean. The distinction between restricted and elaborated codes is in any case a performance distinction, and difference between the users of the two codes may be much less marked at the level of competence. Nevertheless, the fact that non-verbal I.Q. scores and verbal I.Q. scores diverge, with the non-verbal scores being less depressed, again suggests some degree of independence in the relation of language and thought.

D. Bilingualism

The study of bilingualism provides some interesting insights into possible relationships between language and thought. According to one theory, both languages are mapped on to a common, higher-order conceptual system. Operations of thinking take place within this abstract system, and are not identified with either language.

Although in Chapter 4 we noted some evidence that the content and organization of thought is influenced by the particular language being spoken by a bilingual, other studies of bilingual subjects have lent support to the view that thinking is essentially independent of language. Schank (1972) presents a model of natural language processing in which he postulates

> there exists a conceptual base that is interlingual, onto which linguistic structures in a given language map...People fluent in many languages can pass freely from one to another...what they are doing is invoking a package of mapping rules for a given language from the conceptual base. The conceptual base has in it the content of the thought that is being expressed.

Schank's conceptual base is very similar to the conceptual–propositional base of Anderson and Bower (1973) which stores knowledge received from all modalities, including images and any languages, and generates output in any form. The claim that each separate language of the bilingual speaker maps on to a common conceptual base needs some modification in the light of a distinction between two kinds of bilinguals, compound and co-ordinate. Lambert and Preston (1967) define compound bilinguals as those who learned both languages simultaneously, in the same contextual setting, and for whom the symbols of Language A and Language B map on to a single meaning, having exact equivalence. Co-ordinate bilinguals learn their two languages in separate contexts, and the symbols do not have exact semantic equivalence. While compound bilinguals conform to Schank's model in that both their languages have a common conceptual base, this is not true for co-ordinate bilinguals. In practice the compound/co-ordinate distinction is difficult to make. Precise details of the early language learning of bilinguals is not always available. It seems very unlikely that a compound bilingual could acquire all the lexical items of his two languages pairwise, in circumstances of complete parity. Moreover, the distinction hinges on two of the knottiest problems in cognitive psychology—the definition of meaning, and the identification of the relevant elements of context. Nevertheless, it may still be possible for some bilinguals to approximate more closely to the compound type, and others to the co-ordinate type. The distinction generates various predictions, and some of these are borne out by experimental findings. In cases of traumatic aphasia, patients classified as compound bilinguals are more likely to have both languages impaired. Co-ordinate bilinguals, whose two languages are less closely related, are more likely to exhibit specific impairment of a single language. The prediction that compound bilinguals should have greater facility in switching between languages has not been confirmed, and no differences in ease of switching have been detected. In a study which examined only compound bilinguals, Taylor (1971) analysed the responses in a free association test. Responses were predominantly in unilingual clusters, and the probability of switching was lower than for not switching, so that intra-language links were clearly stronger than cross-language links. However, when cross-language switches occurred these reflected semantic associations, which supports the view that cross-language linkage is at a semantic level. Further experiments have tested free recall of mixed-language word lists as compared with unilingual lists. The results are contradictory, and difficult to interpret. Predictions about the performance of bilinguals depend on theoretical assumptions about the mechanisms of storage and retrieval. Glanzer and Duarte (1971) found that lists of words with items repeated in a different language were recalled as well, or better, than lists with items repeated in the same language. A list containing, for example, "horse, neige, cheval, snow" is as easy to remember as "horse, snow, horse, snow". They concluded that in mixed-language lists, both versions of the repeated item were stored as a single meaning. Kolers (1965) also reported that mixed-language lists were better recalled, but Tulving and Colotla (1970) found that, although bi- and trilingual lists were recalled as well as unilingual lists from primary (short-term) memory, recall from secondary (long-term) memory was inferior. They concluded that the semantic organization which is typical of secondary memory is harder to establish for multilingual lists because inter-item links are weaker across language boundaries. One reason for discrepancies between these studies is that subjects may have differed along the compound–co-ordinate dimension.

Lambert and Preston (1967) used the Stroop test to find out how far the two languages of bilinguals are separated, and whether one can be "switched off" while the other is in operation. In the Stroop test, the subject's task is to name the colour of the ink in which a word is printed. When the word is itself the name of a different colour (e.g. the word "blue" written in red ink) the correct response of "red" is delayed by the interference generated by the conflicting word meaning. Lambert and Preston compared the performance of bilinguals naming the ink colour in Language A when the conflicting word was in Language B (saying "red" when the word was "jaune") and naming the ink colour in Language A when the word was in the same language (saying "red" when the word was "yellow"). If the two languages are stored separately, then the interference caused by conflicting information should be less if the conflicting inputs are in different languages, than when they are in the same language. The results showed that interference was reduced when the competing responses were in different languages, which implies a degree of separation, but the fact that some interference did occur in the mixed-language condition indicates that separation is not complete, and subjects could not switch off one language absolutely. To sum up, the experiments with bilinguals suggest that within-language links are stronger than across-language links, but that cross-language links exist, and are mainly at the semantic level, although there is clearly considerable variation between individuals in the way their languages are organized. The existence of high-level semantic links between language does not necessarily confirm the existence of an a-linguistic conceptual base on to which the different languages are mapped. These results are quite consistent with a system whereby the lexical items of the two languages are mapped directly on to each other. Some bilingual verification experiments of the kind described in Chapter 1 testing reaction times to statements like "A bird is *un oiseau*" or "A trout is *un poisson*" might help to shed more light on the semantic organization of the two languages, and show at what points in the semantic network the cross-language links are strongest. The futility of introspection as a source of enlightenment is beautifully, if unintentionally, illustrated by a quotation from George Steiner's *After Babel*. The multilingual Dr Steiner reports:

> From the earliest of memories, I proceeded within the unexamined cognition that ein Pferd, a horse, and un cheval were the same and/or very different or at diverse points of a modulation which led from perfect equivalence to disparity.

E. Cognitive Abilities of Non-human Primates

Studies of animal learning help to define the upper limits of cognitive processes in animals, and the extent of the gap between animal and human cognitive ability. Language is, of course, only one of many factors which contribute to the existence of this gap. Many of the tests employ tasks which penalize animals because they fall outside the naturally occurring repertoire of the animal's behaviour. Physical limitations may be compounded with intellectual ones if the perceptual and motor demands of the task are difficult for the animal to meet. Animals are especially disadvantaged in that the nature of the task cannot be directly communicated to them, and their previous experience may give little clue as to what is required. Because of these problems, we are not entitled to argue that deficits in animal cognition result from the absence of language, but we can point to the achievements of animal cognition as an indication of how effective non-linguistic thought can be. In this section a few studies of non-human primate learning are selected in which the animals solve quite complex problems with a surprising degree of success.

An excellent example of primate cognitive ability is provided by the studies of Viki, a chimpanzee home-reared as described by Hayes (1951). From shortly after birth, Viki's environment and experience were exactly the same as for a pre-school child. Viki did not succeed in learning language, so that her success with non-verbal tasks gives quite a clear indication of how far mental development can proceed independently of language, and how this compares with the performance of a young child. In a series of tests described by Hayes and Nissen (1971), Viki was presented with instrumentation and manipulation problems, similar to the practical problems reviewed in Chapter 3. Viki showed ability to adapt previous knowledge to new situations, and to utilize objects in the environment in new ways. She up-ended a rectangular box to raise a box-stack to the height needed to reach a suspended lure. She spontaneously replaced a defective hook on the rope of her swing by tying a knot, and profited from slight gestural "hints" indicating that box-opening problems could be solved, in one case by using scissors to cut a string, and in another, by inserting a crank into a hole and turning it. Her performance on these tasks was very similar to her child co-subjects, except that Viki did not benefit from seeing pictorial representations of the required responses, but only from the experimenter touching or pointing to the critical elements in the situation. Hayes and Nissen point out that the pictures may not have been meaningful for Viki. In a series of increasingly complex latch-box problems which required two-handed manipulation to depress springs, turn keys etc. her performance was as good as, or better than, the children, and showed rapid improvement through successive problems.

On some well controlled number perception tasks, Viki at the age of three-and-a-half performed at the same level as a three-and-a-half-year-old child. On a number-matching task, in which the card bearing the same number of spots as a target card had to be selected, her accuracy deteriorated as the number of spots increased, especially if the difference between alternative cards was only one spot. In a discrimination task requiring her to remember an absolute number of spots over a series of trials, and respond positively to corresponding cards, she broke down on the four spots *vs.* five spots discrimination. She also failed at a task requiring reproduction of a given number of temporally presented taps. In these tests, Viki's ability is equivalent to that of a child who has not yet learned to count. Children who can count verbally, and, oddly enough, birds, do better.

In concept-discrimination problems, Viki showed ability to discriminate between pictures of animate *vs.* inanimate items, male *vs.* female people, large *vs.* small objects, red *vs.* green, circles *vs.* crosses, and complete *vs.* incomplete pictures (e.g. a dog without legs). The accuracy of Viki's discrimination was within 5% of her child fellow subjects. In sorting tasks, an ingenious method was used to reveal the principles of classification Viki was employing by introducing ambiguous objects. When she was apparently sorting objects into eating tools and writing tools, Viki assigned wooden chopsticks with the writing set and a metal pen with the eating set. She was sorting by material, and not by function. Viki was also tested for "abstraction" as defined by the ability to re-classify the same objects in different ways. A set of buttons could be divided into 40 white and 40 black, or 40 large and 40 small, or 40 square and 40 round. Viki sorted the button collection first by colour, then by shape, and then by size. With other sets, Viki sometimes changed her sorting principle and re-classified spontaneously, sometimes in response to prompting. Viki does not appear to suffer from the rigidity and concreteness which some researchers have claimed to be characteristic of the deaf and aphasic, so that these defects of sorting behaviour do not necessarily stem from linguistic disabilities.

In a conditional matching task Viki achieved 88% accuracy. Pairs of objects had to be matched by colour if presented on a blue tray, and by shape if presented on a white tray. The task imposes considerable demands on memory and attention since the performer must remember the rule, and attend to two dimensions. Another task, which proved beyond Viki's powers, required her to learn arbitrary temporal sequences of string pulling. Eventually, she became distressed and attempts to teach her this task had to be abandoned. Hayes and Nissen noted that three-year-old children succeeded by verbalizing and chanting the sequences, and speculate that "language and sequence behaviour may be intimately related in that language development is dependent upon flexible re-ordering of the same units; and the sequence experience involved in using language may transfer to other sequencing situations". In corroboration, we have already noted that deaf children have difficulty in learning temporal sequences, and that Washoe's signs lack consistently meaningful ordering and other studies of primate learning have also reported very limited memory for sequential order.

It is a general feature of studies of primate learning that performance tends to break down when the memory load, or information processing load, is increased beyond a certain point. Jarrard and Moise (1971) reported that primates could judge two successively presented stimuli to be the same or different when the interval between them was less than 10 s, but response accuracy declined to chance level when the second stimulus was delayed by 30 s. It is reasonable to assume that the greatly superior performance of adult humans is boosted by verbal mediation, which assists them to bridge longer delays. Weinstein (1941) compared four-year-old rhesus monkeys, and three-year-old children, on a delayed matching-to-sample task. A sample object was presented for matching and handling, and then removed. After a delay of 5, 10 or 15 s, choice objects were presented and the subject had to select the one which matched the sample. Both children and monkeys reached an 80% correct criterion at all delays, but showed signs of stress at the longer delay, and the monkeys required more than ten times as many training trials as the children. In classical delayed response experiments, food is placed in one of two identical containers, which are then covered, and after a delay the animal is permitted to make a choice response. Performance on these tasks declines sharply as the delay is increased, but critical delay intervals cannot be taken as an accurate reflection of the duration of the animal's memory, because of the many other variables which govern delayed responses. These include the presence of spatial cues or other perceptual cues, orienting responses made by the animal, motivation, activity and distractability during the delay. The characteristics of the trial sequence are also an important factor. The animal may perform better if the location of the food can be predicted on the basis of previous trials, and find the task more difficult if location is randomly varied from trial to trial. Because there are so many determining factors, different critical delays emerge with different experimental paradigms, different species, and different individuals (Tinklepaugh, 1928). In more natural settings, animals are observed to locate buried food after intervals of days, rather than seconds, so that although experimental procedures yield estimates that compare unfavourably with human memory, they may not be a valid index of the capacity and duration of animal memory.

The ability of primates to learn rules implies that quite complex internal representations must be formed and stored, but little can be inferred about the nature of these representations. Harlow's (1949) studies of problem-to-problem transfer effects revealed that training on a set of problems of one type improved proficiency at learning new problems of the same type. The monkeys' performance over successive problems exhibited a phenomenon Harlow called "learning to learn" or the formation of a "learning set". Typically, the number of trials required to learn a discrimination response shows a dramatic and orderly decrease over successive problems, even though the specific stimuli and the critical cues are changed or reversed. The improvement is not a temporary phenomenon. Braun *et al.* (1952) found that learning sets were retained over a period as long as 8 weeks. What is the nature of cognitive change that takes place when a learning set is formed? According to Harlow, inappropriate error-producing response tendencies are being eliminated. Levine (1965) has derived a Hypothesis Model from a mathematical analysis of patterns of responses. According to this model, the animal progressively adopts a hypothesis, H, which is a mediating process or rule, having general applicability to a group of problems. Examples of hypotheses include a position-alternation rule (e.g. choose the left-hand object on trial n and the right-hand object on trial $n + 1$, in a LRLRLR sequence), or a Win–Stay–Lose–Shift rule (repeat the response if it was rewarded on the previous trial, change the response if it was not rewarded). Some evidence for hypothesis learning comes from an analysis of double alternation problems, in which the correct sequence of responses is LLRRLLRR etc. Systematic patterns of responding can be observed at an early stage, before the correct sequence has been fully mastered. Some of Harlow's monkeys also succeeded in learning a generalized oddity rule, that is, they learned to choose the odd item out of three, two of which were the same and one different, and transferred the principle successfully to new groups of items.

By comparison with adult humans, primates learn very slowly, and require arduous step-by-step training programmes; not all individuals succeed, and learning is less flexible once established. By comparison with pre-linguistic children their cognitive abilities are scarcely inferior. Problems in which humans normally employ verbal mediation, such as learning sequences, delayed matching and counting, appear to be especially difficult for primates. It is a reasonable conclusion that verbalization improves retention, and reduces the information load. How far the achievements of primates can be considered to exemplify "thinking" depends, of course, on how thinking is defined. Probably Viki's performance on the instrumental tasks, and Harlow's rule-learning experiments come closest to the definition of thinking discussed at the beginning of this chapter. There is plenty of evidence that primates possess many of the components of thinking such as memory, some forms of abstraction, concepts, the ability to learn and apply rules and to make judgements, but there is relatively little evidence of the prolonged goal-directed covert mental activity, or of the sequential chains of inferences, that are typical of human reasoning.

F. Cognitive Development in Children

In the course of development a child changes from being a non-linguistic animal to being a linguistic animal, but the expectation that the acquisition of language should produce a clear transformation in cognitive development proves to be naive, and objective causal links between increasing mastery of language and enhanced cognitive ability are elusive. Both theoretical and descriptive accounts of the cognitive development of children are controversial. There is disagreement on the nature of the successive stages, on how far the sequence of development is fixed or variable, and especially on the relative influence of maturation, experience and language. While the view that cognitive development is causally dependent on language development has long been questioned, the opposite hypothesis, which has recently achieved some currency, that basic cognitive structures must be acquired before language can be learned, is also hard to justify empirically. In fact, both those who stress the primacy of language, and those who stress the primacy of cognition, rely on appeals to intuition in the absence of conclusive experimental evidence. In the normal child, cognitive development occurs in parallel with maturation, with increasing experience and education, and with improving linguistic skills, and it is impossible to determine the effect of any one of these factors in isolation. Attempts to establish unidirectional causal links take the form of trying to show the temporal, or logical, priority of either thought or language. Some of these efforts are discussed below.

Macnamara (1972) argues that some cognitive structures are a necessary pre-requisite for the acquisition of language, at least in the early stages. These arguments are mainly of an intuitive kind. For instance, it is suggested that a child could not learn to apply a name to an object, unless he already has a concept of the object. According to this view the child could not learn the correct referents of lexical labels without falling victim to the impasse described by Quine in *Word and Object* (1960). Quine argues that a linguist trying to learn a strange language could not know whether a term like "rabbit" referred to the animal, or some part or attribute of the animal, or some co-occurring feature of the scene. For the child (and, indeed, for the linguist) this problem can be resolved if he is equipped with perceptual biases and constraints similar to those of the rest of the speech community, so that what is perceptually salient for other observers will also tend to be salient for him, and, secondly, with a general inductive learning strategy which allows him to generalize across instances, and to modify or correct his hypotheses in accordance with feedback. If he initially infers that "rabbit" refers to any small furry animal, his misapplications of the term will be corrected, and his overgeneralization will eventually be cut back until his use of the label is confined to acceptable instances. In Chapter 6, evidence that just this kind of strategy does operate in children's concept learning is discussed. Whatever the cognitive basis required for learning the referents of lexical labels, it is clearly also possessed by the chimpanzee linguists. More sophisticated cognitive precursors are required, according to Macnamara, for learning syntax. For example, he states "the child must use his non-linguistic knowledge to arrive at the notions of direct and indirect object". Before he can understand the difference between "John drove the car" and "John drove home", he must understand the nature of the objects and actions mentioned. Similarly, he cannot understand tense usage until he has acquired some understanding of the concept of time. Bruner (1975) has stressed the role of early experience in non-verbal communication and signalling, whereby the child comes to understand concepts such as agent, action, object and recipient, which later emerge in language as case-forms. The intuitive appeal of these arguments receives experimental support from a study by Moeser and Bregman (1973) who found adult subjects unable to learn the syntactic rules of an artificial language, unless they were shown pictured referents for the symbols which provided a semantic basis for learning. If we accept these indications of the primacy of cognitive bases in some of the initial stages of language learning, it is not necessarily true of all the later stages, since many aspects of language which are purely formal and arbitrary, and have no semantic force (such as noun gender in some languages), are nevertheless mastered successfully. The current emphasis on cognitive pre-requisites for language learning comes as a corrective to the imbalance created by the nativist theories of language acquisition, which have tended to treat language as a separate faculty developing independently of cognition. Both are in contrast with the views that were expressed by Vygotsky (1962), which describe the interactive development of thought and language in a complex reciprocal relationship. Vygotsky considered that language and thought originate independently in the very young child. The earliest "thinking" (as, for example, the mental activity involved in reaching for and handling objects) is non-verbal, and the earliest speech is social or emotional, but not intellectual. At the age of about two, thought and language become linked, and for the next few years this interaction is overtly demonstrated in the phenomenon of egocentric speech. Children of this age talk aloud to themselves, as well as communicating with others. The child gives himself instructions, and cautions, or acts out imagined stories. This regulative function of speech is observable in some aphasic patients as well as in young children (Luria, 1967). Vygotsky believed that, at a later stage of development, around seven years of age, this egocentric speech is internalized, and comes to resemble the inner speech of adults, overt speech being restricted to social utterances. The stages of development may not be so clear-cut as Vygotsky represented them. It is quite possible that much of the child's thinking is carried on by means of internal language at an age when egocentric speech is still occurring. The use of egocentric speech by the child may be seen as a form of language-play, rather than as being due to the inability to internalize, and the dropping of egocentric speech is perhaps due to social sanctions, and growing self-consciousness, rather than marking a new stage of cognitive development. In private, egocentric speech persists a good deal later than the age of seven, and is not so very unusual in adults. However, Vygotsky's interpretation is consistent with the observation that egocentric speech changes in character, becoming more elliptical and idiosyncratic before it disappears, in a way that is typical of adult inner speech. Piaget's theory that egocentric speech simply atrophies, and is replaced by social speech (Flavell, 1963), is not so easily reconciled with this observation. Although Vygotsky believed that thought and language merge in inner speech, he maintained "the two processes are not identical, and there is no rigid correspondence between the units of thought and speech". He pointed out that the distinction between a thought and the language in which it is expressed is subjectively apparent when we become aware of a discrepancy, of having failed to capture a thought, and crystallize it in the right linguistic form. Thought and language are still separable in the adult, since thought can be non-verbal, and language unthinking.

Experimental efforts to reinforce the "primacy of cognition" hypothesis aim to show that children can think before they can talk; or can perform a cognitive task before they know the terms in which it would be verbally mediated, if it were verbally mediated; or before they have acquired the habit of verbal mediation; or before they can verbally explain how they do the task. One obvious weakness with this approach is that even when the relevant verbal skills are not overtly present, some rudimentary form of internal verbalization could be available. And, conversely, the presence of well developed verbal skills does not guarantee that a given task is verbally mediated. Adherents of the "primacy of language" hypothesis cite tasks which are performed poorly by children before language is well established, and performed better when language learning is more advanced. The objection to comparisons between subjects with different levels of linguistic skill is that the children who do better are not only better linguists; they are also older and more experienced, with improved memory spans, less distractability, higher motivation and better understanding of the task requirements. In practice, developmental comparisons are just as muddy as the cross-cultural comparisons discussed in the last chapter.

Instead of expounding the major theoretical views on cognitive development, an undertaking which would be beyond the scope of this chapter, some of the tasks that have figured in controversy about the role of language in cognition are selected for discussion. Conservation tasks provide an illustration of the way in which essentially the same empirical findings can be variously interpreted according to the particular theoretical axe which is being ground. In a typical conservation experiment, a child is shown two identical containers, A and B, filled with identical quantities of liquid. The child watches while the liquid in container B is transferred to a third container, C, which is taller and thinner. Below the age of about 8 years, children tend to judge the quantities in A and C to be unequal, and most often state that C, which has the higher level, contains more. For the purposes of the present discussion, the crucial issue is whether the incorrect response is cognitive or linguistic in origin. Piaget and his followers take the view that cognitive development unfolds as a result of the child's experience and interaction with his environment, and that increasing linguistic skill reflects, rather than promotes, cognitive growth. Although he allows that logical reasoning is facilitated by language, language itself cannot bring about understanding of logical principles. Failure in conservation tasks is attributed mainly to the child's inability to grasp the principle of invariance, and to understand that quantities remain unchanged over perceptual transformations. At this age, judgement is dominated by perception rather than by logic. Intervention studies, in which attempts are made to educate the child's judgement by various training procedures, have been used to try to reveal the key factors in the development of conservation. Empirical support for Piaget's interpretation rests on the evidence that training in the use of the relevant linguistic terms (more, same as, bigger than etc.) does not improve performance (Sinclair-de-Zwart, 1969). On the other hand, extensive practical training in variations of the task carried out by Smedslund (1961) also had little facilitating effect. Bruner et al. (1966) suggest that a child has three cognitive modes of representation. The earliest is the enactive mode, which codes actions; the iconic mode is based on internalized perceptions or images; and the verbal or symbolic mode is acquired last. The enactive and iconic modes predominate in the cognition of the younger child. According to their theory, erroneous judgements in conservation tasks are made because attention is focused on perceptual aspects. In the conservation task, the symbolic systems "knows" that the liquid is the same after being poured into the new container, but the iconic system insists that it is different, and the iconic system dominates the response. Bruner's group showed that if the perceptual differences were concealed from the child by a screen which allowed him to see the pouring take place, but not the resulting discrepant levels, he was shielded from misleading perceptions and was more likely to judge correctly that the quantity of liquid poured from one container to another remained the same. While Piaget maintains that the child lacks the necessary understanding, Bruner believes that the principle of conservation is understood, but is overridden by conflicting evidence, so that correct conservation responses emerge only if the perceptual evidence is weakened, or later when the verbal system becomes stronger. In spite of Sinclair-de-Zwart's results, there is some evidence that linguistic confusions are linked to non-conservation. Donaldson and Balfour (1968) studied young children who used "more" and "less" synonymously to mean "not the same as", and whose behavioural responses were similarly confused. They suggested that an underlying competence at a conceptual level is lacking, and that its absence is reflected in both language and behaviour. Correct non-verbal conservation responses can, however, be elicited before linguistic usage has conformed to the established norms. Cohen (1967), in a tea-table experiment, found that four-and-a-half-year-old children who were asked to share out quantities "fairly" were extremely zealous and accurate in compensating for the differences in the shape of the containers provided, although a matched group of children gave the typical erroneous verbal responses in the standard Piagetian versions of the task. This experiment illustrates an important but neglected fact about the concept of invariance. In everyday life, invariance is not a golden rule of logic which, once understood, will serve in any situation. It is a convention which applies in some contexts and not in others. Some objects conventionally retain their identity over perceptual transformations, others do not. A given object after transformation may sometimes be considered identical, and sometimes different, depending on the context, and on the linguistic description which is applied. Green and Laxon (1970), in their delightful paper, *Conservation of number, mother, water and a fried egg chez l'enfant,* point out that quite young infants are able to grasp that mothers and eggs remain invariant over changes of clothing and cooking. But a set of bricks is a tower when the child has built it up, and not when he has knocked it down again. The family puppy, under the description of Fido, retains his identity in spite of changes in size and appearance as he grows older; but when he is described as "the puppy", invariance is not preserved. Learning about invariance is not so much like learning an abstract concept, as like learning a rule of thumb. Decisions about invariance depend on knowing whether the unchanged aspects are more important than the changed aspects, and the child has to learn to extract this information from the context. The acquisition of conservation is liable to be a piece-meal affair, and to involve the gradual accretion of inductive evidence from a variety of different contexts. In Green and Laxon's view "the child learns about quantities of liquid from Baconian experiments conducted in the bath, sink or gutter", a method they describe elsewhere as "suck it and see". To make correct conservation judgements, the child has to learn specific conventions of invariance, rather than an abstract principle; and in order to make correct verbal responses in conservation tasks, he has to learn to apply linguistic terms like "more" and "same" in accordance with these conventions.

Exponents of the verbal mediation hypothesis claim that age-related changes in performance on transposition tasks reflect a growing verbal skill and increasing reliance on verbal mediation. Kuenne (1946) found that four-year-old children, who learned to respond to the larger of two stimuli, could select the larger member of a new pair only when the new stimuli were not much different in size. Older children could select the larger member of a new pair even when these were very different from the originals. She inferred that younger children could not respond in terms of the relation "larger than", and transpose this to the new stimuli, because they lacked the necessary verbal coding. Several horses and carts have since been driven through this interpretation. If younger children are given an initial training with more than one example of a stimulus pair, then they can successfully transfer a relational response to new pairs that are very different in size. Furthermore, relational responding has been elicited in non-linguistic species such as rats, so it clearly does not depend on verbal mediation.

In many tasks, knowing the relevant linguistic terms is by no means a sufficient condition of success. In sorting tasks, the age-related shift from grouping objects by physical features (colour, size

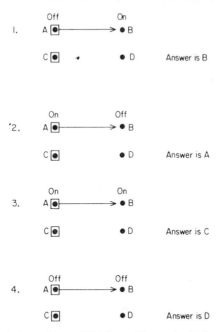

Fig. 2. The light-switch problem. Which position of which switch brings on the light?

etc.), to grouping by function (toys, clothes, things to eat etc.) occurs without any discernibly relevant growth in vocabulary. In an extremely neat experiment, Huttenlocher (1963) confronted 6–12-year-old children with a light-switch problem and found significant age differences. The children saw two light switches, each of which had two possible positions, and a light bulb which was either on or off. From changing the position of one switch only, the children were required to decide how the light was turned on. The problem varies in difficulty through four possible sequences produced by the switch movement (see Fig. 2). Version 1 (Off–On) is easiest. Moving the top switch from A to B brings on the light. In Version 2 (On–Off), moving the top switch from A to B turns off the light, so the child must infer that the initial position A turned on the light. In Version 3 (On–On), the light stays on after moving the top switch from A to B, hence the present position of the other switch must turn on the light. In Version 4 (Off–Off), the light stays off after moving the top switch from A to B, so the other switch must need to be in its other position to bring on the light. Performance varied with the number of steps of reasoning required for solution. The younger children could do the easier versions, but not the harder ones. Although all the children had adequate command of language to formulate the problem, the younger ones could not hold all the relevant information in memory. Memory capacity also emerges as the critical factor in Bryant and Trabasso's (1971) study of young children's performance on transitivity tasks. Piaget *et al.* (1960) reported that after making two length comparisons, A > B and B > C, children below eight years were unable to infer the relationship of A and C. Bryant and Trabasso demonstrated that this failure was not due to either logical incompetence, or linguistic incompetence, but to the inability to retain the information from the original comparisons in memory. With more extensive training, so that the A > B and B > C relations were thoroughly memorized, the four-year-olds could make the correct inference. In some tasks younger children are penalized not only by their poorer memory capacities, but also by the lack of appropriate problem-solving heuristics. Mosher (1962) tested children's performance in a game similar to *Twenty Questions*, and concluded that younger children did not use optimal strategies for seeking and organizing information. Older children asked constraint-locating questions, and accumulated information in an organized sequence. The younger children asked very specific questions such that negative answers yielded little information. They behaved like a player who instead of starting the game by asking "Is it inanimate?", starts by asking "Is it the bottom waistcoat button on the statue of Nelson in Trafalgar Square?". It is hard to judge whether this is because young children do not have their concepts arranged in hierarchies, or because they have not learned the techniques of moving through these hierarchies by successive bifurcations.

The fact that emerges most clearly from these studies of children is that cognitive development has many components: memory, attention, experience and cognitive heuristics are all implicated as well as language. Although the relationship of language and thought proves so complex and confusing, by drawing on the evidence from all the various sources reviewed in this chapter, and in the preceding one, we can advance some tentative conclusions. Language is not a sufficient condition of intellectual success, but the thinker without language is cognitively disabled. Language enables the user to formulate abstract concepts, hypotheses and inferences, rules and general principles at a level of complexity unattainable by the non-linguistic thinker. Language allows the thinker to rehearse mentally, to direct and maintain his attention, and to arrange information in ordered sequences and nested hierarchies. The difference between thinking without language, and thinking with language is rather like the difference between doing mathematical calculations with an abacus, and with a sophisticated electronic calculator. Perhaps the most important advantage conferred by language is that it enables us to acquire information not just from our own personal experiences, but from the accumulated experience of the other past and present language users, giving us access to the entire knowledge pool of our generation.

REFERENCES

Anderson, J. R. and Bower, G. H. (1973). "Human Associative Memory". Winston-Wiley, Washington and New York.

Bernstein, B. B. (1971). "Class Codes and Control", Paladin, St. Albans.

Bernstein, B. B. (1972). A sociolinguistic approach to socialization with some reference to educability. *In* "Directions in Sociolinguistics" (J. J. Gumperz and D. Hymes, eds). Holt, Rinehart and Winston, New York.

Braun, H. W., Patton, R. A. and Barnes, H. W. (1952). Effects of electro-shock convulsions upon learning performance of monkeys: I. Object-quality discrimination learning. *Journal of Comparative Physiological Psychology* 45, 231–238.

Bruner, J. S. (1960). "The Process of Education". Harvard University Press.

Bruner, J. S. (1974–1975). From communication to language: a psychological perspective. *Cognition* 3 (3), 255–287.

Bruner, J. S., Olver, R. R. and Greenfield, P. M. (1966). "Studies in Cognitive Growth". John Wiley and Sons, New York.

Bryant, P. H. and Trabasso, T. (1971). Transitive inferences and memory in young children. *Nature, Lond.* 232, 456–458.

Butcher, H. J. (1968). "Human Intelligence, its Nature and Assessment". Methuen, London.

Cohen, G. (1967). Conservation of quantity in children: the effect of vocabulary and participation. *Quarterly Journal of Experimental Psychology* 19, 150–154.

Craik, K. J. W. (1943). "The Nature of Explanation". Cambridge University Press, Cambridge.

Donaldson, M. and Balfour, G. (1968). Less is more: a study of language comprehension in children. *British Journal of Psychology* 59, 461–471.

Flavell, J. H. (1963). "The Developmental Psychology of Jean Piaget". Van Nostrand, Princeton, New Jersey.

Furth, H. G. (1966). "Thinking without Language". The Free Press, New York.

Getzels, J. W. and Jackson, P. W. (1962). "Creativity and Intelligence". Wiley, New York.

Glanzer, M. and Duarte, A. (1971). Repetition between and within languages in free recall. *Journal of Verbal Learning and Verbal Behaviour* 10, 625–630.

Goldstein, K. (1948). "Language and Language Disturbances". Grune and Stratton, New York.

Green, R. T. and Laxon, V. J. (1970). The conservation of number, mother, water and a fried egg chez l'enfant. *Acta Psychologica* 32, 1–30.

Harlow, H. F. (1949). The formation of learning sets. *Psychological Review* 56, 51-65.

Hayes, C. (1951). "The Ape in our House". Harper, New York.

Hayes, K. J. and Nissen, C. H. (1971). Higher mental functions of a home-raised chimpanzee. *In* "Behaviour of Nonhuman Primates" (A. M. Schrier and F. Stollnitz, eds), Vol. 4. Academic Press, New York and London.

Hughlings-Jackson, J. (1880). On aphasia with left hemiplegia. *Lancet* 1, 637-638.

Huttenlocher, J. (1963). Growth and the organization of inference. Centre for Cognitive Studies Annual Report, Cambridge, Massachusetts.

Jarrard, L. and Moise, S. (1971). Short term memory in the monkey. *In* "Cognitive Processes of Nonhuman Primates" (L. Jarrard, ed.). Academic Press, London and New York.

Kolers, P. A. (1965). Bilingualism and bicodalism. *Language and Speech* 8, 122-126.

Kuenne, M. R. (1946). Experimental investigation of the relation of language to transposition behaviour in young children. *Journal of Experimental Psychology* 36, 471-490.

Labov, W. (1966). "The Social Stratification of English in New York City". Center for Applied Linguistics, Washington, D.C.

Lambert, W. E. and Preston, M. S. (1967). The interdependencies of the bilingual's two languages. *In* "Research in Verbal Behaviour and Some Neurophysiological Implications" (K. Salzinger and S. Salzinger, eds). Academic Press, New York and London.

Lenneberg, E. (1967). "Biological Foundations of Language". Wiley, New York.

Levine, M. (1965). Hypothesis behaviour. *In* "Behaviour of Nonhuman Primates" (A. M. Schrier, H. F. Harlow and F. Stollnitz, eds), Vol. 1. Academic Press, London and New York.

Luria, A. R. (1967). The regulative function of speech in its development and dissolution. *In* "Research in Verbal Behaviour and Some Neurophysiological Implications" (K. Salzinger and S. Salzinger, eds). Academic Press, New York and London.

Macnamara, J. (1972). The cognitive basis of language learning in infants. *Psychological Review* 79, 1-13.

Moeser, S. D. and Bregman, A. S. (1973). Imagery and language acquisition. *Journal of Verbal Learning and Verbal Behaviour* 12, 91-98.

Mosher, F. A. (1962). Strategies for information gathering. Paper read at the Eastern Psychological Association, Atlantic City, New Jersey.

Neisser, U. (1963). The multiplicity of thought. *British Journal of Psychology* 54, 1-14.

Oléron, P. (1953). Conceptual thinking of the deaf. *American Annals of the Deaf* 98, 304-310.

Pavy, D. (1968). Verbal behaviour in schizophrenia: a review of recent studies. *Psychological Bulletin* 70, 164-178.

Payne, R. W. (1973). Cognitive abnormalities. *In* "Handbook of Abnormal Psychology" (J. J. Eysenck, ed.) 2nd edition. Pitman and Sons, Belfast.

Piaget, J., Inhelder, B. and Szemihska, A. (1960). "The Child's Conception of Geometry". Routledge and Kegan Paul, London.

Posner, M. I. (1973). "Cognition: An Introduction". Scott, Foresman and Co., Glenview, Illinois.

Quine, W. V. O. (1960). "Word and Object". Wiley, New York.

Ryle, G. (1949). "The Concept of Mind". Barnes and Noble, New York.

Schank, R. C. (1972). Conceptual dependency: a theory of natural language understanding. *Cognitive Psychology* 3, 552-631.

Sinclair-de-Zwart, H. (1969). Developmental psycholinguistics. *In* "Studies in Cognitive Development" (D. Elkind and J. Flavell, eds). Oxford University Press, New York.

Smedslund, J. (1961). Acquisition of conservation of substance and weight in children. *Journal of Scandinavian Psychology* 2, 71-84.

Steiner, G. (1975). "After Babel: Aspects of Language and Translation". Oxford University Press, Oxford.

Stengel, E. (1964). Speech disorders and mental disorders. *In* "Disorders of Language" (A. V. S. de Reuck and M. O'Connor, eds), CIBA symposium. Churchill, London.

Taylor, I. (1971). How are words from two languages organized in bilinguals' memory? *Canadian Journal of Psychology* 25, 228-240.

Tinklepaugh, O. L. (1928). An experimental study of representative factors in monkeys. *Journal of Comparative Psychology* 8, 197-202.

Tulving, E. and Colotla, V. A. (1970). Free recall of trilingual lists. *Cognitive Psychology* 1, 86-98.

Vernon, P. E. (1970). "Creativity". Penguin, Harmondsworth, Middlesex.

Vygotsky, L. S. (1962). "Thought and Language". MIT Press, Cambridge, Massachusetts. (First published in 1934).

Weinstein, B. (1941). Matching from sample by rhesus monkeys and by children. *Journal of Comparative Psychology* 31, 195.

Zangwill, O. L. (1964). Intelligence in aphasia. *In* "Disorders of Language" (A. V. S. de Reuck and M. O'Connor, eds), CIBA symposium. Churchill, London.

6

Concepts and Concept Formation

Until recently, work on concept formation provided a prime target for many common criticisms of cognitive psychology, since it was open to charges of being too narrowly restricted, and too artificial to have much relevance for problems about conceptual behaviour outside the laboratory. Arguably, many researchers confined their studies to types of concept which are relatively trivial, and represent only the tip of the iceberg of conceptual knowledge. They erected elaborate models of concept formation based on findings which have little generality. In spite of decades of experimental studies carried out with great industry, technical ingenuity and expertise, not much ground seemed to have been gained since Bruner *et al.* analysed the issues in 1956. However, important new developments in the last few years have changed the whole trend of research on concepts and concept formation. The new work focuses on the structure of natural, everyday concepts acquired during normal life experience, rather than on artificial concepts acquired by experimentally controlled procedures. This approach, instantiated in the work of Eleanor Rosch, is reviewed in Section VI, and represents a promising alternative to the traditional studies. Obviously, it is of great pragmatic importance to understand how best to impart concepts to other people. In education, and in any kind of information dissemination, we need to know how to structure and present a concept (1) so that it is readily and thoroughly understood; (2) so that the learner's newly acquired concept corresponds closely to the teacher's; and (3) so that the concept is well retained, is clearly and consistently related to other elements in the conceptual system, is unambiguous but modifiable, and can be utilized in thought and action. How much has the study of concept formation so far contributed towards these goals?

I. THE NATURE OF CONCEPTS

Most of the definitions of a concept which are offered in the literature are very broad. According to Bourne (1966):

> a concept exists whenever two or more distinguishable objects or events have been grouped or classified together, and set apart from other objects on the basis of some common feature or property characteristic of each.

In a later version Bourne (1974) elaborates this definition to include the relationship between the critical features as integral to the concept. Thus a concept is defined by the relationship which governs the set of critical features or properties. Others define concepts in terms of their behavioural effects. For Bruner *et al.* (1956):

> to categorize is to render discriminably different things equivalent, to group objects and events and people around us into classes, and to respond to them in terms of their class membership rather than their uniqueness.

Hayes and Nissen (1971), aiming for a definition generous enough to permit animals to have concepts, formulated a rather similar version:

> a consistent response to a constant aspect of a variety of stimuli regardless of the specific context in which this aspect occurs.

When we come to examine the traditional studies of concepts, as opposed to their definitions, it is hard to see what has happened to these liberal and all-embracing concepts of concepts. In the earlier work, what we find is a dedicated concentration on red triangles and blue squares, with series of experiments after experiments devoted to yet more red triangles and blue squares, and a widespread neglect of the vast range of conceptual knowledge which is not devoted to simple geometric figures. This situation is quite understandable, but the consequences are unfortunate. The psychologist who studies concept learning, and concepts, faces the usual dilemma. That is, he has to make a choice between relevance and rigour. If he elects to study real-life natural concepts, he will find them impossible to standardize and specify very precisely, and many uncontrolled factors such as the life experience of the individual contribute a great deal of variability, so that his research may lack rigour. If, instead, he selects a limited range of highly simplified and well standardized concepts for study under controlled laboratory conditions, the experiments may achieve considerable precision, but will have only limited relevance. The most common choice has been to opt for rigour and sacrifice relevance, but more recently there has been a reversal of this trend (see Sections V and VI).

We can see more clearly where these limits lie if we analyse the differences between the kind of concepts used in laboratory experiments, and the kinds of concepts we acquire in everyday life, in more detail. Experimental stimuli can be exactly specified. The red triangles and blue squares have a specifiable number of relevant dimensions (e.g. size, colour and shape), with a specified range of possible values on each of these dimensions (e.g. large/small, red/blue, triangle/square). Irrelevant dimensions (e.g. position) are also designated and controlled. The relationship between the relevant attributes is established by the experimenter, so that, for example, the concept is based on a conjunctive relation (red and small and triangular) or a disjunctive one (either red or triangular). The most important aspect of experimental concepts is their well-definedness, and in everyday life not many kinds of concept possess this characteristic to anything like the same extent.

Everyday concepts vary along a continuum ranging from concrete to abstract. It is also possible to discern similar continua ranging from simple to complex, and from non-verbal to verbal. At the concrete end of the continuum lie those concepts that are defined in terms of their physical characteristics, like a particular kind of flower or make of car. While these belong to the type of everyday concept which is most similar to the experimental concepts, they are nevertheless much less specific. The defining attributes of everyday concepts in so far as they can be identified, tend to consist of an open-ended disjunctive set of possible values. For example, a tulip may be red, pink, white, yellow or blackish. Other defining attributes may have a continuous range of possible values, so that the tulip may be between 6 and 15 inches in height, and flower between March and May. Non-criterial, irrelevant attributes may be numerous, variable and unspecified. Consider the irrelevant attributes of a class like "flowers". These comprise characteristics which vary within the class, and include highly salient dimensions such as colour, size and shape. Moreover, as new varieties develop, the set of irrelevant attributes may change. As Smith *et al.* (1974) pointed out in their model for classification, which was outlined in Chapter 1, not all the features which define a class carry equal weight, and the features which are used for classifying instances that are typical of the class, may be different from those used when the instances are a-typical. In practice, we select the defining features most appropriate for the context in which classification takes place. While we might use the feature "winged" to classify birds in a zoological context, we would need to choose some other features in a context which included angels and aeroplanes. The defining features of everyday concepts are not fixed, and the borderline between relevant and irrelevant dimensions is often hazy. Many of these difficulties are overcome by Rosch's account of concepts, discussed in Section VI, because, in her view, concepts are represented as prototypes, rather than as sets of discrete critical features. Hence classification of an instance need not be carried out by means of matching defining features; instead, an instance can be classified by comparison with the prototype. As was noted in Chapter 1, it seems implausible that classification should always require feature comparisons. The recognition of a rose as a flower, and an apple as a fruit seems to be instantaneous and holistic. Brooks (1976) has suggested that concept identification in everyday life is more often intuitive, implicit and non-analytic, and that, in contrast to analytic feature-testing models, class membership of an instance is inferred from its overall similarity to another known instance of the class. If we know that one particular rose is a flower, we can infer that other similar examples are also flowers without recourse to feature comparisons.

Many everyday concepts cannot be defined in terms of physical characteristics at all. Functional concepts like vehicles, tools, toys, weapons and Wittgenstein's famous "games" (Wittgenstein, 1953) are only loosely related by a common use or associated activity. A boot and a hat are both instances of the concept "clothing", but may have no physical features in common whatever. The classification of functional concepts may also depend on context, so that a dagger may be an ornament in one situation, and a weapon in a different context. When classification is dependent on context, and on the intentions, actions, and previous experience of whoever is making the classification, considerable ambiguity creeps in, and the correct classification is often doubtful. For everyday concepts, the category boundaries tend to be indeterminate. Chairs shade off into stools, benches, thrones, seats and sofas, and there may be different opinions as to how a particular object should be classified.

When we come to consider concepts that lie toward the abstract end of the concrete-abstract continuum, there may be even less consensus of opinion. There is liable to be disagreement as to the critical features of abstract concepts like "democracy" or "freedom", and disagreement about what is, or is not, an instance of such a concept. Many people have idiosyncratic or incomplete mental representations of abstract concepts. Concepts of this kind have three characteristics which contribute to the lack of uniformity. Firstly, they are higher-order concepts which rest on a substrate of underlying concepts in terms of which they are defined. So we cannot understand the concept of democracy unless we first understand something of the concepts of voting, and of the nature of government, and something of alternative systems of government with which democracy is contrasted. Secondly, while concrete concepts can be learned either by ostensive definition, or by verbal definition, or by a mixture of both, many abstract concepts can only be acquired verbally. Since there is no object which can be pointed out as an example of "democracy", we depend on verbal descriptions, definitions and explanations. While the uniformity of human sense organs ensures that perceptually defined concepts are fairly similar for everyone, verbally defined concepts are more liable to be distorted by misunderstanding and misinterpretation. Finally, abstract concepts are also more liable to be dependent on context than physical and functional ones. Concepts like "aggression" and "freedom" are relative rather than absolute, and depend on the scale of values previously established in the experience of whoever is making the judgement, and on the current social and political context.

All these considerations emphasize the extent of the gap that divides natural, everyday concepts from the red triangles and blue squares of the laboratory experiment. Although the studies of semantic memory reviewed in Chapter 1 have been concerned with some more natural concepts, they have focused on the structural relationships between concepts that have already been acquired, and not on the process of acquisition. We still know very little about the way people learn to categorize the real world around them.

II. CONCEPTUAL BEHAVIOUR

Besides employing rather limited and simplified kinds of concepts, laboratory studies typically examine only a very restricted kind of conceptual behaviour. A typical experimental paradigm requires the subject to "learn" a concept like "a large red square". In fact the subject's task is not one of concept learning, concept formation or concept acquisition as these terms are normally used, because the subject already *has* the concept of a large red square. His task resembles problem solving more than concept formation. He has to discover which of the possible alternatives the experimenter has designated as positive instances for the purpose of the experiment. He has to identify the relevant attributes, and the relationship in which they are combined. How well does this experimental task correspond to conceptual behaviour in everyday life? The first stage in natural concept acquisition is often one of perceptual learning. Although we may be innately endowed with the perceptual capacity to discriminate between exemplars and non-exemplars of the concept, experience enhances this discriminatory power as we learn to identify, attend to and organize the relevant attributes of the stimulus. Subjectively, we have this experience when we learn to recognize the symbols of a foreign alphabet, to interpret the properties of cells seen under a microscope, or tell the difference between a genuine and a fake work of art. But when we "learn a concept" in everyday life, we usually learn a great deal more than the relevant attributes and how they are organized. We learn something about the relative importance of the defining attributes, so that we can still make a tentative classification of deviant or atypical instances. We learn how the context in which an instance is encountered may alter the weighting of defining attributes, and this will also help us to classify ambiguous or borderline cases. A pile of bricks is more likely to be considered as a work of art when encountered in a reputable gallery than on a building site. Also, instead of learning to differentiate a concept from a limited set of alternatives, we learn how it relates in terms of similarities and differences to all the other concepts we have already acquired. Everyday concepts are not learned in isolation. To learn a concept is to "place" it in our conceptual network, so that it relates, closely or distantly, to all the other concepts in the knowledge system. This is why we should hesitate to allow that someone has understood a concept like "inflation" if he could define it, and cite instances, but could not state the causes or the consequences.

Conceptual learning usually, but not necessarily, involves learning verbal labels. In the normal course of development children learn the appropriate names for the concepts they are in the process of acquiring. However, when we examined the conceptual behaviour displayed in sorting tasks in Chapter 5, it was evident that, although grouping into functional classes, and grouping into superordinate classes appeared to be associated with verbal labelling ability, grouping into concrete classes distinguished by physical features was independent of verbal ability. Both animals and language-handicapped humans could utilize simple physical concepts, and could learn conceptual relations like oddity rules, and conditional rules. To insist on restricting the term "concept" to verbal concepts is to create too sharp a dividing line in the continuum which runs from simple physical concepts to complex abstract ones.

Just as there is a continuum of types of concept, so there is also a range of conceptual behaviour, which includes both non-verbal and verbal responses. When we acquire a concept we do not just learn to recognize and name instances, we may also develop emotional responses, and we learn to behave appropriately towards instances of the concept. So a cat which has the concept of "dog" can not only discriminate dogs from non-dogs, but may also experience fear, and respond with flight. The human who has learned the concept of "dog" can, in addition, make a variety of verbal responses including naming, defining and describing. The full repertoire of conceptual behaviour is not always present, so that we may sometimes be able to recognize and name an instance of a concept, but not give an adequate definition. In everyday life we have many concepts which are only partially acquired in this way, and the criteria for "having a concept" are ill defined. It is not at all clear which forms of conceptual behaviour should be taken to constitute evidence of conceptual learning. It is just this kind of confusion, which makes it difficult to decide (as we saw in Chapter 5) when children have attained the concept of conservation. A more analytic approach to concept learning, which separates out different forms of conceptual behaviour, is likely to be helpful in dispelling some of the confusion.

III. TRADITIONAL EXPERIMENTAL STUDIES OF CONCEPT FORMATION

There are two serious drawbacks to the traditional experimental studies of concept formation. The first of these is the limited range of concepts and conceptual behaviour which have been examined, and the consequent limitations on the applicability of the findings to more natural situations. The second is that although experimental work has yielded lengthy lists of variables which have been shown to affect performance in concept-learning tasks, these variables are so numerous, and so interactive that, even within the highly restricted framework of the laboratory experiment, it has proved difficult to formulate law-like relations, and to predict the outcome of any given combination of variables.

A. Methods

The experimental findings are reviewed below in order to assess how far these criticisms are justified. Methodologically, researchers have concentrated on two experimental paradigms, which have been extensively used to study concept formation. In the reception paradigm, the experimenter presents a single stimulus item: the subject is asked to judge whether it is, or is not, a positive instance of the concept. Following his response, he is told whether or not he was correct. The experimenter then presents the next stimulus, and so on. Each sequence of stimulus, response and feedback constitutes a discrete trial. Trials continue until the subject is consistently responding correctly. In the selection paradigm, the entire population of stimuli is displayed simultaneously to the subject, and one item is designated as a positive instance of the concept. In order to discover how the concept is defined, the subject can select any other item in the display, and ask whether it is a positive instance of the concept or not. He continues selection until he can state the concept correctly. The main measure of performance, common to both methods, is the number of trials taken to reach solution. Solution is defined as the trial following the last error trial, or the trial preceding a correct statement of the concept. It is common practice to amalgamate the scores of groups of subjects, and plot the average number of errors made on each successive trial. Sometimes the speed of response on each trial is measured, and sometimes confidence ratings for successive trials are obtained by asking the subject to state the degree of his confidence in each response. If the researcher is interested in knowing what mental operations direct and accompany concept formation, then none of these measures gives much clue as to the subject's strategy; what hypotheses he has formed, and how he revises them in the light of the information he receives. The selection paradigm, however, does allow the experimenter to form some idea of the subject's strategy by observing the pattern of his selections. Bruner *et al.* (1956) detected four different strategies. In conservative focusing, the subject adopts an initial hypothesis that all the attributes of the positive instance are relevant, and tests it by selecting stimuli that differ in one attribute at a time. If the first positive instance is a small green square, then a large green square may be selected next, and if it also proves positive, then the subject can infer that size is not relevant. In focus gambling, instances are selected that differ in more than one attribute, e.g. a large red square may be selected. A lucky gamble results in quick accumulation of information. If the large red square is positive, then both colour and size are irrelevant, and shape emerges as the critical dimension. If the large red square proves negative, the gamble does not come off. Either size or colour must be relevant, and further tests are necessary to determine which. In scanning strategies, instead of testing for the relevance of the attributes, the subject entertains either a single hypothesis (successive scanning) or several hypotheses (simultaneous scanning) consistent with the positive instance, and revises these hypotheses in the light of the information yielded by confirming or disconfirming instances. Scanning strategies impose a heavy load on memory, and require quite complex inferential reasoning. However, although the selection paradigm will reveal the general pattern of the subject's choices, this is often not sufficient to allow us to infer his strategy in detail (Dominowski, 1974). Suppose, for example, that on Trial 1 the subject selects a large unfilled red circle, and is told "positive", and on Trial 2 he selects a small unfilled red circle. This response sequence is consistent with any or all of the following hypotheses: (1) size is the relevant dimension; (2) the concept is "any red circle"; and (3) the concept is "red unfilled figures". A potentially more informative technique is to ask the subject to report his current hypothesis after each trial, and do his thinking aloud, but this requirement often changes a subject's performance, forcing him to be more consistent and orderly. So we are still left with the problem of detecting what strategy the subject would employ if a vocal self-commentary was not required. To characterize performance in conceptual tasks adequately, measures of efficiency like the number of trials to solution, need to be combined with observations and inferences about the subject's hypothesis formation, so that it is clear not only what he is doing, but how and why he is doing it.

B. Experimental Variables: Stimulus Factors

A major determinant of performance in concept formation is the complexity of the concept, defined as the number of relevant dimensions, and some studies have reported a linear relationship between number of relevant dimensions, and number of trials to solution (Bulgarella and Archer, 1962). It takes longer to learn the concept of a large red tilted triangle, than to learn the concept of a red triangle. But further experiments have demonstrated that several other factors interact with the number of relevant dimensions in determining ease of learning. The number of irrelevant dimensions is important, because responses based on these have to be eliminated before the concept is learned. If increasing the number of relevant dimensions produces a corresponding decrease in the number of irrelevant dimensions, then the problem may be made easier.

The effect of the number of relevant and of irrelevant dimensions will also depend on whether or not some of these dimensions are redundant. Bourne and Haygood (1961) found that if the dimensions are co-varying instead of being independent, learning is not impeded by additional dimensions. That is, if shape and size co-vary so that triangles are always large, and circles are always small, then one of the two dimensions is redundant, and only one need be considered. If any shape can take any size, then the two dimensions are non-redundant, and both must be taken into account. Redundancy of either relevant or irrelevant dimensions can improve performance, provided, of course, that the subject perceives the redundancy.

Another variable that interacts with the number of relevant dimensions is the number of values on each relevant dimension. Battig and Bourne (1955) found that adding more values, say six colours instead of three, increased the task difficulty; but this variable did not interact with the number of irrelevant dimensions.

Yet another important aspect of the concept which influences ease of learning is the type of relevant dimension, or cue, which defines the concept. Some cues are easier to utilize because they are more salient or attention-attracting. In the sorting tasks discussed in Chapters 4 and 5 it was evident that physical cues are easier to employ than non-physical ones, like functional characteristics, or superordinate class. The saliency of a particular physical dimension is increased if the different values of the dimension are highly discriminable. Size is more likely to be an effective cue if size differences are very marked (Shepp and Zeaman, 1966). Trabasso (1963) used line drawings of flowers in a concept-learning task, and found the shape of the flowers and the shape of the leaves were more salient for the subjects than the critical cue, which was the size of the angle between the main stem and the leaf stem. It was necessary to widen the angle or to colour the angle red in order to increase its salience, and attract the subject's attention to this cue. In practice, salience probably depends on discriminability, and also on biases acquired through previous experience of cue utility.

Many of these stimulus factors are also likely to interact with the subject's strategy. Although this has not been systematically explored, the effect of number of dimensions, for example, would depend on whether the subject was trying to test the relevance of each dimension separately, or adopting a holistic strategy.

Another variable which is a powerful determinant of ease of learning is the type of rule, or conceptual principle whereby the attributes are combined. If two attributes, A and B, are relevant to the concept, the rule may be conjunctive (A and B), disjunctive (A or B) or conditional (If A then B). More complex rules are relational ones (e.g. A above B, or the odd one of a set); rules containing negations (e.g. A and not B); or multiple rules [e.g. (A and B) or (A and C)]. The usual finding is that conjunctive rules are easiest to learn, and disjunctive and relational rules are about equally difficult (Bruner *et al.* 1956; Hunt and Hovland, 1960). Probabilistic concepts (sometimes but not always, A and B) are also more difficult than deterministic ones. Multiple concepts increase in difficulty with each increment in structural complexity (Neisser and Weene, 1962). Differences in rule difficulty may be partly attributable to biases established in everyday experience, which appear to favour the conjunctive principle, and these tend to lessen with practice (Haygood and Bourne, 1965). Rule difficulty also varies with the subject's strategy, and the order in which he encounters positive and negative instances.

If we try to relate these experimental findings to a real-life example and predict what factors would make a particular model of car especially easy to identify, we can make the following points, all of which accord well without intuitions. It should differ from other cars in colour, size, shape and as many other features as possible (fewer irrelevant dimensions). It should always be the same colour, same size and same shape (redundancy of dimensions). The colour, size, shape etc. should be easily distinguishable from the colours, sizes and shapes of other cars (saliency). Yet it is paradoxical that although we can construct an optimal concept of this kind, the interactive relationships of the stimulus factors are too complex for us to predict the relative difficulty of two different concepts when some of the stimulus characteristics which facilitate identification are possessed by one, and some by the other.

C. Experimental Variables: Procedural Factors

Especially in the reception paradigm, concept learning is affected by procedural factors such as sequence effects, timing, informative feedback and memory load.

The sequence in which stimuli are presented may make it easier for the subject to identify the concept. Learning is faster if positive instances of the concept are encountered early in the sequence, and are in close temporal contiguity, rather than being widely spaced. Since the subject must retain the information gained from positive instances in order to abstract the relevant attributes, temporal contiguity assists him by minimizing the memory load, and reducing interference effects (Bourne and Jennings, 1963). Generally speaking, positive instances convey more information than negative instances, and this finding is consistent with the difficulty in processing negative information discussed in Chapter 3. Negative evidence requires conversion to a positive form and in non-binary situations, when there are more than two alternatives, the appropriate conversion is not apparent. The information "not A" does not imply "B" when C and D are also possible alternatives. Bruner *et al.* (1956) remarked that in teaching natural concepts to children, we tend to point out positive instances rather than negative ones. However, while the superiority of positive instances generally holds good for learning conjunctive concepts, Bourne and Guy (1968) found that this was not the case for other types of conceptual rule, and, even for conjunctive concepts, a sequence in which positive and negative instances occur in contrasting succession may be optimal (Wells, 1967).

Both the quantity and the quality of informative feedback have been shown to affect performance. Not surprisingly, the subject does better if he is told after each response whether he was right or wrong, and omitting feedback on some trials delays solution. Equally unsurprisingly, misinformative feedback is detrimental. When misinformative feedback is given, the concept becomes a probabilistic one rather than a deterministic one. (For example, if a red triangle is sometimes, but not always designated a positive instance.) Pishkin (1960) found that subjects eventually learned to identify this kind of probabilistic concept, even with 40% misinformative trials, but solution was substantially delayed. Early in the sequence, subjects tend to engage in guessing, but later learn to ignore the misinformation. Studies have also been carried out to compare the effectiveness of positive and negative feedback. Positive feedback confirms a correct response; negative feedback disconfirms an error response. Buss and Buss (1956) viewed feedback as reinforcement, "rewarding" a correct response, and "punishing" an incorrect one, and found that negative feedback had more effect. A similar finding could be predicted if feedback is considered simply as a source of information, since in some cases more information is provided by negative feedback, in spite of the greater difficulty of processing negative information. If the concept is "a small red triangle", and the subject's hypothesis is "any red figure" his responses to red triangles will be correct and receive confirmation, but this positive feedback gives him no further information, and does not help him to revise his hypothesis. On the other hand, if he responds "yes" to a red square, and is told "wrong", then he has information which should lead him to revise his hypothesis. Later, conflicting results (Bourne et al., 1967) have shown that both positive and negative kinds of feedback can help subjects to identify the concept. Obviously, the value of each will depend on the nature of the subject's hypothesis, his stage of learning, his strategy, the sequence of stimulus items, and the number of alternatives. When a child is learning a new concept, he needs to know that he is right in calling a dog a dog, as well as wrong in calling a cat a dog, but the larger the number of non-dogs around the less information can be derived from mistakes. This is probably why we rarely give a child negative feedback without amplification. We don't say "No, it's not a dog" without adding "It's a cat".

The effectiveness of the type of feedback also varies with the nature of the response. Dominowski (1974) probed the effectiveness of four different kinds of trial outcome in eliciting appropriate behaviour (keeping a correct hypothesis, or changing an incorrect one). He found that the order of effectiveness was Positive Confirming (the subject says yes and is right), Positive Infirming (the subject says yes and is wrong), Negative Confirming (the subject says no and is right) and, by far the least effective, Negative Infirming (the subject says no and is wrong). Dominowski's results are shown in Fig. 1. The similarity between these results and the verification tasks

Trial Outcome	Correct use of feedback (%)
Positive Confirming	96
Positive Infirming	83
Negative Confirming	83
Negative Infirming	51

Fig. 1.   Percentage of responses consistent with the feedback information after different types of trial. From Dominowski (1974).

described in Chapter 3, suggests that feedback effectiveness is a function of processing biases, as well as the subject's strategy.

Temporal factors are also known to affect ease of learning. In the reception paradigm, the timing of the sequence of events can either be too rapid to permit adequate processing of the feedback and reappraisal of hypotheses, or it can be too slow, so that forgetting occurs. While increasing the interval between response and feedback exerts little, if any, effect, the delay between feedback and the next trial is critical. Bourne *et al.* (1965) found that the optimal inter-trial interval is about 9 s for simple concepts, and about 17 s for complex ones. The more difficult the task, the more mulling time is required. Theoretical accounts of concept learning are outlined in the next section, but it is worth noting that these effects of inter-trial interval are more consistent with an information processing theory of concept learning, than with a stimulus-response reinforcement theory, since S–R theory predicts that delays should weaken reinforcement and retard learning.

The difficulty of concept learning is partly attributable to the memory load imposed by the task. In the reception paradigm, the subject must retain the information derived from each trial over the succeeding trials. When the method is modified to allow previous stimuli to remain on view, the memory load is lightened, and the solution is reached earlier. In the selection paradigm, although all the stimuli remain available for inspection, the subject still has to remember which have been classified as positive instances, and which as negative ones. Bruner *et al.* (1956) forced subjects to solve a selection problem in their heads, without being able to view the array. Significant changes in performance occurred. Selections were less systematic, and sometimes repetitive. The scanning strategy, which imposes a greater memory load, was, under these conditions, less efficient than the focusing strategy. Cahill and Hovland (1960) showed that incorrect responses are more likely to be incompatible with information from trials early in the sequence, than with information supplied by immediately preceding trials, so that errors can be attributed, in these cases, to forgetting.

In addition to stimulus factors, and procedural factors, concept learning is also affected by the nature of the learner. Besides individual differences in strategies, which are discussed in more detail later, differences of age, sex, I.Q., motivation, stress, previous experience, species and language ability are all known to influence the efficiency of concept learning. Thus even when the researcher restricts his studies to laboratory experiments in which the stimulus variables and procedural variables are controlled as carefully as possible, these individual differences contribute a further source of variability, making it difficult to discern any general laws of concept learning.

IV. THEORIES OF CONCEPT LEARNING

While the theories of concept learning that have been proposed are in principle testable, and open to refutation, in practice it is difficult to decide which is most acceptable, because each will fit some of the data some of the time. Enough has already been said about the large number of variables that affect concept-learning tasks for it to be evident that any single theory of concept learning will be unlikely to account for all of them. The general applicability of any theory is further limited by the individual differences in concept learning which are described in more detail in the section on hypothesis-testing models. A broad distinction can be made between earlier associationist theories which view the concept learner as passively undergoing a series of experiences which bring about changes in behaviour reflecting learning, and later hypothesis-testing theories which characterize the concept learner as actively engaged in processing information, forming, testing and revising hypotheses, sifting possibilities, rejecting and deciding. While the former provide a mechanistic account of the concept-learning process in quasi-physiological terms, the latter give a mentalist description. Since the two kinds of theory are thus at different levels of description, direct comparisons between them can hardly be formulated. The passive *vs.* active distinction is really based on a confusion of these levels. We are all "passive" at the neuronal level, and we are all "active" at the mentalist decision-making level. The choice of a particular level of description, and so the theoretical bias of a given researcher, has been largely influenced by the psychological climate of the era in which his opinions were formed. Those nurtured in the post-1950s tradition of "cognitive" psychology, whose interest is predominantly in human performance, have tended to prefer the active hypothesis-testing models. Prior to this date, those working in a more physiological tradition were concerned to study mechanisms of learning common to humans and to animals, and adopted the passive associationist account.

A. S-R Associationist Theories

According to this type of theory, concept learning is a form of discrimination learning whereby the relevant attributes of positive instances of the concept are progressively associated with a positive response, and the attributes of negative instances are associated with a negative response. The process is complicated by the presence of irrelevant attributes which may sometimes be associated with positive examples, and sometimes with negative examples. Since these attributes receive inconsistent reinforcement they are gradually neutralized (Bourne and Restle, 1959), while, because all positive instances have some degree of similarity to each other, the S-R connections generalize to novel examples of the concept. If stimulus generalization is the underlying mechanism of concept learning, then learning should occur more rapidly if the positive instances are very similar to each other, and very different from the negative instances, especially if the negative instances also form a fairly homogeneous class. Empirical findings confirm this prediction. Difficulties with the S-R account of concept learning centre around the nature of the stimulus, and the nature of the reinforcement. Many of the kinds of natural concepts discussed earlier in this chapter do not appear to possess any common attributes which could become associated to a common response. This is true of functional, superordinate and abstract concepts, and also of the rule-based concepts like "the odd item in a set". This problem has led to a revised version of S-R associationism, which introduces an internal mediating stage intervening between the stimulus and the response. Some of the experimental findings concerning the effects of informative feedback are also difficult to accommodate within the S-R theory. If feedback functions as reinforcement, then it is surprising that delaying the feedback has little effect on rate of learning. The effects of the order of positive and negative trials are also more in keeping with an information processing account, than with an S-R model.

Mediation theory is a more complex form of associationism, designed to overcome the problem of finding a common factor to link physically disparate stimuli to the same conceptual response. A common internal mediating response is postulated to link the various instances of, say, food, to a common response. Mediators may be non-verbal, like the "fractional eating response" which, according to Osgood (1952) is elicited by any type of food, and is in turn associated with an overt behavioural response. More commonly, mediators are characterized as covert verbal labels. Fractional responses, and other internal symbols, such as images, are less

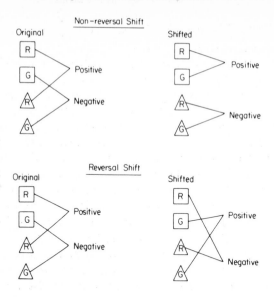

Fig. 2. *Above.* The concept shifts from Red = Positive to Square = Positive (an extra-dimensional shift). Half the stimuli change from positive to negative or vice versa. *Below.* The concept shifts from Red = Positive to Green = Positive (an intra-dimensional shift). All the stimuli change.

S-R theory → Reversal shift is harder, because more pairs are changed.

Mediation theory → Non-reversal shift is harder, because the mediator (the dimension name) is changed.

plausible as mediators for concepts such as "oddity" or "equivalence". A striking advantage of mediation theory is that the internal mediators can substitute for external stimuli, and so allow the possibility of de-contextualized conceptual behaviour in the absence of physical stimuli. We can think and talk about cabbages and kings quite as well when none are around.

Mediation theory and simple unmediated S-R theory generate different predictions about the effect of changing an experimental concept. In Fig. 2, two kinds of change, or shift, are shown for stimuli which vary in colour and shape. In the non-reversal shift, the critical attribute shifts from red to square. This is called an *extra-dimensional shift*, since the relevant dimension changes from colour to shape. In this case some, but not all, the stimuli change from positive to negative, or vice versa. The reversal shift changes the relevant value from red to green within the same dimension, and so is called an *intra-dimensional shift*. The red stimuli become negative, and the green ones positive. This produces a situation in which all the originally positive examples change to negative and vice versa. Mediation theory predicts that the extra-dimensional non-reversal shift should be more difficult, because the name of the critical dimension mediates the response, and the shift necessitates a change of mediator. In the intra-dimensional reversal shift, the same mediator, "colour", can be retained. Unmediated S-R theory predicts the opposite. The intra-dimensional shift should be more difficult, because each individual S-R connection has to be undone and re-made. The experimental results show that animals, young children and slow learners behave according to the unmediated S-R theory prediction. Adult humans and older children behave as if they use verbal mediation (Kendler and Kendler, 1962). The difference in the relative difficulty of the two kinds of shift has been attributed by the Kendlers to the development of language ability which allows verbal mediation to be used, but Slamecka (1968) has pointed out that the extra-dimensional shift may be harder for reasons not connected with the use of verbal mediation. He pointed out that when only a sub-set of the stimuli change from positive to negative it is harder to detect that a shift has occurred, and the post-shift pattern of reinforcement is more inconsistent. However, if extra-dimensional shifts are intrinsically more difficult, this is hard to reconcile with the fact that younger children find them easier than intra-dimensional shifts. It is not at all clear whether these age-related changes in conceptual behaviour are due to language development, or to some other aspect of cognitive growth.

B. Hypothesis-testing Models

These models assume that subjects form hypotheses about the concept, but in fact such hypotheses may not be very different from mediating responses, since a simple hypothesis might be "shape is the critical attribute". Since people cannot always state what hypotheses, if any, they are currently entertaining, it is further assumed that hypothesis testing may occur at an unconscious level, and this provision makes the distinction between hypothesis testing and verbal mediation somewhat hazy. However, according to H-testing models, people pursue a definite information-seeking strategy which is guided by their current hypotheses. This assumption can be partially justified because, at least some of the time, subjects can describe their strategies, and, at least some of the time, their responses show a consistent pattern, most clearly evident in the selection paradigm. H-testing may be a more difficult strategy in the reception paradigm, especially if the concept is complex, and the memory load is excessive.

Bruner *et al.* (1956) described the focusing and scanning strategies that subjects apparently were adopting in their selection task. More precise versions of these strategies have since been formulated. Restle (1962) distinguished several possibilities. A subject may select one hypothesis from the total pool of possible hypotheses, and operate on the principle of Win–Stay–Lose–Shift. That is, he retains the hypothesis if his response was correct, but discards it and selects another if his response turned out to be an error. Alternatively, he may test several hypotheses simultaneously. There are also different views as to the fate of the discarded hypotheses. A disconfirmed hypothesis may be returned to the pool of hypotheses remaining to be sampled, or it may be eliminated from the pool. Restle has shown that these two possibilities yield the same mathematical predictions as to the probable number of errors before solution.

Intuitively, a no-memory model whereby people fail to eliminate disconfirmed hypotheses is unconvincing, and evidence for the role of memory in concept learning has already been cited. Bower and Trabasso (1964) developed a no-memory model of sampling-with-replacement, the disconfirmed hypotheses being replaced in the pool, so that they are still available for re-sampling. Data from a simple concept learning task showed that the probability of error responses remained stationary up until the last error, and so appeared to reflect an abrupt transition from no-learning to learning, that is, an all-or-none type of learning, rather than a gradual incremental progress from chance responding towards complete solution. This all-or-none pattern is consistent with a total pool of alternative hypotheses remaining constant in size, because no progressive elimination occurs. The probability of selecting the correct alternative therefore remains constant, whereas if the pool steadily diminished as each disconfirmed hypothesis was eliminated from it, then the probability of sampling the correct hypothesis would steadily increase. Later experiments (Levine, 1962; Trabasso and Bower, 1966) refuted the all-or-none sampling-with-replacement model by showing that misinformative feedback prior to solution did delay learning. If the subject had learned nothing during the pre-solution trials, random reinforcement at this stage should have no effect. This finding has necessitated modification of the original sampling-with-replacement model. In the modified version, subjects do reject disconfirmed hypotheses, but, because of the limited capacity of working memory, they fail to keep track of all the discarded alternatives, which may therefore, after an interval, creep back into the pool of hypotheses remaining to be sampled. That is, the subject forgets which hypotheses he has already tested and found to be wrong. The size of the pool may then still be fairly constant since it would consist of the number of untested hypotheses, plus the reinstated hypotheses, minus those discarded hypotheses that can be held in memory. A model which incorporates a limited and imperfect memory is much more plausible than one which permits memory to play no part at all. In general, the all-or-none model applies best to identification of very simple unidimensional concepts. When concepts are multidimensional it is possible to have a partial solution— to have learned some, but not all, of the critical attributes, and so be progressing towards the solution. When several hypotheses are tested simultaneously, it may be possible to reject several at once, so that the probability of solution is increased. Erikson *et al.* (1966) showed that response latencies decrease as the subject nears solution, and inferred that this reflected the decreasing size of the set of hypotheses remaining to be tested, selection of a new hypothesis being faster from a smaller pool. More detailed scrutiny of response patterns also has suggested that Win–Stay–Lose–Shift is too simple a way to characterize the subject's strategy. The models of Restle (1962) and of Bower and Trabasso (1964) assumed that learning occurred only on error trials, because a current hypothesis was unchanged after a correct response. Levine (1966) showed that subjects did use the information gained from positive feedback after a correct response to eliminate other hypotheses, as yet untested, that were inconsistent with this information. So what appears to be a simple example of Win–Stay can involve covert changes, with consequences on trials later in the series. Erikson *et al.* (1966) also found that response latencies continue to decrease in post-solution trials, when all the responses are necessarily correct, as the subject grows more confident.

Dominowski (1974) has pointed out that the empirical evidence is too inconsistent to give conclusive support for any one model of concept learning, and that model builders have tended to make two false assumptions. One is the assumption that the same strategy would be employed by different subjects; and the second is that the same strategy would be employed in different situations. By monitoring the performance of individual subjects, Dominowski was able to detect a striking variety of strategies between different subjects, and also strategy-shifting by individuals in the course of the task. Asking subjects to think aloud revealed that some subjects reached solution by guessing, without adequate evidence. Some tested one hypothesis at a time, and others reported they were trying to test multiple hypotheses simultaneously. Some subjects ignored negative feedback, and behaved like those in Wason's number series experiment (Chapter 3, p. 63) persisting in re-testing hypotheses that had been disconfirmed. Others tried with varying success to use both positive and negative feedback.

Commenting on the lack of uniformity exhibited by his subjects Dominowski concludes "This state of affairs not only casts doubt on any theory assuming a common strategy for all subjects, but also raises the question of whether this kind of theory is useful". As a result of his salutary observation it seems likely that future research on concept learning will abandon the attempt to produce general models, and will yield alternative models for different strategies, and different types of task.

Hypothesis-testing behaviour, as described in these models, may be an experimentally induced phenomenon, which is not representative of everyday concept learning. Brooks (1976) reported that subjects may learn concepts intuitively and unconsciously, and be able to identify instances without being able to verbalize the categorization rules, or specify the defining attributes. His subjects learned to pair structured letter strings with names of cities or animals (e.g. VVTRXRR—Paris, MRRRRRM—bison). They were unaware that these stimuli could be classified as New World or Old World items, yet when new letter strings were presented, and they were asked to classify these as New World or Old World, they performed with 60–65% accuracy. They had apparently learned the basis of the classification incidentally and unconsciously.

V. DEVELOPMENTAL STUDIES OF CONCEPT LEARNING

Some studies of concept learning in children have been less constrained by prior theoretical assumptions than the experimental work on adults, and have generated some interesting observations about children's conceptual behaviour in natural learning situations. Brown (1958) in his paper *How shall a thing be called?* tackled the problem of the relationship between the child's use of names, his conceptual categories, and the objects in the world. The complexity of this relationship has also been pointed out by Olson (1970), who noted that a single word may have multiple referents (e.g. the word "eye" can be applied to visual sense organs, needles, potatoes etc.), and that a single referent may have several possible labels (e.g. a person may be labelled as George, father, husband, lawyer, man etc.). Brown's informal observations suggested to him that the particular labels which are learned first by the young child are selected for him by adults, and the choice is governed by a number of factors. In general, brief words that are easier for the child to reproduce are preferred to longer ones (so "dog" would be supplied in preference to "quadruped"). The brevity principle may ·be over-ridden by frequency. Since bananas are more often referred to as bananas than as fruit, or food, the label "bananas" is supplied. Other principles are utility and economy. The child is· taught "flower" before he learns to distinguish daffodils and tulips, and "money" before he learns the names of individual coins. He does not need to make fine botanical distinctions or financial reckonings. The growth of vocabulary may therefore proceed from subordinate to superordinate class labels (bananas and apples before fruit), or from superordinate to subordinate (car before Ford and Mercedes). Labels for the highest superordinate classes like "substance" or "artefact" do not appear in the young child's vocabulary, though Brown's argument that they are ruled out on grounds of non-utility and infrequency may be only partly correct, and the major factor that dictates their late acquisition could be their complexity and abstractness. Brown's observations do undermine both the view that children's conceptual development proceeds from initially wide, undifferentiated categories by progressive differentiation and refine-ment towards the acquisition of narrower specific sub-categories; and the opposite view that children begin with specific lower order categories, and by progressive abstraction of similarities build upwards to acquire general higher-order categories. His examples demonstrate that vocabulary growth can proceed in either direction.

Olson (1970) lists some additional factors which govern the choice of the most suitable lexical label for making unambiguous reference. Important among these are the context of perception, and the context of communication. "Flower" is an adequate label for a given item when all the other items in the perceptual context are non-flowers, but it is not an adequate identifying label in a garden full of flowers. If the label is to serve a communicative function, the set of alternatives for the listener must be inferred by the speaker. The child who says that he lives "in the white house" may succeed in conveying his home location to a listener who lives in the neighbour-hood, but not to a stranger.

Brown also points out that there is often a disparity between the category names the child uses, and the cognitive categories he has in mind. This is apparent in the errors of overgeneralization that commonly occur in child speech. When children are learning concepts, they seem to operate with a strategy of inductive generalization, so that, for example, the name "clock" is generalized and applied to a variety of clocks. Overgeneralization is apparent when children call all men "Daddy", or all large four-legged animals "cows". In these cases, the cognitive categories are more general than the names.

Baron (1973) provides an account of overgeneralization in terms of the componential acquisition of meaning. The overgeneralizing stage reflects global undifferentiated concepts, but as more components of meaning are accumulated, they become more specific and refined, and overgeneralization is gradually restricted. Terms like "before" and "after", and "more" and "less" are initially confused because they reflect the undifferentiated concepts of "not now" and "not equal", and in the discussion of conservation experiments in Chapter 5, a similar tendency to use terms like "bigger" without distinguishing separate components of height and width was also evident. Ervin-Tripp and Foster (1966) similarly observed that children treated words like "good", "happy" and "pretty" as synonymous when describing faces.

Overgeneralization is not simply a reflection of imperfect concept learning, but a reflection of a very well adapted strategy. By overgeneralizing, wrong responses get corrected, and the information from errors characterizes the negative instances, so that critical differences become apparent, and the overgeneralized concept can be cut back to the positive instances. The child as concept learner is seldom operating in the reception paradigm. He is not presented with a sequence of positive and negative instances of a single concept. Nor does his learning situation resemble the selection paradigm very closely, since he will be trying to master many concepts contemporaneously over quite a long period of time, and the set of alternatives from which he can select items to test his hypothesis is constantly shifting as the perceptual scene around him changes. Overgeneralization is not wholly unrestricted, but occurs only within a limited range of semantic distance. "Daddy" is overgeneralized to "man" but not to "people". Not all features are valid cues for generalization. No instances have been recorded of children overgeneralizing on the basis of colour, for example. They do not assume that fire-engines and cherries belong to the same class because both are red. If the child failed to generalize, or generalized only to examples very similar to the first positive instance, rather like a conservative focuser, acquisition of concepts would be very slow. Because everyday concepts have very many irrelevant features, which vary independently, it would be difficult to extract the defining features by this method. The same objection applies to Rosch's (1975) view (see Section VI) that children learn concepts by constructing a prototype. A prototype does not represent the defining features of a concept, but instantiates the features most commonly associated with instances of the concept. Building a prototype of this kind would also require extensive experience. Brooks' (1976) theory of implicit, non-analytic concept learning provides a more plausible account of how children acquire concepts. Having learned to identify one instance of a concept, the child generalizes from this known instance on the basis of overall similarity. Having learned that "Rover" is an instance of "dog", he generalizes, or overgeneralizes, the concept to similar dog-like animals. Overgeneralization is a strategy which defines the boundaries of concepts, and is likely to produce rapid learning, and minimize the load on memory. Making naming errors does not carry severe penalties, especially when the perceptual context helps to make the reference clear. It is probably more important to acquire some means of communication, however inaccurate, as rapidly as possible, so that a strategy which produces errors of overgeneralization is likely to be the concept-learning strategy which is best adapted to the child's needs and capacities.

In contrast to the traditional experimental studies of concept learning in adults, which were criticized for the artificiality of the task, and the narrow range of concepts studied, these observations of children's concept learning are based on the natural situation, but are largely anecdotal. A compromise between the two approaches which achieves a degree of formality and rigour without diverging too far from natural concept learning is now beginning to emerge.

VI. THE NEW APPROACH: STUDIES OF THE INTERNAL STRUCTURE OF NATURAL CONCEPTS

This new approach to the study of concepts is currently spearheaded by the work of Rosch (Rosch, 1975; Rosch and Mervis, 1975). It is concerned to probe the structure of natural concepts, and is guided by, *a priori*, rational considerations and supported by formal experiments. This work derives from two sources, drawing together, in what has proved a fruitful combination, ideas generated by two different areas of research. Firstly, Rosch has been concerned to question and revise some of the assumptions underlying the models of semantic memory and semantic processing described in Chapter 1. Although these models have mainly concentrated on describing the structural relations *between* concepts, they also make some assumptions about the internal structure of these concepts. Both the network, and the set-theoretic models, assume that concepts consist of lists or sets of features. We noted that models such as that of Smith *et al.* (1974) make the further assumption that these features can be divided into those that are criterial or defining, and those that are merely characteristic. One difficulty in applying this model to natural concepts is that the defining features of many common categories are unknown or non-existent. We classify chairs, toys and puddings without being able to produce a list of defining features. Rosch's proposal that natural concepts are represented as prototypes, rather than as lists of features, avoids this paradox. This line of thinking owes much to a second source— the work on schema formation carried out by Posner and Keele (1968, 1970). They showed that people are able to abstract and store a schema, or prototype, representing the central tendencies of a set of patterns. Their experiments involved random forms such as dot patterns, and showed that subjects could accurately classify prototypes which they had never seen, but which exhibited the central tendencies of sets of patterns they had previously learned to classify. Moreover, subjects tended to believe that they had actually experienced the prototype patterns before, and recognized them better than the patterns they had seen. Posner and Keele also demonstrated that the nature of the stored prototype varies. When the subjects had learned a classification over a set of patterns that were highly variable (a loose concept), they were better able to recognize new deviant instances. Initial experience with a set of patterns of low variability produced a tight concept, and high rejection of deviant instances. The authors speculate that the learned memory representation involves both a central tendency or prototype, and a boundary. The concept boundaries may be more or less generous. The novel aspect of Rosch's work is the application of prototype theory to natural concepts, and the way in which it is related to models of semantic processing.

There are several important points which have emerged from her research. One series of experiments confirms the existence of reference points or prototypes for natural categories, with instances being arranged in order of deviation from the prototype. In one paradigm, subjects were asked to place pairs of stimuli into the empty slots of sentence frames consisting of linguistic "hedges" (see Lakoff, 1972). Examples of such hedges are "—— is essentially ——", "Loosely speaking, —— is ——". The hedges express varying degrees of relatedness between two items whereby the first is classified in terms of the second, which thus constitutes the reference point. In Rosch's experiment, stimuli were drawn from the categories of colour, line orientation and number. Placing of pairs drawn from within these categories revealed four colours as focal (e.g. the placing *"orange* is roughly *red"* shows red to be the focal reference point); horizontal, vertical and diagonal as focal orientations; and multiples of ten as focal numbers. The results were consistent across large numbers of subjects. Indeed, focal colours appear to be the same for many different cultures and languages, although the boundaries of the colour names vary. Rosch believes that basic physical categories of colour and form, which are physiologically determined, are universal and invariant for all cultures. Another experiment in which subjects placed stimuli at a physical distance from each other, so as to represent their psychological distance, revealed continua of resemblance as in the semantic space models of Chapter 1. Rosch has also shown that the mental representations of colour categories as prototypes have psychological reality by a series of "priming" experiments. Colour judgements can be facilitated if the name of a focal colour is given first as a prime and the colour subsequently presented for judgement is a "good" example of the category (that is, one that closely resembles the prototype). Similar results were obtained for other semantic categories such as furniture and fruit. Pre-priming the prototypes facilitated classification of "good" instances. According to Rosch, the psychological reality of prototypes is reflected in children's concept learning. Rosch claims that good examples of categories are learned earlier, and that children have initially tight category boundaries, being reluctant to include poor examples, but this sequence of development is inconsistent with the overgeneralization phenomenon noted in Section E. In scaling experiments, subjects could reliably rate the extent to which an instance fitted their idea of a category, so that they could rate different examples of chairs as being more or less close to their "idea" or prototype of a chair. A series of experiments explored the nature of these prototypes and within-category relationships, which Rosch, borrowing Wittgenstein's terminology (Wittgenstein, 1953), has called Family Resemblances. Positive correlations were found between high ratings of prototypicality for an item, and a wide distribution of that item's features throughout the set. Negative correlations were found between a high rating of prototypicality, and the distribution of an item's features in *other* categories. Thus prototypes have a high family resemblance within their own category, and a low degree of overlap with the attributes of contrasting categories. The category of chair is defined, not by a set of criterial features, but by a distribution of overlapping features which are shared by most instances, and are incorporated in the prototype. If concepts are stored as prototypes, then models which assume that classification takes place by checking criterial features need to be revised. However, if, instead, classification takes place by comparison with the prototype, the boundaries need to be specified. To date, Rosch has not tackled the problem of concept boundaries.

She has, however, offered some interesting speculations about basic levels of categorizing, which amplify Brown's suggestions about the factors which govern whether subordinate or superordinate terms appear first in child speech. Rosch proposes that divisions between levels of categorization have perceptual and functional origins, and preferred levels are those where there is an optimum amount of overlap within and between categories. At a superordinate level like "furniture", there are few shared overlapping features within the class. At a lower-order subordinate level such as "dining chair", there is high overlap within the category, but too great an overlap with contrasting classes like kitchen chairs and desk chairs. The preferred level, or basic category, is the intermediate level "chair", where the within-class overlap is maximized, and the between-class overlap is minimized. Basic level categories are learned first developmentally, according to Rosch, although Brown's observations suggest that this is not always true. She also maintains that in condensed systems, such as sign languages, basic levels predominate, and the super- and subordinate class names are sometimes missing. Rosch believes that basic level categories such as "chairs" are also distinguished behaviourally. Objects belonging to these categories invoke similar actions such as "sitting on", while higher-level categories such as "furniture" do not produce common motor responses. She asserts that visual shape similarities are greater within the basic level categories, all chairs being roughly similar in shape, while different pieces of furniture can be highly dissimilar. Although in experiments subjects' ratings have confirmed her views, the results are very dependent on the particular categories and examples selected for testing. It is not difficult to think of counter-examples. Objects from different categories like oranges, balls and globes are more similar in shape than oranges and bananas. A motor response such as "polishing" may be common to most instances of furniture for some people. While Rosch's general theory of conceptual structures has great intuitive appeal, more extensive testing may yet reveal that not all concepts are represented as mental prototypes, and the distinction between basic level categories, and other, non-preferred levels is not so uniform and clear-cut as she supposes.

Nevertheless, this new approach to the study of concepts marks a turning point in that it illustrates a new willingness to combine intuitive, philosophical, cross-cultural and linguistic analysis with a wide variety of experimental methods in trying to explore the natural concepts which are naturally acquired in the course of everyday life.

REFERENCES

Baron, J. (1973). Semantic components and conceptual development. *Cognition* 2/3, 299–317.

Battig, W. F. and Bourne, L. E. (1955). Concept identification as a function of irrelevant information and instruction. *Journal of Experimental Psychology* 49, 153–164.

Bourne, L. E. (1966). "Human Conceptual Behaviour". Allyn and Bacon, Boston.

Bourne, L. E. (1974). An inference model for conceptual rule learning. *In* "Theories in Cognitive Psychology" (R. L. Solso, ed.), The Loyola Symposium. Laurence Erlbaum, Potomac, Maryland.

Bourne, L. E. and Guy, D. E. (1968). Learning conceptual rules, II. The role of positive and negative instances. *Journal of Experimental Psychology* 77, 488–494.

Bourne, L. E. and Haygood, R. C. (1961). Effects of redundant relevant information upon the identification of concepts. *Journal of Experimental Psychology* 61, 259–260.

Bourne, L. E. and Jennings, P. (1963). The relationship between contiguity and classification learning. *Journal of General Psychology* 69, 335–338.

Bourne, L. E. and Restle, F. (1959). Mathematical theory of concept identification. *Psychological Review* 66, 278–296.

Bourne, L. E., Guy, D. E., Dodd, D. and Justesen, D. R. (1965). Concept identification: the effects of varying length and informational components of the inter-trial interval. *Journal of Experimental Psychology* 69, 624–629.

Bourne, L. E., Guy, D. E. and Wadsworth, N. (1967). Verbal reinforcement combinations and the relative frequency of informative feedback in a card sorting task. *Journal of Experimental Psychology* 73, 220–226.

Bower, G. H. and Trabasso, T. R. (1964). Concept identification. *In* "Studies in Mathematical Psychology (R. C. Atkinson, ed.). Stanford University Press.

Brooks, L. (1976). Non-analytic concept formation and memory for instances. S.S.R.C. 1976 Conference of Human Categorization.

Brown, R. W. (1958). How shall a thing be called? *Psychological Review* **65**, 14-21.

Bruner, J. S., Goodnow, J. J. and Austin, G. A. (1956). "A Study of Thinking". Science Editions, New York.

Bulgarella, R. and Archer, E. J. (1962). Concept identification of auditory stimuli as a function of amount of relevant and irrelevant information. *Journal of Experimental Psychology* **63**, 254-257.

Buss, A. H. and Buss, E. H. (1956). The effect of verbal reinforcement combinations on conceptual learning. *Journal of Experimental Psychology* **52**, 283-287.

Cahill, H. E. and Hovland, C. I. (1960). The role of memory in the acquisition of concepts. *Journal of Experimental Psychology* **59**, 137-144.

Dominowski, R. L. (1974). How do people discover concepts? *In* "Theories in Cognitive Psychology" (R. L. Solso, ed.), The Loyola Symposium. Laurence Erlbaum, Potomac, Maryland.

Erikson, J. R., Zajkowski, M. M. and Ehrmann, E. D. (1966). All or none assumptions in concept identification: analysis of latency data. *Journal of Experimental Psychology* **72**, 690-697.

Ervin-Tripp, S. M. and Foster, G. (1966). The development of meaning in children's descriptive terms. *Journal of Abnormal and Social Psychology* **61**, 274-275.

Hayes, K. J. and Nissen, C. H. (1971). Higher mental functions of a home-raised chimpanzee. *In* "Behaviour of Nonhuman Primates" (A. M. Schrier and F. Stollnitz, eds), Vol. IV. Academic Press, New York and London.

Haygood, R. C. and Bourne, L. E. (1965). Attribute and rule learning, aspects of conceptual behaviour. *Psychological Review* **72**, 175-195.

Hunt, E. B. and Hovland, C. I. (1960). Order of consideration of differential types of concepts. *Journal of Experimental Psychology* **59**, 220-225.

Kendler, H. H. and Kendler, T. S. (1962). Vertical and horizontal processes in problem solving. *Psychological Review* **69**, 1-16.

Lakoff, G. (1972). Hedges: a study in meaning criteria and the logic of fuzzy concepts. Chicago Linguistics Society. Eighth regional meeting, Chicago.

Levine, M. (1962). Cue neutralization: the effects of random reinforcements upon discrimination learning. *Journal of Experimental Psychology* **63**, 438-443.

Levine, M. (1966). Hypothesis behaviour by humans during discrimination learning. *Journal of Experimental Psychology* **71**, 331-338.

Neisser, U. and Weene, P. (1962). Hierarchies in concept attainment. *Journal of Experimental Psychology* **64**, 644-645.

Olson, D. (1970). Language and Thought: aspects of a cognitive theory of semantics. *Psychological Review* **77**, 257-273

Osgood, C. E. (1952). The nature and measurement of meaning. *Psychological Bulletin* **49**, 197-237.

Pishkin, V. (1960). Effects of probability of misinformation and number of irrelevant dimensions upon concept identification. *Journal of Experimental Psychology* **59**, 371-378.

Posner, M. I. and Keele, S. W. (1968). On the genesis of abstract ideas. *Journal of Experimental Psychology* **77**, 353-363.

Posner, M. I. and Keele, S. W. (1970). Retention of abstract ideas. *Journal of Experimental Psychology* **83**, 304-308.

Restle, F. (1962). The selection of strategies in cue learning. *Psychological Review* **69**, 329-343.

Rosch, E. (1975). Cognitive reference points. *Cognitive Psychology* **7**, 532-547.

Rosch, E. and Mervis, C. B. (1975). Family Resemblances: studies in the interval structure of categories. *Cognitive Psychology* **7**, 573-605.

Shepp, B. E. and Zeaman, D. (1966). Discrimination learning of size and brightness by retardates. *Journal of Comparative and Physiological Psychology* **62**, 55-59.

Slamecka, N. J. A. (1968). A methodological analysis of shift patterns in human discrimination learning. *Psychological Bulletin* **69**, 423-438.

Smith, E. E., Soben, E. J. and Rips, L. J. (1974). Structure and process in semantic memory: a featural model for semantic decisions. *Psychological Review* **81**, 214-241.

Trabasso, T. R. (1963). Stimulus emphasis and all or none learning in concept identification. *Journal of Experimental Psychology* **65**, 398-406.

Trabasso, T. R. and Bower, G. H. (1966). Presolution dimensional shifts in concept identification. A test of the sampling with replacement axiom in all or none models. *Journal of Mathematical Psychology* **3**, 163-173.

Wells, H. (1967). Facilitation of concept learning by a simultaneous contrast procedure. *Psychonomic Science* **9**, 609-610.

Wittgenstein, L. (1953). "Philosophical Investigations". Basil Blackwell, Oxford.

7

Computer Simulation

The purpose of this chapter is not to attempt a comprehensive review of computer simulation (CS) studies, but rather to try to evaluate the power of machine analogies as a technique for investigating the nature of human thought, and for testing models of cognitive processes. To do this, it is necessary to clarify the aims of computer simulation, the assumptions underlying this technique, and the conditions that need to be satisfied before valid inferences can be made about human performance from the data derived from machine performance. All these issues are critically involved in the fundamental problem of functional equivalence. In general, the aim of computer simulation is to make machines perform tasks in ways that are functionally equivalent to the ways in which humans carry out the same tasks. But what is to count as functional equivalence?

I. THE PROBLEM OF FUNCTIONAL EQUIVALENCE

The criteria which are appropriate and sufficient to permit a claim of functional equivalence will necessarily depend on how complete, detailed and exact a reproduction of human behaviour the CS worker is aiming to create. Because this has not always been made clear, misunderstanding and confusion have arisen, and computer simulation has been severely criticized (e.g. Dreyfus, 1972) for failing to attain levels of equivalence that are not strictly necessary or relevant. Pylyshyn (1975) makes this point when he comments:

> The relation of model to system-being-modelled must be partial and incomplete in important ways. As Sellars (1963) has put it, the interpretation of the model as some kind of analogue of a system is possible only if the model is accompanied by a commentary which tells the user which

aspects of the system are mapped onto the model, and which aspects of the model are relevant to its analogy with the system. Dreyfus wants the relation of 'representing' to be so complete and transparent that no such commentary would be necessary. But this is impossible unless the model and the system are so close to being identical that the model can no longer serve as an instrument for understanding the system—which, in the case of CS, is its sole purpose.

Given, then, that the object of CS is not to produce entities which are virtually identical with human beings, but only to produce analogies which are equivalent in some respects, it is vital to specify the kind of equivalence which *is* essential if computer models are to prove an informative method of investigating human behaviour. Some of the problems which have made this a difficult and confusing issue are discussed below. It is perhaps surprising to find that these are exactly the same problems that arise when we try to formulate general theories of human performance on the basis of experimental testing of human subjects.

A. Equivalence with Whom? The Problem of Individual Differences

Should a CS program yield a result which is equivalent to the best human performance, to the average human performance, or to the performance of some individual of normal intelligence? Should it be equivalent to a skilled and practised human performer, or to an untutored beginner? Since the range of human performance at complex tasks like chess playing, mathematics or logical problems is very wide, this question needs to be answered. Dreyfus cites one CS worker (Gruenberger, 1962) as aiming for a program that plays chess better than any man, and regards the achievement of only "reasonably competent" chess playing programs as evidence for the failure of CS. However, if the aim of the programmer is to reproduce the mental operations involved in the chess playing of an average or novice player, then a reasonably competent machine performance might well constitute a successful simulation. Attempts to simulate "average" performance might fail for the reason that the average performance in tasks like problem solving and concept formation does not necessarily reflect the performance of any single individual. Why should the computer mirror average performance if no individual subject in the experimental task does? If the gap between machine performance and average human performance is no greater than the differences between one human individual and another, it is hardly justifiable to conclude that the simulation is unsuccessful.

Turing's test (Turing, 1950) evades the problem of individual differences by requiring that the output of a computer simulation should be such that an observer could not distinguish it from the output of a human performer; that is to say, it should be equivalent to the output of *some* human individual. Even so, it might be necessary to instruct Turing's observer that some aspects of the comparison were relevant and others irrelevant. In judging the equivalence of mathematical calculations, for example, it might be desirable for him to confine his comparison to the accuracy of the solutions, and ignore differences in speed. Arguably, the most satisfactory equivalence would be achieved if systematic variations in the program produced variations in the machine performance so as to mimic the whole range of human individual differences.

B. General Equivalence or Specific Equivalence? The Problem of Task Differences

Humans possess cognitive abilities which enable them to perform a wide range of different tasks. Most CS programs are designed to carry out only a limited set of specific tasks. This limited generality has led some critics, such as Bolton (1972) to assert "A computer which performs one specialist task very well, but is helpless at any other problem is not therefore representative of human problem solving". A number of arguments can be advanced for not accepting Bolton's stricture. Lack of versatility is not necessarily a fatal flaw in computer simulation. Even if we accept Spearman's (1927) conclusion that there is a general ability factor in human intelligence, as well as specific ability factors, common sense insists that human versatility is not unlimited. People can be excellent scientists, and poor bridge players. It is not clear what degree of general ability a CS program ought to manifest if it is to be analogous to human intelligence.

Some CS programs have in fact achieved a measure of generality, notably the *General Problem Solver* of Newell *et al.* (1959), a sequentially organized program which proceeds by setting goals, detecting differences between the prevailing state and the goal, and generating moves to reduce these differences, in the manner of the TOTE unit of Miller *et al.* (1960) (described in Chapter 3). Technological difficulties of incorporating sufficient specific data to cope with a wider range of problems have proved to be one of the main limitations to the generality of this program. It did succeed in solving a variety of logical and mathematical problems, and was in principle extendable to other problems. However, there are serious theoretical, as well as technological, problems in trying to expand the data base of a CS beyond a certain point. These theoretical problems centre on the organization of the computer's stock of knowledge as it becomes increasingly complex. But, even if a single CS program can represent only a sub-set of human cognitive abilities, CS work taken as a whole does exhibit considerable generality, in that many different programs employ the same basic design principles.

It is also reasonable to question the assumption that a CS program needs generality if it is to be a useful analogy to human performance. Whether this is so, or not, depends on the aims of the simulation, and the claims that are based on it. If the aim of a CS program is to test a model of letter recognition by simulating the hypothesized stages of processing, and comparing them with human performance, the validity of the simulation is not affected if the program cannot also recognize faces. The lack of generality would be crucial only if the program claimed to exemplify a general mechanism of pattern recognition; or, if we could assert as an empirical fact that humans employ the same processing stages in all pattern recognition tasks. In fact, the whole trend of the experimental work on human information processing over the last decade or so has been to reveal that processing stages are task specific, rather than being uniform across different tasks. It is hardly fair to castigate computer simulation for failing to display a generality which is also lacking in theoretical models of cognition, and in experimental results. Most CS workers are far from claiming a generality and completeness that their programs do not possess. Anderson and Bower (1973) explicitly state that they "try to abstract from the real world significant components of the phenomena at hand". Whether or not they manage to identify the significant components is a much more important issue than generality *per se*.

C. Equivalence and the Problem of Strategy Differences

Besides applying different processing operations in different tasks, a single human performer typically has a range of possible strategies available for any single task. To take a simple example, he may choose any one of several methods in order to multiply 346 by 24. Computer programs do not usually have this flexibility. However, there is in principle no obstacle to programming a simulation with alternative strategies. The *Logic Theorist* of Newell *et al.* (1958), for example, has three heuristics available for proving theorems. The fact that different strategies can be used to perform the same task does, however, raise some serious problems for computer simulation. Firstly, it is extremely difficult to identify and represent the factors which incline a human performer to prefer one strategy over another, or to abandon one strategy and shift to another. Individual preferences are liable to be determined by past experience, intelligence, practice, the relative values placed on speed and accuracy, and the cost in terms of cognitive load. These determinants of strategy selection are not sufficiently well understood, and are too complex and variable to be accurately simulated. Secondly, it is difficult to judge whether functional equivalence between human and computer has been achieved if different strategies can yield the same result, or to infer non-equivalence if the same strategy could yield different results. It should be noted, though, that the tendency to assume uniformity of strategy is not confined to CS work. Many models of human performance (for example, models of memory) based on experimental data also make this assumption, and are open to the same criticism.

D. Competence Equivalence or Performance Equivalence?

Critics of CS, including Dreyfus (1972) and Neisser (1963), have argued that the man–machine analogy breaks down in so far as machines fail to incorporate the performance factors which influence human processing, and so lack "psychological reality". Again, this criticism could equally well be levelled at information processing models which ignore emotional, motivational and experiential factors just as much as CS does. The criticism may be justified either if a model claims to be a performance model, when in fact it is a purely competence model; or, if competence models are considered too restricted to be illuminating. In practice, most models, whether they take the form of computer simulation models, or theoretical models based on experiments with human subjects, select and incorporate some performance factors and ignore others. Early versions of the Collins and Quillian model of semantic memory described in Chapter 1 failed to incorporate effects of familiarity and experience. The *Logic Theorist* of Newell *et al.* (1958), on the other hand, does include effects of experience, being biased towards choosing moves which gave successful solutions in previous problems. What needs to be justified is the criterion for selection of some performance factors and the omission of others.

A major plank in Dreyfus's critique is his contention that it is *a priori* impossible to formalize in CS the phenomenological aspect of human performance. Human problem solving is accompanied by subjective feelings such as boredom, fatigue, interest, frustration and understanding. Neisser (1963) also emphasized the motivational differences between man and machine. A man playing a game of chess is seldom motivated solely by the desire to win the game. More commonly he has a multiplicity of motives, and may be concerned with the elegance and novelty of his strategies, the quality of social interaction with his opponent, and the time within which he would like to conclude the game so that he can go away and do something else. The values he attaches to these various goals may shift throughout the game and change his behaviour. Human goals are multiple, interactive and flexible. Computer goals are more often simple and fixed. Computer output does not exhibit the fluctuations caused by feelings of boredom, fatigue and lack of perseverance, and in these respects, is not, according to the phenomenologist view, equivalent to man.

The phenomenologist attack on CS also claims that the man-machine analogy is invalid because the machine does not "understand" what it is doing. In answer to this objection, Wilks (1976) remarked that:

> if I am asked for the phenomenology of anyone else's understanding, I have, of course, no feelings and immediate assurance to fall back on, and I am out in the cold world of watching his behaviour for appearances of understanding. ...What kind of criteria of phenomenological reassurance about the understanding of another can I have that I do not have for a machine—the criteria are and must be behavioural in both cases.

In other words, the existence of subjective understanding is just as much a problem for the human experimental psychologist as it is for the CS worker. Admittedly, the cross-cultural comparisons of cognitive tasks reviewed in Chapter 5 showed how difficult it can be to ensure uniformity of understanding across human subjects. Nevertheless, it is arguable that the problem of understanding is an order of magnitude greater in machine–human comparisons than in human–human comparisons. It is usually possible to test human understanding by examining a much more varied and extensive repertoire of verbal and non-verbal behavioural responses than a machine can produce. The importance of the question of "understanding" is illustrated by the specific examples discussed in Section IV.

Dreyfus also claims that the exercise of human intelligence is critically dependent on having a body because it is based on knowledge acquired by means of the perceptual and motor systems. This objection is only partly countered by Pylyshyn (1975) who, while admitting that the body is necessary for the acquisition of knowledge, maintains that there is no reason why the formal conceptual structures so acquired cannot be represented in a machine. According to this view, the machine could accurately represent human capacities at the point in time when a task was begun. But most human performance involves continuous processing of perceptuo-motor feedback during the task, so the bodiless machine would not be equivalent in this respect. In fact, since it is now possible to equip machines with sensor and effector mechanisms, there is no reason why perceptuo-motor modifications of ongoing performance cannot be programmed to occur during the course of the task. When this is done, it turns out to enhance the "understanding" of the machine in important ways (see Section IV).

Some performance factors such as familiarity, set, practice, intentions, distractability and limited persistence can be incorporated in CS systems in so far as they can be defined in formal terms. If intentions are defined as the selection of operations so as to produce a predetermined goal state; or familiarity is defined as the occurrence of a positive match between a new input and a stored representation of a previously encountered input, these factors can be adequately represented in CS, although the subjective emotions that accompany them are absent.

The extent to which a CS model needs to incorporate performance factors, and the selection of which ones should be included, is again dependent on its aims and claims. If the aim is to represent one of the possible sets of operations that a human could employ in carrying out the task (a weak equivalence), it would be important for the CS model to incorporate human performance factors that are fairly fixed and uniform such as limited memory and limited information processing capacity. It would be less necessary to incorporate performance factors like values and motives that are more variable. If the aim of the CS is to mimic the *actual* performance of a human subject (a strong equivalence), then failure to include the variable performance factors would be more damaging.

E. What are the Criteria for Equivalence?

Selection of the appropriate criteria will depend on whether the aim of the CS is to demonstrate a weak equivalence or a strong equivalence. It might seem that a claim of weak equivalence, that is, that the machine represents a possible model of human performance, is justified if the machine succeeds in performing the task. But this is only true if certain *a priori* criteria are also fulfilled. A machine which plays a passable game of chess, but selects its moves by testing the outcomes of many thousands of possible moves, cannot be even weakly equivalent to the human player, since we know *a priori* that such a method is beyond the capacities of the human information processing system. If the CS is designed to test for strong equivalence, and to represent the operations actually employed by human performers, much more stringent criteria are required. In addition to performing the task successfully, and having a processing capacity that falls within the range of human abilities, the machine should also give some further evidence of using the same operations as human subjects. Such evidence may be forthcoming if, for example, a set of problems yields the same order of difficulty for the machine and for man, and if the errors made by the machine are qualitatively similar to the errors of the human subject. A claim of strong equivalence would be further reinforced if the steps of the CS program are reflected in the protocols of human subjects. Although "thinking aloud" may provide only an incomplete record of the stages of human reasoning, it does indicate some of the processes of hypothesis selection, testing, revision and rejection which occur before solution is reached, and comparison of protocol and program provides one of the most powerful tests of man–machine equivalence.

When these criteria are not satisfied, are we entitled to claim non-equivalence, and to infer that the model of human behaviour being tested in the CS must be rejected? In making a judgement of non-equivalence it is necessary to locate the source of the difference. Does the CS differ from the human performer because it does not incorporate the same sequence of operations? Or does the difference lie in the performance factors such as differences in speed, memory capacity, motivation and past experience? While comparison of test outputs may fail to shed any light on the source of non-equivalence, comparison of protocol and program is more likely to pinpoint the difference and show whether the model being tested is wholly mistaken, or only wrong in certain details.

In this discussion it has become clear that, while some of the objections raised by critics of CS are not very relevant, there are serious problems of interpretation when CS studies are used to test psychological models. It is also apparent that most of these same problems arise when the psychological models are tested against experimental data derived from human subjects. Here the difficulties of interpretation arouse less chauvinistic passion, and too little attention, but are just as acute.

The remainder of this chapter is devoted to consideration of particular examples of CS in different cognitive tasks, and to the specific limitations of CS in each of these.

II. COMPUTER SIMULATION OF PATTERN RECOGNITION

Computer simulation of pattern recognition illustrates many of the problems and limitations that beset other kinds of simulation. Human pattern recognition has several characteristics that are especially hard to simulate mechanically. Sutherland (1968) has listed some of the conditions that a theory of visual pattern recognition must fulfil if it is to be satisfactory, and the same conditions apply to a CS program if it is to be an adequate representation of human pattern recognition. These include the ability to recognize patterns successfully over variations of size, position and brightness; the ability to extract the pattern from a redundant or noisy background; the ability to use context-generated expectancies to identify novel, ambiguous or ill-defined patterns, and the ability to recognize complex patterns at a global level without consciously processing individual details.

The majority of CS programs have concentrated on the recognition of alphanumeric characters, and, in consequence, cannot claim to represent more than a fraction of normal human pattern recognition ability. The preference for simulating character recognition has been dictated partly, no doubt, by the utility of having machines to process written inputs, and partly by the fact that printed characters, because they can be specified in terms of a fairly small set of well defined features, are easier to handle in a CS program than patterns with more numerous, ill defined and variable features. It is an example of what Anderson and Bower (1973), in McLuhan's words, call "the medium determining the message". They rightly emphasize the importance of realizing "how often technological capabilities and constraints have determined theoretical decisions in this field".

Template matching models work by matching the input to an identical stored representation of the character. These models work well enough so long as the characters are invariant (like the standardized forms used by banks), but cannot operate over variations of size and rotation, differences in type-face, and distortions, since a mismatch is registered if input and stored template differ in any respect. Such a model is clearly quite dissimilar to human pattern recognition which operates successfully over a wide range of variability. Attempts to improve template matching by inserting smoothing, or pre-processing operations which normalize size and orientation have made it more effective, but the range of variability which can be tolerated is still limited (Selfridge and Neisser, 1960).

Computer simulation programs which test for specific features, and combine results of these tests into a total pattern, have been more successful. One such program is described by Unger (1959). The system tests for the presence or absence of specific features (like a vertical stroke, a diagonal stroke or a closed loop). The feature tests are arranged in a sequential branching tree, and a binary decision is made at each node. The result of each test determines which test is applied next, so that the final outcome specifies the identity of the character. Other programs (e.g. Uttley, 1958; Uhr, 1963) incorporate hierarchically arranged units, the firing of the higher-order units being determined by inputs from the lower-order feature analysers. Another hierarchical model is Selfridge's *Pandemonium* (1958) diagrammed in Fig. 1. The lowest-level units, which Selfridge calls "data or image demons", transmit the pattern to the next level of "computational demons", which analyse the component features. This information is combined at the level of the "cognitive demons", and the decision is based on the relative amplitude of the firing of the cognitive demons. The one firing with the

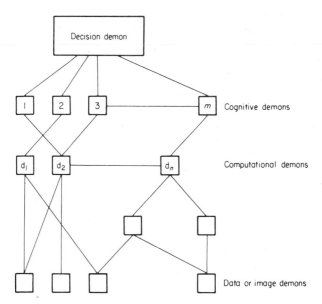

Fig. 1. The essential stages in *Pandemonium*. From Selfridge (1958).

greatest amplitude determines the response. This model has several properties which reflect important principles of human pattern recognition. One problem in the design of CS programs for pattern recognition has been the selection of features. What feature tests should be incorporated in the model? Computer simulation programs, unlike humans, are initially programmed with a small set of feature tests arbitrarily selected by the programmer. Models like the *Pandemonium*, and Uhr's model, are able to modify this initial selection. In the *Pandemonium*, the selection of computational demons, and the weightings attached to their outputs, can be changed by feedback procedures. Incorrect decisions result in the rejection of misleading feature tests, or reduced weight being given to their outputs. In Uhr's program the feature analysers are initially selected at random from an operating set, and unsuccessful feature analysers are discarded and new ones adopted. Both these models therefore reflect, to some extent, the self-modifying properties of the human system. When we find that not all Ford cars are green, we stop applying colour tests in identifying makes of car.

The *Pandemonium* model also has a second property which has been considered essential for man–machine equivalence. The output of the feature analysers is in an analogue rather than a digital form. That is, the output is a continuously graded quantity rather than an all-or-none, yes–no, discrete state. Most computers operate on the digital principle, with elements assuming the discrete states of 0 or 1, whereas the human nervous system can transmit continuously graded analogue information. Dreyfus (1972) has made especially heavy use of this particular stick for beating machine simulation, on the grounds that computers cannot operate in analogue form, and that their failure to do so invalidates claims of equivalence. Several arguments can be advanced in refutation of this objection. Firstly, it is not impossible to incorporate analogue devices in computers, although it may be complex and time-consuming to do so. Secondly, if the size of the discrete steps is sufficiently small the difference between analogue and digital forms becomes negligible (Pylyshyn, 1975). Thirdly, Sutherland (1974) has pointed out that, while analogical functioning is typical of physical processes in the human brain, it is not typical of cognitive processes. Humans are poor at categorizing analogue information, since we can only identify about seven different pitches in a range of tones, while our ability to categorize discrete information such as verbal stimuli is virtually unlimited. It is more accurate to describe the brain as an analogue-to-digital transformer than a strictly analogue processor, since continuously graded signals such as speech sounds are transformed to digital responses. Finally, the analogue–digital difference between man and machine would only be important if physical equivalence rather than formal equivalence was required.

Another feature of the *Pandemonium* model is that it allows simultaneous processing of features. Experimental work with human subjects suggests that some features of patterns can be processed simultaneously in parallel, at least when the patterns have become familiar (Corcoran, 1971).

Although computer simulation of pattern recognition has been largely concerned with printed alphanumeric characters, some success has been achieved with handwritten characters as well. In handwriting the features are much less well-defined. While a printed N may be defined by two parallel vertical strokes linked by a diagonal stroke running from the top of the left-hand vertical to the bottom of the right-hand vertical, in a handwritten N, the strokes may be neither vertical nor parallel, and the diagonal may fail to join them. Computer simulation programs like Doyle's (1960) extract the most reliable features during a learning phase, during which various examples of the letters are presented, together with their correct identifications. After learning, Doyle's program achieved 90% accuracy for a small set of letters. Other programs (see Eden, 1968a, for a review) have improved their performance by a limited use of contextual constraints. The program of Mermelstein (1964) used inter-stroke constraints to help identify handwritten words. Since the identity of a given stroke is partly determined by its neighbours, the use of this contextual information makes the identification easier.

The use of context is a corner-stone of human cognition, and a major stumbling-block for computer simulation. The important differences between the ways in which men and machines are able to utilize contextual cues are best illustrated in the recognition of speech and handwriting. In both cases human recognition maintains a high standard of accuracy in spite of distortion, variability or ambiguity. Just as two examples of a handwritten letter may have no single feature in common, two versions of the same phoneme spoken by different speakers, in different words, may have no acoustic features in common. Yet the human pattern recognizer can identify them with remarkably little difficulty. Consider what happens when we encounter a badly written letter in a word, and cannot immediately identify it. We can use local contextual cues such as the letter sequences within the word, and the word length; or we can use more wide-ranging contextual cues such as syntactic and semantic constraints within the sentence or a longer segment of the text. We can use our knowledge of the subject matter and of the writer's intentions and literary style. If these cues fail, we can search for another occurrence of the unidentifiable symbol in the text, and try to use contextual cues to identify this example. If we achieve a tentative identification of the symbol, we can test the plausibility of this identification in different occurrences, and if the identification is confirmed we can formulate a set of defining features for future use.

The same strategies apply in speech recognition. If we are confronted with an unintelligible utterance, we can draw on our knowledge of phonemic, syntactic and semantic constraints; of the situational context of the utterance, and on the gestures, facial expression and personal character of the speaker. Two important points emerge from these illustrations. The human recognizer can apply past experience and general knowledge of any kind. His entire life experience is potentially available, and no bounds are set to the range of contextual cues he can employ. The computer can only apply a limited range of contextual information which has been pre-selected as specifically relevant to the particular task. The human recognizer is not confined to a "bottom-up", part-to-whole processing strategy of testing component features, and building upwards to a recognition of the whole pattern. He can shift flexibly to a "top-down", whole-to-part strategy of tentatively identifying larger units, and then filling in the details. Hill's (1968) idealized automatic speech recognizer (ASR) which is diagrammatically represented in Fig. 2, gives some impression of the number and complexity of the processing operations it would need to incorporate. Hill emphasizes that a basic structure for the recognition of the acoustic properties of speech needs additional "procedures which utilize inbuilt knowledge of the general structure of the speech signal at all levels". At present automatic speech recognition of this degree of sophistication is no more than an ideal. It is not yet technologically feasible to incorporate a comparable wealth of knowledge and experience in a computer. Probably the most advanced of current speech recognition programs is SPEECHLIS (Nash–Webber, 1975), which utilizes stored syntactic rules and semantic information. The system has a vocabulary of 250 words, and is restricted to the semantic domain of lunar geology. An input sentence is recognized by first making preliminary, tentative matches of individual words. A provisional hypothesis is generated in accordance with the stored rules of syntactic legality and semantic acceptability. The hypothesis is compared with the input sentence, checked, and revised until a complete match is achieved. The use of higher-level knowledge of linguistic

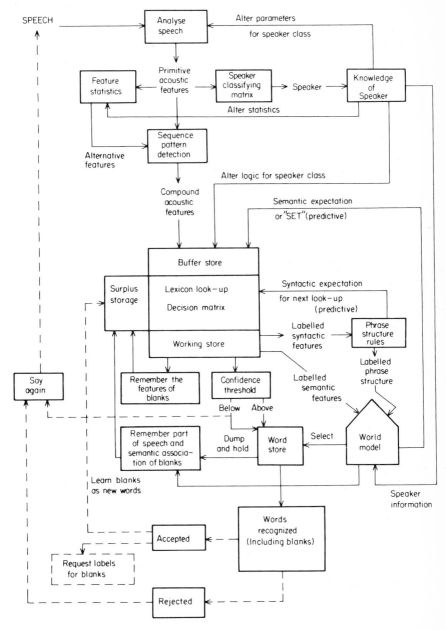

Fig. 2. A hypothetical ASR machine.

structure enables SPEECHLIS to recognize spoken sentences with much greater accuracy than systems which operate only at the phonemic level, but a speech recognition program of this kind can only perform effectively within its own restricted semantic domain. It can cope with lunar geology, but lacks the semantic information necessary to handle other topics. The scope of the program is limited by its own data base, and, unlike the human perceiver, it is not equipped to expand its own stock of knowledge and so extend its scope to include other semantic domains.

Some attempts have been made to programme computers to recognize what Eden (1968b) calls "natural patterns", such as electro-cardiograms, clouds, fingerprints and blood cells. These patterns resemble the natural concepts discussed in Chapter 6, in that it is difficult or impossible to supply a list of defining properties. Computer simulation is handicapped by our inability to make explicit the criteria we ourselves apply in recognizing natural patterns. Computer recognition of diseased blood cells, or cardiac irregularities can only succeed if the physician can give a precise description of the critical properties. Human recognition of natural patterns tends to be probabilistic, and this raises the further problem of specifying how such probabilistic decisions are determined. Ledley (1964) has described a technique for high-speed automatic analysis of biomedical pictures. The machine scans a picture of blood cells and locates the points within it that exceed a pre-deter-mined level on a black–white scale. The objects thus located are analysed in terms of curvature, and the position of holes within the objects. Alternative forms of the program analyse nerve endings in terms of the angle of branching and the degree of taper. Programs like this employ a limited set of parameters to extract particular aspects of the pattern which have been previously selected as critical. Their function is usually to classify patterns as normal or abnormal, rather than to make a precise identification. In medical diagnoses made by humans, decisions tend to be influenced by past experience, and subjective knowledge of the patient's history and personal qualities, in ways that cannot be accurately described. The scope of these contextual influences can again be very wide-ranging.

Biederman (1972) has experimentally demonstrated the effects of context on recognition of natural objects by human subjects. He studied the perception of natural objects which were embedded in real-world scenes. He found that even if the subjects knew before-hand what object to look for, and whereabouts in the scene it would be located, their ability to perceive the object was impeded by jumbling other areas of the scene, so that they were clearly using the global context of the whole scene, rather than confining their processing to the designated local area. Recent "scene analysis" programs (e.g. Guzman, 1968) have achieved considerable success in identifying and describing lay-outs of 2D and 3D blocks using various kinds of line junction as cues, but have difficulty in identifying natural objects in pictorial scenes. The identification of a cat in a drawing may require wide-ranging contextual knowledge and is not wholly based on determinate visual cues. For example, it may depend on the real-world knowledge that an animal depicted as chasing a mouse is liable to be a cat, even though its visual appearance is a-typical or ambiguous. Since we are not as yet able to say exactly how contextual factors influence recognition, or even what stage of the recognition mechanism is affected, our ability to represent contextual effects in computer simulation is necessarily inadequate.

III. COMPUTER MODELS OF MEMORY

Most of the earlier CS models of memory attempted to represent only a circumscribed set of sub-processes of memory. More recent models, which have greater generality, are considered in the next section. Reitman's (1970) Waiting-room Model represents a simple version of input processing in short-term memory, and provides a useful illustration of the way in which a detailed comparison of computer output and human data can suggest which properties of the original model are wrong, or oversimplified. In this case, the non-equivalence of man–machine outputs reveals the shortcomings of the CS model. According to the Reitman model, items are processed by a coder before being stored in permanent memory. Processing time is fixed, and when items arrive at the coder at a rate exceeding the speed of processing, they must queue up in the "waiting-room" in order of arrival. During waiting time, decay takes place at a fixed rate, and items are lost after a fixed amount of decay has occurred. When the queue length (the number of items waiting to be processed by the coder) exceeds the fixed capacity of the waiting-room, new items "bump out" old items on the principle of first in, first out (the oldest items are lost first). For recall of serial lists, the model generates a primacy effect that is governed by the rate of presentation. Items from the first part of the list are well recalled because these have been processed by the coder; but when the rate of presentation is fast, items have to queue in the waiting-room, and are bumped out by succeeding items. With a slow rate of presentation, more items can be recalled from the early part of the list, because the waiting-room fills up slowly, and fewer items are lost through bump-out. The model also predicts a stable recency effect. Items from the end of a serial list are the ones most recently presented, and these are well recalled. The items from the end of the list correspond to the contents of a full waiting-room, and the same number can be recalled however long the list. The model also predicts that if recall is delayed, the waiting-room contents will have been lost through decay, and only the coded items will be recalled, so that, after a delay, the primacy effect remains intact, but the recency effect disappears. In all these respects, there was good agreement between the computer results, and the human data, but the simulation was defective in several other features. Because the program treats individual items as equal and independent, it yields a regular cyclical pattern, successfully recalling every third or fourth item from the middle part of the list. Human subjects do not display such regularity: for them, items differ in ease or difficulty, interact with each other, take varying lengths of time to process, and may be given queuing priority. Coding time is not fixed, but varies with the particular item, or group of items. Forgetting is not all-or-none, and partial information is often available. The non-equivalence of the CS in these respects serves to highlight the importance of interactive processes and variable strategies in human memory.

EPAM, the Elementary Perceiver and Memorizer (Feigenbaum, 1963) was designed to mimic a stimulus–response learning system. Another model called SAL, the Stimulus and Association Learner (Hintzman, 1968) works on a similar principle. Incoming stimuli are sorted through a branching discrimination network. At each node, a feature test is carried out, and the result of the test determines which branch the stimulus is routed along, and which test is applied next. The number of test nodes is the minimum necessary to differentiate the stimulus from others in the set, and the stimulus is stored at the terminal node. A stimulus is therefore defined by its pathway through the sorting tree, as in Unger's letter recognition model. The system models acquisition and forgetting through interference, since errors will be made when a new stimulus is similar to an old one, and the tests in the existing network are insufficient to distinguish it. A new test node is then constructed, and the network is expanded locally as new items are learned. Responses associated with the stimuli are stored at the terminal nodes. One version of SAL permits multiple responses to be associated with a single stimulus instead of just one. It incorporates a push-down stack of responses, with the most recent responses having priority at the top of the stack. This enables the system to mimic retroactive interference effects, since the most recently learned responses occur as intrusion errors. How far does this model achieve functional equivalence with human performance? It displays some of the same forgetting characteristics, but the sequential feature analysis employed in these models is more error prone than the human system, which can test multiple features simultaneously. There is no provision for improvement in performance with increasing familiarity of the stimuli, and no context effects operate. Whether the model could, in principle, be extended to the learning of larger units such as sentences or propositions is doubtful. EPAM and SAL have only a weak equivalence to human memory. They represent a model for a limited sub-set of memory functions which could possibly correspond to one of the strategies the human learner has at his command for this kind of task.

IV. LANGUAGE UNDERSTANDING AND QUESTION ANSWERING

These simulations attempt to produce systems that will analyse and store linguistic inputs, and operate on them by retrieving facts and answering questions. For the most part, their aim has been to create systems that have psychological plausibility rather than psychological reality. These simulations have been especially valuable in highlighting those aspects of language processing that are least well understood. They have explored the difficulties of precisely specifying an adequate mechanism for analysing and representing meaning; they have exposed the limitations of systems that do not have access to a wide range of contextual and real-world information; and they have directed the attention of psychologists, not before time, to the need to define more carefully what we mean by "understanding".

Most CS models of language analysis operate by parsing the input and representing it in an associative network of nodes and links, corresponding to the component items and the relations between them (Frijda, 1972). The organization of the network, and the variety of the types of relation specified by the links varies from model to model. The construction of a parsing mechanism has come up against the same problem that confronted some of the programs for the recognition of patterns. The global pattern, or the global meaning of a sentence cannot easily be derived from an analysis of

the parts. The parser cannot begin by analysing word–word relationships, because these frequently depend on higher-order relationships
between larger units of the sentence. Hence a simple left to right
processing will not work, any more than bottom-up processing can
be relied on in pattern recognition. In a sentence like "the woman
who bought the ring was cheated by the jeweller", the fact that
"the woman" is the logical object does not emerge until the passive
verb construction has been analysed. Another difficulty is that the
parser cannot operate on syntax alone, since the analysis may depend
on semantic constraints as well. In "he said he would give her a ring
in the evening after he had been to the jeweller", we do not know
whether to interpret "ring" as a telephone call or an article of
jewellery until the reference to "the jeweller" makes the latter
interpretation more plausible. To overcome these problems, models
may opt for multiple parsings, backtrackings, or tentative parsings
which are subject to revision. Schank's (1972) program illustrates one
approach to the modelling of natural language analysis. Schank's
system employs a verb-based parser guided by a conceptual analyser.
It parses sentences by a method which is intuitively rather similar
to the way we understand foreign languages, when we have only
an imperfect or halting grasp of the grammar. The model has a
conceptual base consisting of stored knowledge about conceptual
relationships, for example, the knowledge that the word "go"
implies movement by an actor or object and a change of location.
This stored knowledge is used to guide the parser in interpreting the
input, and to generate expectations. The parser begins by isolating
the main verb, and refers this to the conceptual dependency
network. The conceptual relations associated with the verb are used
to determine the role of other words in the sentence. The output of
the parser is a network with the components of the sentence mapped
on to an abstract representation of labelled nodes and links. In one
of Schank's examples, the sentence "the big man took the book" is
mapped as:

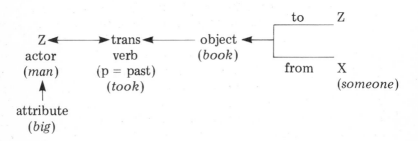

The parser has added the inference that the act of taking involves transfer of possession from someone (X) to the actor.

Schank's model is limited by the extent of its stored conceptual knowledge, and it operates only over a restricted range of sentence types. It cannot spontaneously expand its conceptual base. In practice, the initial verb-finding process might be expected to run into difficulties, since it employs syntactic cues to identify the verb such as inflections, and these may not always be present. As a model of human understanding it is not entirely plausible, since it is intuitively obvious that in reading, or listening to speech, comprehension is not suspended until the arrival of the main verb.

The remaining programs discussed in this section are chosen to illustrate the problem of understanding. Weizenbaum (1968) describes a program called DOCTOR which performs the role of psychiatrist in a conversation with a patient. Weizenbaum supplies a transcript of a conversation with a human subject acting as patient. The machine responses are given in italics.

Men are all alike.

In what way.

They're always bugging us about something.

Can you think of a specific example.

My boyfriend made me come here.

Your boyfriend made you come here.

He says I'm depressed much of the time.

I am sorry to hear you are depressed.

The program operates by selecting a key word in the input, and applying a transformation rule contextually associated with that key word. In the absence of a key word, a standard filler type of output is supplied, or an earlier transformation is reiterated. Weizenbaum asserts that in human–human interaction "there can be no total understanding and no absolute test of understanding". In his simulation, the "naturalness" of the conversation is the test of the machine's understanding. We need not be phenomenologists to feel there is something unsatisfactory about DOCTOR's understanding. DOCTOR's success seems to stem mainly from the choice of format in which the machine plays the traditionally restricted, and somewhat unresponsive, role of the psychiatrist. Clearly, as a dinner-table conversationalist he would be much less acceptable. Weizenbaum admits that DOCTOR's conversation breaks down if the human participant deviates from the role of patient, but he claims that human–human conversations degenerate similarly when contextual assumptions are not shared. This parallel is hardly sufficient to conceal the vast difference between ordinary human-human conversation, and the DOCTOR–patient conversation. Most humans share enough cultural context to be able to converse satisfactorily over a wide range of topics and, most importantly, misunderstandings can usually be remedied by explanations, or by backtracking until a common ground is found, and establishing a new shared framework from that point. Indeed, if this were not so, it would hardly be possible for teachers to impart new ideas to their pupils.

The understanding of computers is limited not only by the restricted context available to them, but also by the restriction of their input and output modalities. In relation to understanding, there is some point to the argument that functional equivalence cannot be achieved by machines lacking some kind of a body. Human–human understanding is not dependent solely on linguistic interchanges, but is also mediated by shared sensory information, and demonstrated by appropriate actions. Two recent programs manifest a deeper level of understanding because they simulate some perceptual and motor functions as well as language processing. In the philosopher's terms their use of language has reference as well as sense. Winograd's program operates within its own real world, which is composed of a table-top array of blocks of different sizes, shapes and colours (Winograd, 1972). It is equipped to perceive and manipulate these objects, and can store information and answer questions about the state of this world, and also carry out commands to move the objects around. It can use the perceptual context to identify the referents in the questions and commands, and can infer the intended referent when the description is ambiguous. A command like "Put it on top of the red one" identifies the referent of "it" as the last mentioned object, and searches the scene for the most likely referent to fit the description "the red one". This kind of behavioural evidence of understanding is more satisfactory than a purely verbal output, and is the kind of evidence we often demand from children and pupils when we suspect that parrot-like replies may conceal a lack of understanding.

A more satisfactory level of understanding is also demonstrated by Scraggs's attractive kitchen-hand LUIGI, a robot with a data base called "kitchenworld" (Scraggs, 1975). LUIGI can perceive the utensils and food items that compose his world; answer questions about them; perform simple tasks like picking up, cleaning, sandwich-making; describe his own procedures and give recipes. LUIGI stores real-world descriptions of physical objects, and also has a mental world of abstract concepts, and conceptual relations such as the set/super-set relation. Scraggs believes that Luigi is in principle extendable to other environments, although the data base required to make him more versatile would be impracticably large and complex. A sample of LUIGI's conversation is given below so that the reader can judge whether it seems more rewarding than DOCTOR's.

Where are the cookies?

Perhaps the cookies are on the shelf. Should I check?

Yes.

No the cookies are not on the shelf. Maybe they are on the counter. No they are not on the counter. I can't find the cookies.

I ate the cookies.

O.K.

Where are the cookies?

There are none.

Indeed, in this sample, LUIGI seems a good deal more rational than his questioner.

Norman (1973) has listed a number of types of question which are typically handled in different ways by men and machines, and so serve to show where equivalence breaks down. One is the Telephone Number Problem. If asked to give the telephone number of Charles Dickens, a human subject would most probably reject the query outright as a stupid question. The computer would search its memory and eventually signal "Not known". Humans apply general knowledge of literature, and the history of technological progress, and can reject this anomalous input at an early stage of processing. The Three Drugstores Problem is rather similar. Given the input sentence "I went to three drugstores" the computer stores this information. The human would ask "Whatever were you looking for?". The input is not rejected outright, but some further clarification is requested because the original statement does not make complete sense on its own. In another example, The Empire State Building Problem, the question "Where is the Empire State Building?" elicits different answers from humans depending on whether the questioner is two blocks away from the Empire State Building, or in the middle of Europe, and on whether his intentions are interpreted as a wish to go there, or to know the approximate location, or the postal address. The human answer is adapted to the contextual setting of the question and the inferred purposes of the questioner, whereas the computer's answer would be a standard one. What is apparent in these three examples is that the range of knowledge that the human thinker can bring to bear on the question spans his entire life experience, not just the immediate local context: that he is able to perceive what, in all his stock of information, is relevant to the question being asked, and that his responses are flexibly determined, not fixed. It is the restricted use of contextual information which is the chief source of non-equivalence in the understanding of computers. It is worth noting, however, that the ability to modify responses in accordance with contextual information is typical of *adult* human question answering, and that young children behave rather more like computers. The child who gets lost at a football match, and tells the policeman that his name is Johnny and he lives at number 29, is behaving like the computer answering the Empire State Building Problem.

V. PROBLEM SOLVING

Computer simulation of problem solving has had some success with logical, algebraic and geometric problems, and with the so-called Move problems. All these problems are characteristically well defined, and solution can be reached by application of a limited set of rules. The *Logic Theorist* of Newell *et al.* (1963) succeeded in proving 38 of the first 52 theorems of Whitehead and Russell's *Principia Mathematica*. It proceeded by first describing and classifying the axioms, and then applying rules of replacement, detachment, substitution and chaining to find the proof. The heuristics were guided by the outcome of previous problems. When a new problem was perceived as similar to an earlier one, previously successful operations were selected. How far this is analogous to human insight, as Newell *et al.* claimed, is doubtful. The organization of operations was strictly sequential, and success was dependent on the order in which the problems were presented. The *Logic Theorist* could not "learn" in the sense of finding new solution procedures, or modifying old ones, although it could use its accumulated experience to select from its existing repertoire the operations most likely to succeed. Because of its sequential organization, it could not consider several possible solutions simultaneously, in the way that Neisser (1963) maintains that humans do.

Man–machine equivalence is quite close in simulations of the class of problems known as Move Problems. These include the Water-jug Problem described in Chapter 3; the Tower of Hanoi Problem in which discs have to be transferred between pegs to produce a stipulated arrangement; the Monster Problem (Simon and Hayes,

1976) in which three different sizes of monster each hold a different-sized globe, and the task is to re-allocate the globes so that the large monster holds the large globe, the medium-sized monster holds the medium globe and the small monster holds the small globe; and the Missionaries and Cannibals Problem (Simon and Reed, 1976) which requires that five missionaries and five cannibals be moved from the left bank of the river to the right bank, with a boat that holds a maximum of three persons, and with the constraint that cannibals must never outnumber the missionaries, neither on a bank, nor in the boat. Recent studies comparing computer performance, and human performance on these problems have been useful in revealing the similarities and differences. Simon and Hayes computer program UNDERSTAND was tested on the Monster Problem. Human solver protocols showed that the humans engaged in preliminary efforts to understand the problem thoroughly, before attempting any moves, often requesting clarification of the instructions and querying the legality of possible moves. This stage was not represented in computer simulation. Both humans and computer were able to select the relevant information in the initial presentation of the problem, and discard the irrelevant information, such as the colour of the monsters. Human subjects appeared to use feedback from error moves to modify their interpretation of the problem, and this ability was also not represented in the computer program. Although both humans and computer showed a similar order of difficulty for various versions of the problem, the interesting feature of this study is that differences emerged from the protocol–program comparisons, even though performance, in terms of number of moves to solution, was quite similar. Clearly, equivalent results do not guarantee equivalence of procedures. Atwood and Polson's simulation of the Water-jug Problem (Atwood and Polson, 1976) leads to the same conclusion. Again, equivalent orders of difficulty over a series of problems were obtained, but move-by-move comparisons showed that human subjects selected their moves in accordance with a familiarity principle not represented in the computer program. Subjects preferred moves which brought about states familiar from previous experience. In their simulation of the Missionaries and Cannibals Problem, Simon and Reed (1976) compared the frequency with which particular moves were made. Quite close agreement of human and computer data was found. Task manipulations such as providing a sub-goal (e.g. get three cannibals alone on the far bank at some point), produced similar shifts in the move selection strategies of both the computer and the human solvers. These studies underline the importance of detailed stage by stage comparisons in judging the equivalence of man and machine performance. Grosser comparisons can conceal underlying differences.

Chess playing has been more difficult to simulate because the chess game is a much more complex and ill-defined problem. The number of possible strategies is far greater, and the heuristics used by the human player are not sufficiently well understood to be exactly specified and reproduced. Chess-playing computers are programmed with heuristics for the selection of a sub-set of possible moves, but many aspects of human chess playing are not represented. It is characteristic of human chess playing that, as in pattern recognition, the human can shift freely back and forth between an atomistic processing, considering individual pieces, and a more global processing of whole areas of the board. Skilled players tend to perceive the positions of the pieces in an holistic fashion, in terms of the overall pattern, and seem to have a mental library of such patterns which are associated with likely moves and possible outcomes (De Groot, 1965). The human player's thinking may involve both verbalization and visualization. He is able to simplify the problem by selecting the most essential elements, and focusing attention on these. The past experience of the human chess player also enables him to assess his opponent's temperament, level of skill and style of play, and to use this knowledge to predict probable counter moves, and to select his own strategy. In short, the heuristics of human chess playing are multiply determined, flexible, and to some extent inaccessible to consciousness. Although computers have been programmed to play chess more successfully than the average human, their operations are not strongly equivalent to human chess playing.

Many of the limitations of computer simulation that have been noted throughout this chapter are both technological and theoretical. There are limits on the size of the data base that is practicable, so that the computer can only store and access a restricted local context. This handicap imposes limits on the versatility, flexibility and depth of understanding that the simulation can attain. It follows that the computer cannot simulate the human thinker, but only an arbitrarily defined sub-set of thinking operations. The extent to which computers succeed in simulating human thinking forces us to reconsider questions about the relationship of language and thought discussed in Chapters 4 and 5, and to acknowledge that the language of the computer program can be adequate for many kinds of thinking.

Besides these limitations of scope and complexity, the main barrier to successful computer simulation is our ignorance of many aspects of human performance. We cannot simulate processes which we cannot describe. We cannot specify, for example, exactly how practice and familiarity bring about improvement in performance, nor how conscious rule-following gives place to automatic unmonitored skilled performance. We don't understand how we decide which are the essential features of a pattern or a problem, and which are inessential or irrelevant; or how we decide what aspects of past experience, and what kinds of contextual information, are applicable to a new problem. We don't understand what governs shifts between verbal and visual coding, or serial and parallel processing, or how attention operates to produce in-depth processing of focused information, and rough monitoring of objects and events outside the focus. We are not able to say very precisely what we mean by creative thinking, or insight. The kind of thinking which is most difficult to formalize is the kind that is not language based. In all these areas, the success of computer simulation is curtailed by the shortcomings of theoretical psychology, rather than the shortcomings of CS techniques.

Ideally, experimental testing of human subjects, machine simulation and theory building ought to constitute a three-way interaction. Rumelhart and Norman (1975) express this policy in describing their methods:

> We postulated a procedure: then we put the components together, modifying the parts to make this possible: then we used the system for a while, discovering the strengths, weaknesses and conceptual errors. We then repeated the entire process, each time learning more about our underlying theoretical conceptualizations.

Their initial postulates are derived from theories which in turn are based on human data. The computer simulation provides a method of discovering whether the theory is fully specified, since the exercise of formalizing the theory exposes any vagueness or inconsistency, and the results of the computer simulation are a test of the predictive power of the theory. Thus experimental testing of human subjects, and machine simulation provide two complementary ways to test the validity of psychological models. By comparison with human testing, the CS method is better controlled, and, although the problem of equivalence makes the interpretation of the findings more difficult, the methodology of cognitive psychology gains in power and precision from the technique of computer simulation.

REFERENCES

Anderson, J. R. and Bower, G. H. (1973). "Human Associative Memory". John Wiley and Sons, New York.

Atwood, M. E. and Polson, P. G. (1976). A process model for water jug problems. *Cognitive Psychology* 8, 191-216.

Biederman, I. (1972). Perceiving real world scenes. *Science, N.Y.* 177, 77-80.

Bolton, N. (1972). "The Psychology of Thinking". Methuen, London.

Corcoran, D. W. J. (1971). "Pattern Recognition". Penguin Books, Harmondsworth, Middlesex.

De Groot, A. D. (1965). "Thought and Choice in Chess". Mouton, The Hague.

Doyle, W. (1960). Recognition of sloppy handprinted characters. *Proceedings of the Western Joint Computer Conference*, San Francisco.

Dreyfus, H. L. (1972). "What Computers Can't Do". Harper and Row, New York.

Eden, M. (1968a). Handwriting generation and recognition. *In* "Recognizing Patterns: Studies in Living and Automatic Systems" (P. A. Kolers and M. Eden, eds). The M.I.T. Press, Cambridge, Massachusetts.

Eden, M. (1968b). Other pattern recognition problems and some generalizations. *In* "Recognizing Patterns: Studies in Living and Automatic Systems" (P. A. Kolers and M. Eden, eds). The M.I.T. Press, Cambridge, Massachusetts.

Feigenbaum, E. A. (1963). Simulation of verbal learning behaviour. *In* "Computers and Thought" (E. A. Feigenbaum and J. Feldman, eds). McGraw-Hill, New York.

Frijda, N. H. (1972). Simulation of long term memory. *Psychological Bulletin* 77, 1-31.

Gruenberger, F. (1962). "Benchmarks in Artificial Intelligence", p. 2586. The RAND Corporation.

Guzman, A. (1968). Decomposition of a visual scene into three-dimensional bodies. *In* "Proceedings AFIPS 1968 Fall Joint Computer Conference". Spartan Books, New York.

Hill, A. (1968). Automatic speech recognition: a problem for machine intelligence. *In* "Machine Intelligence" (N. L. Collins and D. Michie, eds), Vol. I. Edinburgh University Press.

Hintzman, D. L. (1968). Explorations with a discrimination net model for paired-associate learning. *Journal of Mathematical Psychology* 5, 123-162.

Ledley, M. (1964). High speed automatic analysis of biomedical pictures, *Science, N.Y.* 146, 216.

Mermelstein, P. (1964). Computer recognition of connected handwritten words. Sc.D. Thesis. Dept. of Electrical Engineering, M.I.T.

Miller, G. A., Galanter, E. and Pribram, K. H. (1960). "Plans and the Structure of Behaviour". Holt, Rinehart and Winston, New York.

Nash-Webber, B. (1975). The role of semantics in automatic speech understanding. *In* "Representation and Understanding: Studies in Cognitive Science" (D. Bobrow and A. Collins, eds). Academic Press, London and New York.

Neisser, U. (1963). Imitation of man by machine. *Science, N.Y.* 139, 193-197.

Newell, A., Shaw, J. C. and Simon, H. A. (1958). Elements of a theory of general problem solving. *Psychological Review* 65, 151-166.

Newell, A., Shaw, J. C. and Simon, H. A. (1959). Report on a general problem solving program. In *Proceedings of the International Conference on Information Processing*. Paris, Unesco House.

Newell, A., Shaw, J. C. and Simon, H. A. (1963). Empirical explanations with the logic theory machine: a case study in heuristics. In "Computers and Thought" (E. A. Feigenbaum and J. Feldman, eds). McGraw-Hill, New York.

Norman, D. A. (1973). Memory, knowledge and the answering of questions. In "Contemporary Issues in Cognitive Psychology" (R. A. Solso, ed.). The Loyola Symposium. V. H. Winstons and Sons, Washington.

Pylyshyn, Z. W. (1975). Minds, machines and phenomenology: some reflections on Dreyfus' 'What computers can't do'. *Cognition* 3, (1), 57-77.

Reitman, J. S. (1970). Information processing model of STM. In "Models of Human Memory" (D. A. Norman, ed.). Academic Press, London and New York.

Rumelhart, D. E. and Norman, D. A. (1975). The Computer Implementation. In "Explorations in Cognition" (D. A. Norman and D. E. Rumelhart, eds). W. H. Freeman, San Francisco.

Schank, R. C. (1972). Semantics in conceptual analysis. *Lingua* 30, 101-140.

Scraggs, G. W. (1975). Answering questions about processes. In "Explorations in Cognition" (D. A. Norman and D. E. Rumelhart, eds). W. H. Freeman, San Francisco.

Selfridge, O. G. (1958). Pandemonium: a paradigm for learning. In "The Mechanization of Thought Processes". HMSO.

Selfridge, O. G. and Neisser, U. (1960). Pattern recognition by machine. *Scientific American* 203, 60-68.

Sellars, W. F. (1963). "Science, Perception and Reality". The Humanities Press, New York.

Simon, H. A. and Hayes, J. R. (1976). The Understanding process: problem isomorphs. *Cognitive Psychology* 8, 165-190.

Simon, H. A. and Reed, S. K. (1976). Modelling strategy shifts in a problem solving task. *Cognitive Psychology* 8, 86-97.

Spearman, C. (1927). "The Abilities of Man: Their Nature and Measurement". Macmillan, London.

Sutherland, N. S. (1968). Outlines of a theory of visual pattern recognition in animals and man. *Proceedings of the Royal Society Bulletin* 171, 297-317.

Sutherland, N. S. (1974). Computer simulation of brain function. In "Philosophy of Psychology" (S. C. Brown, ed.). Macmillan, London.

Turing, A. M. (1950). Computing machinery and intelligence. *Mind* 59, 433-460.

Uhr, L. (1963). Pattern recognition computers as models for form perception. *Psychological Bulletin* 60, 40-73.

Unger, S. H. (1959). Pattern detection and recognition. *Proceedings of the I.R.E.* 47, 1737-1752.

Uttley, A. M. (1958). Conditional probability computing in the nervous system. In "Mechanization of Thought Processes", HMSO.

Weizenbaum, J. (1968). Contextual understanding by computers. In "Recognizing Patterns: Studies in Living and Automatic Systems" (P. A. Kolers and M. Eden, eds). The M.I.T. Press, Cambridge, Massachusetts.

Wilks, Y. (1976). Dreyfus's Disproofs. *British Journal of the Philosophy of Science* 27, 177-185.

Winograd, T. (1972). Understanding natural language. *Cognitive Psychology* 3 (1), 1-191.

8

Hemisphere Differences

It has been known since the nineteenth century that the two cerebral hemispheres are functionally asymmetrical. Broca (1865) and Hughlings Jackson (1880) noted the tendency for language disorders to occur following left hemisphere damage, and since then a growing body of clinical evidence has accumulated confirming their observations, and also revealing a right hemisphere specialization for a variety of non-verbal visuo-spatial cognitive processes. Currently there is a marked upsurge of interest in cerebral asymmetry among cognitive psychologists. Several factors have triggered this development. The intrusive effect of hemisphere differences have to be taken into account whenever experimental procedures involve the presentation of visual or auditory material which is spatially extended to the left or right of the subject. In dichotic listening or tachistoscopic recognition experiments, performance differences between left and right ears, or left and right sides of the visual field reflect differences in the processing capacities of the two hemispheres, and researchers must necessarily take account of this factor in interpreting their results. There has also, perhaps, been some unease at the extent of the gulf between theories of higher mental processes abstractly represented in flow-chart models, and the underlying brain mechanisms. In some ways, the study of hemisphere differences represents an attempt to bridge this gulf and to forge closer links between cognition and neurophysiology. It holds out the fascinating prospect of mapping the words, images and conceptual processes of human thinking on to actual physical locations in the brain. As a result, a great deal of recent research has been devoted to the detection and characterization of functional differences between the hemispheres in normal intact subjects, and there are now three main sources of evidence for hemispheric specialization in humans. Firstly, the study of the brain-injured allows comparisons to be made between the performance of patients with localized damage in one hemisphere, and patients with similar damage to the opposite hemisphere. Alternatively, patients with unilateral damage can be compared with normal intact subjects. Secondly, studies of a group of split-brained patients, who have had the two cerebral hemispheres surgically disconnected, have yielded comparisons of the performance of each of the isolated hemispheres. Thirdly, studies of normal intact subjects employ procedures whereby information is channelled so as to reach one hemisphere before the other. Comparisons can then be made between performance in conditions when the input is directed to the left hemisphere, and conditions when it is directed to the right. In all these comparisons, problems of methodology and of interpretation of the findings arise, so that the evidence from each of these three sources can be criticized. Nevertheless, the results have converged to a considerable extent, and produced a consensus such that, although some of the details may be disputed, the general conclusions that different cognitive processes are subserved by different hemispheres are not in doubt. This chapter will review the particular difficulties that attend each method of investigating hemispheric specialization, summarize the findings, and assess the theories.

I. STUDIES OF THE BRAIN-INJURED

When unilateral brain damage is sustained the effects are specific to the side of the lesion, and the kinds of deficit that are observed following lesions of the left hemisphere are different from those that are associated with lesions of the right hemisphere. This relationship between the side of the lesion, and the type of disorder, provides evidence of the functional specialization of the hemispheres, but there are numerous reasons why the pattern does not always emerge very clearly and consistently.

In many cases the nature, locus and extent of the damage cannot be very accurately ascertained. When the observations are based on the effects of tumours, cerebro-vascular damage or closed head injuries, the lesions tend to be diffuse, and to have quite widespread secondary consequences such as oedema, infection and intra-cranial pressure, so that it is more difficult to establish a precise relation between the site of the damage, and the kinds of deficit that result. Another problem arises when patients have been suffering from pathological conditions, such as focal epilepsy, prior to surgical inter-vention. In these cases the epileptic condition may have produced changes in cerebral organization, and the post-operative deficits cannot be taken as a reflection of normal brain organization.

Newcombe (1969) has pointed out that these problems are minimized in studies of brain injuries resulting from gunshot or missile wounds. The lesions are usually quite circumscribed; they receive early treatment, so that the possibility of infection and generalized damage is reduced; and they are usually incurred by soldiers, who are young healthy adults of normal intelligence at the time of injury.

Further problems arise in choosing a standard of comparison in order to assess the degree of deterioration following brain injury. It is desirable to have pre-morbid performance scores so that pre-post comparisons can be made for each individual case, but in practice this data is rarely available. Patients may not come to the notice of the clinician until their condition has progressed to a stage at which intellectual deterioration is already present. Comparison of the effects of right- and left-side lesions is also complicated by the fact that patients with left hemisphere pathology tend to seek treat-ment earlier, because the attendant language disorders are more obvious and more disturbing than the disorders that result when the right hemisphere is affected. Again these problems are less severe in studying missile-injured soldiers, since the records of army intelligence tests carried out prior to the injury may be available. Failing pre-post comparisons, it is possible to compare the performance of the brain-injured with normals, or to compare the performance of groups with brain injuries that are similar in locus and extent but in different hemispheres. Comparison of right-brain-injured with left-brain-injured requires careful matching, not only of the lesions, and the time elapsed since they were incurred, but also of characteristics such as age, sex, I.Q., handedness, health and medica-tion which are likely to affect performance. Because of the limited numbers of cases available, in many studies the matching falls short of these requirements, and the groups compared are too small and ill-assorted. The time elapsing since the injury or operation is an important variable, because a considerable amount of recovery of function may take place. The initial deficits cannot be wholly attributed to the loss of function in the damaged area, since post-traumatic shock and secondary consequences contribute to the impairment of performance. When these effects have dissipated, some restoration of function may have already begun. The mechanism of recovery is not well understood. It is not clear how far there is take-over of function by undamaged brain areas, or how far recovery can be accounted for by compensating strategies (Zangwill, 1947). Different individuals appear to have different powers of recovery. In individuals with mixed dominance a bilateral representation of function seems to permit a greater recovery, and a high level of pre-traumatic intelligence, combined with perseverance in retraining, enhances the prospect for recovery. As a result, the extent of the deficit observed following a lesion will vary considerably as a function of the post-traumatic interval, and the recuperative powers of the individual.

The effects of unilateral brain injuries are in any case different for left- and right-handers. There are individual differences in the direction and degree of lateralization of brain function, which are linked, to some extent, with hand preference. While the majority of individuals have language ability lateralized in the left hemisphere, and visuo-spatial abilities in the right, this pattern is not universal. Rossi and Rosadini (1965) used sodium amytal injections to anaesthetize a single hemisphere. With this technique a temporary disruption of language occurs if the anaesthetized hemisphere is the one which is functionally specialized for language. Their results indicated that approximately 90% of right-handed subjects had language lateralized to the left hemisphere, while only about 64% of left-handers conformed to this pattern. It appeared that, of the remaining 10% of right-handers and 36% of left-handers, some had the reversed pattern of organization, with language functions represented in the right hemisphere, while some showed a much greater degree of functional symmetry (sometimes called bilaterality, mixed dominance or mixed-brainedness) with language being represented in both hemispheres. Different methods of assessing laterality have produced different results. Zangwill (1960), basing his estimates on the occurrence of speech disorders following head injuries, suggested that only 35% of left-handers have the left hemisphere dominant for language, while 40% are mixed dominant, and 25% are right dominant. Because of these variations in cerebral organization, it is difficult to predict the effects of lesions even when hand preference is clear. In fact neither of these estimates is likely to be very accurate, because labelling an individual as left- or right-handed is itself an imprecise and oversimplified classification. Oldfield (1971) has shown that handedness is a graded characteristic, and scores from questionnaires used to determine a measure of handedness range along a continuum from extreme left-handedness to extreme right-handedness. According to Oldfield's criterion, 10% of males and 5.9% of females are left-handed. Using a stricter criterion, Annett (1970) has reported a J-shaped binomial distribution of handedness in the population with the proportions of left, mixed- and right-handers being 4%, 32% and 64%, respectively. Because of these disparities, apparently anomalous effects of brain lesions may be due to misclassification of handedness, as well as variations in the pattern of cerebral organization.

Cerebral asymmetry also varies with age. In early childhood the localization of function is not "fixed", and both hemispheres are equipotential (Lenneberg, 1967). During the first 2 years of life a lesion of either hemisphere delays the acquisition of language, so that both hemispheres seem to be involved in the early stages of language development. There is a progressive decrease in the role of the right hemisphere, and after language is established, although left hemisphere lesions continue to produce speech disorders in 85% of cases, a right-hemisphere lesion only has this effect in 45% of the cases. All these speech disorders caused by early lesions disappear within about 2 years. When a hemisphere is diseased in early childhood, the language function is re-located in the other hemisphere, so that if the diseased hemisphere is removed at a later stage, no disturbance of language ensues. In early childhood cerebral organization is flexible, but the ability of the right hemisphere to take over the language function effectively diminishes with age and is lost by the early teens.

In spite of these difficulties and discrepancies, there is good general agreement that, in the majority of cases, different kinds of deficit are associated with lesions of the left and right hemispheres. Newcombe's study of missile injuries reveals a dichotomy between left-brain-injured and right-brain-injured persisting many years after the injuries were incurred. The left hemisphere group were consistently poorer at tasks requiring learning and retention of verbal material, and in tests of verbal skills such as vocabulary, spelling and word fluency, while the right hemisphere group showed no impairment on these tasks. Instead, the right hemisphere group were consistently poorer at learning visually guided mazes, at drawing or reproducing block designs, at estimating the number of cubes in a diagrammatic arrangement, and at recognizing incomplete patterns, especially fragmented faces. A double dissociation of the site of the lesion and the nature of the deficit emerges clearly from the data, and is complemented by the observations of many other researchers. Patients with unilateral right-sided damage typically show deficits in visuo-spatial tasks including face recognition (De Renzi *et al.*, 1968), discriminating the position and slopes of lines (Warrington and Rabin, 1970), estimating a number of dots, and recognizing nonsense figures (Kimura, 1966). Corsi (cited in Milner, 1971) designed a verbal and a non-verbal version of a memory test, and found that patients with left fronto-temporal lobectomies were poor at recognizing recurring words in a series of words, but could recognize recurring pictures in a series of abstract pictures. The right fronto-temporal group could recognize words, but not pictures.

Disorders of verbal information processing are associated with left-hemisphere damage whether the material is represented in a visual or an auditory form. Milner (1962) has reported evidence showing that auditory functions are lateralized in a way that corresponds to the verbal/non-verbal dichotomy in visual tasks. Normally, verbal material is better perceived by the left hemisphere, and non-verbal material, such as musical and environmental sounds, is better perceived by the right hemisphere. Kimura (1961) found deficits in the auditory perception of verbal material after left temporal lobe damage, and Milner (1962) found recognition of melodies, timbre and tonal patterns was impaired after right temporal lobectomy.

Recent emphasis on hemisphere differences, and on asymmetry of function, has tended to obscure the existence of hemispheric interaction. While the evidence from unilateral lesions indicates that each of the two hemispheres is specialized for the performance of particular tasks, the normal brain does not function as two isolated units, but as a closely integrated system. The interactive nature of hemispheric organization is shown by the fact that uni-lateral lesions may have bilateral consequences, and the results of bilateral lesions do not simply represent the sum of the effects that would arise from each of the lesions alone. Teuber (1962) has reported that the effects of unilateral lesions may not be confined to the contralateral visual half-field, and subtle changes may occur in both halves of the visual field. Similar changes may occur in the tactile sense of both hands, and are not confined to the hand contra-lateral to the lesion. In hearing, unilateral lesions impair binaural judgements of localization, and binaural synthesis of sounds of different frequencies. In these tasks the normal interactive operation of the hemispheres is disturbed. Newcombe and Ratcliff (1973) studied the effects of bilateral brain injuries, and noted some specific deficits which had not been detected with unilateral injuries of either hemisphere. In object naming and judgements of left–right orientation, the bilateral group took significantly longer to respond than those with unilateral injuries, as if the rate of processing was slowed by the bilateral injuries. Paradoxically, Teuber (1962) reported that while unilateral injury of either hemisphere slowed down the rate at which ambiguous figures like the Necker cube reverse, bilateral injuries speed up the reversal rate. Even if the effects of bilateral injuries are not very consistent, they do provide evidence of a mutual influence of one hemisphere on the other.

Anatomical differences between the hemispheres are not marked, and the results of morphological studies are not always in good agreement, probably because different methods of measurement have been employed. Von Bonin (1962) summarizes results indicating that the left hemisphere has a slightly greater volume than the right, and the fissures are slightly deeper. Hyde *et al.* (1973) found the right superior temporal gyrus to be significantly wider than the left in adult brains, and Geschwind (1972) reported that the planum temporale was larger on the left side in both infant and adult brains.

Electrical stimulation of the exposed cortex has also yielded some observations which support the conclusion that visuo-spatial functions are localized in the right hemisphere, since patients reported that right-sided stimulation produced vivid visual experiences (Penfield and Perot, 1963). Another method of investigating hemisphere differences has been discovered as a by-product of the use of electroconvulsive therapy (ECT) in the treatment of depressed psychiatric patients. When applied unilaterally, ECT produces a temporary malfunction of the hemisphere to which it is directed. Differential effects of left- and right-sided placement of the electrodes has been reported. Fleminger *et al.* (1970) found verbal paired associate learning was more impaired in right-handed patients by application of ECT to the left hemisphere, while Miller (1974) found that recognition of geometrical and nonsense figures was relatively more impaired when the ECT was administered to the right hemisphere.

II. STUDIES OF SPLIT-BRAIN PATIENTS

The evidence for functional specialization of the hemispheres which comes from the effects of lesions is complemented and reinforced by the results of studies of patients who have undergone cerebral commissurotomy, so that the two hemispheres are disconnected (Gazzaniga *et al.*, 1962; Gazzaniga, 1967). In these cases, it is possible to examine the functions of each single hemisphere in isolation, by testing the response capacities when sensory inputs have been confined to one hemisphere.

Disturbances of sensory–motor integration in these patients have been observed when the response must be made with the hand contralateral to the side stimulated. For example, when sensory information is presented on the right side and so transmitted to the left hemisphere, responses can be made with the right hand since this is primarily controlled by the left hemisphere. Responses by the left hand (controlled by the right hemisphere which did not receive the sensory information) are impaired. The patient is typically able to point to body areas that have been touched, using the right hand to point to locations on the right side of the body, and the left hand to indicate locations on the left side of the body, but he has difficulty in using the hand opposite to the body location. Similarly, the patient can point to the location of a light source in the right visual field with his right hand, or in the left visual field with his left hand, but the crossed integration proves more difficult. Individual patients vary in their ability to mediate crossed responses.

The lateralization of language functions to the left hemisphere, and visuo-spatial functions to the right, is reflected in the patterns of deficit exhibited by the split-brain patients. Figure 1 shows how left and right visual fields project to right and left hemispheres, respectively. The patient cannot name or describe objects or words presented in the left visual field, nor can he name objects which are placed in the left hand. The right hemisphere appears to be mute, and, after disconnection, has no access to the speech mechanisms of the left hemisphere. Further tests have shown, however, that the right hemisphere is not wholly a-linguistic, and is capable of analysing and encoding verbal material to some extent. When simple words are presented in the left visual field to the right hemisphere, the patient can point with his left hand to a corresponding object or the corresponding word in a display. More sophisticated language comprehension has been shown by the ability to select the word "clock" out of five words presented to the left visual field after hearing a definition such as "used to tell the time", and this suggests that the right hemisphere is capable of some semantic analysis. Even so, the linguistic abilities of the right hemisphere are restricted to fairly rudimentary processing of concrete words in simple choice situations. Levy and Trevarthen (1977) showed that while the right hemisphere was capable of carrying out visual word matches (when a word was presented in the left visual field, the identical word could be correctly selected from a set of alternatives), the ability to carry out a phonological match was lacking (when a word was presented

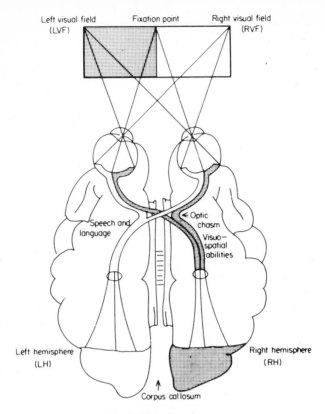

Fig. 1. Visual pathways.

in the left visual field the patient could not select a rhyming word from the alternatives). These findings necessitate some modifications in the view that the language function is lateralized in the dominant hemisphere. To regard language as a single unitary function is clearly an oversimplification. Instead, the split-brain results force us to consider language as a set of interrelated component functions, which can be lateralized to varying extents. While speech and phono-logical encoding are reserved to the left hemisphere, the right is capable of some verbal analysis. However, a recent study of aphasic patients (Kinsbourne, 1971) has shed a different light on the language capacities of the right hemisphere. Kinsbourne's patients were suffering from aphasia following lesions of the left hemisphere, and were producing fragmentary and disordered speech. In order to decide whether this aphasic speech was the output of the damaged left hemisphere, or of the undamaged right hemisphere, the left side was anaesthetized. Since the speech showed no changes as a result of anaesthesis, it was possible to conclude that the right hemisphere was mediating the aphasic speech. So, although in the split-brain patients the right hemisphere appeared totally incapable of speech, in Kinsbourne's aphasics, the right hemisphere was producing disordered speech.

The specialization of the right hemisphere for visuo-spatial functions has been confirmed by the performance of the split-brain patients. Geometric designs are copied better by the left hand after commissurotomy, and Milner and Taylor (1972) found that the left hand was strikingly superior in matching complex tactile patterns. With the left hand, patterns could be correctly matched after intervals of up to two minutes, while with the right hand, five out of seven patients could not match the patterns even with a zero delay interval.

In spite of the good agreement of the results of the split-brain studies with the conclusions based on unilateral lesions, there are serious problems in the interpretation of these results. The capacities of the disconnected hemispheres may not give an accurate indication of the lateralization of functions in the normal intact brain for various reasons. Firstly, the commissurotomy patients had suffered from severe long-standing epilepsy prior to surgery, which may have caused abnormal re-organization of their brains. Levy and Trevarthen (1977) have argued that the uniformity of the patterns of deficit exhibited by these patients is not consistent with a pathological origin. They claim that if the epileptic condition had caused re-organization, more diverse patterns of deficit would have been produced. In their view, the similarity of the observed disorders is more plausibly attributed to the surgical intervention which was the same for all these patients. A closer look at the individual data casts some doubt on this argument, since the performance of the split-brain patients is not in fact very uniform, and a considerable range of individual differences is apparent. The possibility that the functioning of the disconnected hemispheres is not representative of normal hemisphere specialization cannot be altogether dismissed. Secondly, the possibility that some information can still be transmitted from one hemisphere to the other via remaining pathways in the midbrain cannot be wholly ruled out. Thirdly, since the disconnected hemispheres are not subject to the mutual facilitation and inhibition that occurs in the intact brain, their functioning must necessarily be different. And, finally, the ability of these patients, after years of testing, to "cross-cue" between hemispheres, bypassing the severed callosal route, and transmitting information by bodily gestures and orienting responses, has been noted by most researchers, although it is difficult to assess the effectiveness of such methods of inter-hemispheric communication. However, it does mean that the two hemispheres in the split-brain are not totally isolated from each other and can communicate indirectly to some extent. For all these reasons, the study of split-brain does not itself provide definitive answers to questions about hemispheric specialization in normals, but it does strengthen and amplify the evidence from other sources.

III. STUDIES OF HEMISPHERE DIFFERENCES IN NORMAL SUBJECTS

A. Techniques and Methodological Problems

Techniques have been developed to explore functional differences between the hemispheres in normal subjects by channelling sensory inputs so that they are projected primarily, or most directly to one or other hemisphere. In visual perception (see Fig. 1) stimuli are placed to the left or right of a central fixation point, so that they are projected to the contralateral hemisphere. Stimuli in the left visual field fall on the nasal hemiretina of the left eye and the temporal hemiretina of the right eye, and project to the right hemisphere. The right visual field stimulates the temporal hemiretina of the left eye and the nasal hemiretina of the right eye and projects to the left hemisphere. With auditory perception, material presented to the left ear is projected primarily to the contralateral right hemisphere and the right ear transmits primarily to the left hemisphere. Each ear has pathways to both hemispheres, but the contralateral paths are stronger, and when both ears receive input simultaneously the ipsilateral paths are inhibited (Kimura, 1967; see Fig. 2). Accordingly, superior performance, in terms of accuracy or latency response, is predicted when the material is projected directly to the hemisphere specialized for processing that type of material. For example, we predict that verbal material should be better perceived when presented to the right visual field or the right ear, and non-verbal material should be better perceived when presented to the left visual field or left ear. Of course, in normals the two hemispheres are not disconnected and information can be rapidly relayed across the corpus callosum from one hemisphere to the other. These

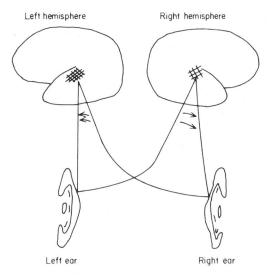

Left hemisphere   Right hemisphere

Left ear   Right ear

Fig. 2. Auditory pathways.

techniques do not therefore allow the functioning of each hemisphere to be examined in isolation, and we cannot tell whether
stimuli are processed within the hemisphere to which they were
initially projected, or whether the input has been transmitted across
the transcallosal route for processing in the other hemisphere. When
hemisphere differences are obtained, two interpretations are usually
possible. If, for example, verbal inputs are processed faster and
more accurately when projected to the left hemisphere, and more
slowly and inaccurately when presented to the right, the inferior
performance of the right hemisphere may be due to the less efficient
language-processing capacities of the right side. Alternatively, it may
be explained on the assumption that the non-specialist right
hemisphere sends the information across to the language hemisphere
for processing, and some delay and loss of information is incurred
in transit. So obtained hemisphere differences might be due either
to the unequal efficiency with which the input is processed within
each hemisphere, or to the crossing-over between hemispheres.
Experimental data does not usually discriminate between these
alternatives. Two questions need to be asked in considering this
issue. If we favour the unequal efficiency explanation, we need
to ask whether the evidence from unilateral lesions suggests that the
non-specialist hemisphere would have the capacity to perform the
task at the observed level of efficiency. If, on the other hand, we
prefer the crossing-over explanation, we need to ask whether the

estimates of the time required for transcallosal transmission are consistent with the differences in reaction times obtained for left and right hemisphere presentation. Filbey and Gazzaniga (1969) found that vocal responses to dots presented in the right visual field were 33 milliseconds (ms) faster than vocal responses to dots presented in the left visual field, and concluded that this represents the amount of time taken for the information to cross from the right hemisphere to the speech mechanisms of the left, but other experiments have produced differences varying from about 4 ms to about 60 ms. The magnitude of the difference varies from task to task, from individual subject to individual subject, and from trial to trial. This variability can only be reconciled with a crossing-over explanation by making the additional assumptions that more complex stimuli would take longer to transmit, and that loss of information during crossing may make the final processing more difficult. This latter assumption is supported by some animal studies which have indicated that memory traces established by interhemispheric transfer lack precision and stability (Myers, 1962). Nevertheless, Carmon *et al.* (1972) have pointed out that the anatomical distribution of transcallosal fibres is such that, for stimuli presented further out in the periphery of the visual field, the inter-hemispheric path would be longer than for stimuli presented closer to the fixation point, and should therefore produce larger left–right differences. They found no change in the left–right difference when the stimuli were presented 8° of visual angle off-centre, and when they were presented at only 1° off-centre, and this is difficult to account for in terms of the crossing-over explanation.

Further methodological problems in the techniques for studying hemisphere differences in normal subjects have been reviewed by White (1972). In presenting visual stimuli, it is essential to ensure that the subject maintains fixation on the central point during the stimulus presentation so that the stimulus falls outside the foveal area of vision. If the subject shifts his eyes, the stimulus may not be uniquely projected to the contralateral hemisphere. Although subjects are instructed to fixate the central point they may not succeed in doing so all the time. In order to ensure maintenance of fixation, it is best to allocate stimuli randomly to left and right visual fields on successive trials, so that the subject cannot antici-pate the stimulus location and move his eyes to fixate the expected position. In some experiments this precaution was neglected (e.g. Moscovitch and Catlin, 1970), and stimuli were presented in the same visual field for whole blocks of trials, so that anticipatory eye movements were likely to occur. It is desirable to monitor eye position continuously by means of a television camera which records the position of the eyes during each stimulus presentation, so that trials on which fixation shifted can be discarded, but this control has only been used in relatively few studies. The technique is also dependent on the stimulus being placed at the correct degree of eccentricity from the fixation point to ensure non-foveal vision. Foveal and parafoveal vision extends as far as 2.5° either side of the fixation point, and acuity falls off quite markedly at distances greater than 5° off-centre (Bouma, 1976). Stimuli should therefore be positioned between 2.5° and 5° from the centre, and many studies can be criticized for failing to fulfil this requirement.

The exposure duration of the stimulus should also be limited to a time less than the latency of eye movement, which is estimated at about 180 to 200 ms, depending on the extent of the movement. When longer stimulus durations are employed, eye movements may take place after the stimulus onset with the result that the stimulus is not confined to the contralateral hemisphere.

The predicted hemisphere asymmetries will depend on whether the stimulus is classified as verbal or as non-verbal. Although it may seem a simple matter to decide whether or not a given task is a verbal one, in practice it is not so easy. Subjects often transform or recode the stimuli from one form to another. They construct images for words, and give names to faces or nonsense figures. Different subjects may adopt different strategies for coding or recoding stimulus material, and may evolve new strategies at different stages of practice. Recoding strategies therefore contribute both to inter-subject variability, and to intra-subject variability in the magnitude and direction of hemisphere asymmetries.

When reaction times are used to measure hemisphere differences, problems relating to the statistical significance of the results arise because of the large variance that is inevitably associated with reaction times. The effects of practice, fatigue, fluctuations of attention, false or correct anticipation, repetitions, and stimulus–response compatibility all contribute to produce this variability in the speed of response, and the relatively small effects of functional differences between the hemispheres are easily obscured. When accuracy measures are employed instead of reaction times there may be other problems. It is usual to examine the performance of left and right visual fields for recognition of stimuli exposed very briefly at near-threshold durations and to compare the number of errors for left and right presentations. Recognition thresholds vary from subject to subject, and tend to decrease as the subject becomes more practised, so that it is hard to select an exposure duration that will produce a uniform level of difficulty. An additional factor, which can influence the recognition or processing of visual stimuli, is the directional scan which takes place when a horizontally extended display is presented in the left or right visual field. A left-to-right attentional scan, established by reading habits, favours material in the right visual field (White, 1969), since scanning proceeds leftwards directly from the fixation point, while for material in the left visual field the focus of attention must first be shifted from the centre to the leftmost element in the display. In order to eliminate scanning effects, which may obscure the effects of hemispheric specialization, some researchers present stimuli in vertically extended displays, instead of horizontal rows, but this method also has disadvantages. If the stimuli are words, vertical presentation is so "unnatural" that subjects would be forced to change their normal processing strategies.

Whatever form of measurement is adopted, the observed hemisphere differences may originate at any stage intervening between stimulus input and response output, and experimental designs do not always allow the critical stage to be identified. Hemispheric asymmetries could be reflecting differences in perception, in analysis, in judgement, or in control of the voice or hand making the response. Asymmetries at the analysis stage and at the response stage may cancel each other out.

Figure 3 gives a diagrammatic representation of some alternative models for the recognition of faces, with either manual or vocal responses. Model A represents the way Geffen et al. (1971) interpreted their finding that reaction times for face recognition were faster for left field, right hemisphere presentation, when a manual response was required. They assumed that processing took place within the hemisphere of presentation, the right hemisphere being superior, and that the manual responses could be mediated by either hemisphere. Model B represents their interpretation of the results obtained when a vocal response was required. Here the superiority of the right hemisphere at processing faces is cancelled out, because the results of the processing have to be transferred across to the left hemisphere, which has sole control of the vocal response mechanism. Model C represents another possibility whereby face processing is confined to the right hemisphere, and vocal responses to the left. This version is not consistent with the results obtained by Geffen et al. (1971), but is included here to illustrate

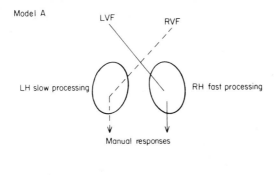

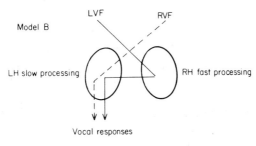

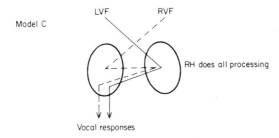

Fig. 3. Models for processing and responding to faces. Model A—no crossing, LVF is faster; Model B—single crossing, LVF = RVF; Model C—double crossing, LVF is faster.

the way in which models can be arbitrarily constructed to explain whatever experimental results are obtained. Most researchers assume that responses made with the whole hand can be mediated by either hemisphere, but that responses requiring fine control of individual fingers can only be mediated by the contralateral hemisphere. In the split-brain patients, however, the isolated hemispheres could not control ipsilateral responses made with the whole hand, so it may be wrong to assume, as in Model A, that the manual responses could be initiated equally well by either hemisphere. Since we cannot be certain whether the processing mechanisms, or the response mechanisms, are completely lateralized or only partially lateralized, the researcher is not constrained in his choice of assumptions. In consequence, a general weakness of this kind of model-building is that by making *ad hoc* assumptions about crossing, re-crossing and differences in processing efficiency, it is possible to "save" the hypothesis of lateralization of function whether the predicted asymmetry is found or not.

In experiments which use dichotic listening to explore hemispheric differences in processing auditory material, there are also some methodological problems. The assumption that an input is primarily transmitted to the hemisphere contralateral to the ear of presentation is only justified if it is exactly synchronized with the competing input in the ipsilateral ear. Asymmetries in auditory processing have sometimes been obtained with monaural stimulation, but only in a few tasks with a high level of difficulty (Bakker, 1970; Cohen and Martin, 1975). It is also essential that the subjective intensity of the signals be equated for both ears, so that differences are attributable to functional specialization rather than to differences in acuity.

The variability in hemisphere differences which is often found in experiments with normal subjects may be due to lack of precision in the techniques of testing, strategy differences, or individual differences in the degree and direction of lateralization. It is common to find that not all the subjects in an experiment exhibit the predicted asymmetries of performance, or that asymmetries shift at different stages of practice, or with small changes of instructions, type of material and experimental design. Although considerable consensus of results seems to have been achieved, the extent of this apparent agreement may be misleading, since results that run counter to predictions are seldom reported. The predictions are largely based on the clinical findings and the practice of discarding negative results means that an artifically high level of support has been claimed.

IV. THEORIES OF HEMISPHERIC SPECIALIZATION

A. Functional Specialization Theories

These can account for many of the observed hemispheric asymmetries, but cannot explain the variability of the results. These theories differ in the degree of specialization which is attributed to the hemispheres. On an absolute specialization theory, a given function is considered to be absolutely reserved to one hemisphere and differences are attributed to crossing-over. On a partial specialization theory, a given function is considered to be performed more efficiently by one hemisphere, and differences are attributed to unequal efficiency. The experimental findings on the whole confirm the results of the clinical and split-brain studies. In vision, there is typically a left hemisphere advantage for alphabetic material and familiar objects, and a right hemisphere advantage for slopes of lines, patterns of dots, faces and nonsense figures. In dichotic listening, there is generally a left hemisphere advantage for verbal material and speech sounds, and a right hemisphere advantage for non-speech sounds, melodies and pitch discrimination. Theories of functional specialization have recently been amplified and extended to try to account for the variability and lack of consistency that prevails in the laboratory studies.

B. The Attentional Theory

Kinsbourne (1970) argues that a structural determinant such as functional specialization should produce more robust and consistent asymmetries. Kinsbourne also maintains that the observed asymmetries are too large to be accounted for by crossing time, which he estimates at 4 ms. According to his theory, a basic asymmetry arising out of the functional specialization of the left hemisphere for verbal material, and the right hemisphere for non-verbal material may be either enhanced or obscured by attentional factors. For example, when the left hemisphere is primed or activated, its superiority in processing verbal material becomes more marked, but if the right hemisphere is activated, its advantage diminishes. Concurrent verbal activity or the expectation of verbal stimuli activates the left hemisphere, while concurrent non-verbal activity or the expectation of non-verbal stimuli serves to activate the right. Whenever one hemisphere is more highly activated than the other, there is an attentional bias toward the contralateral side of space, resulting in enhanced processing of material presented on that side. The theory also postulates that activation of one hemisphere exerts an inhibitory influence on the functioning of the other. Thus, observed asymmetries may shift in accordance with the subject's expectations or cognitive "set", and with whether or not he is engaging in covert verbalization. This theory has received some experimental support.

Kinsbourne found that when subjects were required to locate the position of a gap in a square, no difference between left and right visual field presentation was obtained, but when a concurrent verbal memory load was imposed (priming the left hemisphere), a right field advantage emerged. Spellacy and Blumstein (1970) reported that when subjects were expecting speech sounds, there was a right ear, left hemisphere advantage for identification of dichotically presented vowels, but if the subjects were expecting non-speech sounds, there was a left ear advantage. Cohen (1975) also found that no visual field differences were evident when words, digits and dots were presented in a randomly mixed sequence, but when the subject received a pre-trial cue, indicating which kind of stimulus would follow, a clear right field advantage for words, and a small, though not significant, left field advantage for dots, were obtained. Kallman and Corballis (1975) have invoked Kinsbourne's attentional theory to explain their finding that the predicted left ear advantage for musical sounds waned as testing proceeded, and they have suggested that the right hemisphere became fatigued, or could no longer maintain a state of activation. On the other hand, Berlucchi *et al.* (1974) found a left field superiority for discrimination of faces, and a right field superiority for letters even when these were randomly interspersed so that no expectations could be formed. On Kinsbourne's view, asymmetries should be insignificantly small if no cognitive set is formed, and no concurrent activity is imposed. Another discrepant result has been reported by Geffen *et al.* (1973) who found that a right visual field advantage for naming digits disappeared when a concurrent verbal task was imposed, and a left field advantage emerged. They concluded that left hemisphere capacity was overloaded by the concurrent task, thus reducing its efficiency in processing the digits. If concurrent tasks may either activate a hemisphere and so facilitate performance on the primary task, or overload it and so depress performance, it becomes impossible to make unequivocal predictions. Goodglass *et al.* (1971) examined the effects of concurrent verbal and non-verbal tasks on the recognition of both verbal and non-verbal items, and found only very small shifts. They suggested that attentional effects may magnify existing lateral asymmetries, but are not powerful enough to reverse them. To sum up, although there is some experimental evidence which favours the attentional theory, it is not clear how strong attentional effects are, relative to the effects of the underlying functional specialization; it is not clear at what point a concurrent task ceases to activate and starts to overload, or at what point activation degenerates into fatigue. Because of these uncertainties, the effects of attentional determinants of hemispheric asymmetry are unpredictable.

C. The Component Stages Theory

This approach can account for some of the variability in hemisphere differences, but it is only applicable to verbal tasks. The theory begins with the hypothesis that laterality effects in processing verbal information might be the joint product of underlying asymmetries in different components of the task. Small changes of task, of paradigm, or of strategy might change the relative importance of the component stages, and so shift the overall asymmetry. In processing verbal information, it is possible to distinguish between a stage of physical analysis, and later stages of nominal or phonological analysis, and semantic analysis. A task originally devised by Posner and Mitchell (1967) allows the physical and nominal stages of letter recognition to be decomposed. When subjects are asked to judge whether a pair of letters is same or different, pairs in the same case (AA or aa) can be judged the same on the basis of physical shape (a physical identity match), but pairs in different cases like Aa can only be judged the same on the basis of name (a nominal identity match). The left hemisphere appears to be functionally specialized for the naming stage, since nominal identity matches have reliably produced a right visual field advantage, whereas physical identity matches yielded either no difference or a small left field advantage (Cohen, 1972; Geffen et al., 1972; Ledlow et al., 1972). In the auditory modality somewhat similar results have revealed a left hemisphere superiority in the recognition of stop consonants (phonemes which cannot be identified by a defining set of acoustic properties); again, both hemispheres performed equally well in the recognition of vowels, which could be identified at the level of simple physical analysis (Studdert-Kennedy and Shankweiler, 1970). These results are also compatible with findings reported by Cohen and Freeman (1976) in a lexical decision task. In this task, letter strings were displayed in left and right visual fields, and the subject was required to decide if a given string was a word or a non-word. Some of the non-words were homophones of real words (e.g. mone, hirt, werk). It is usually assumed that homophones take longer to reject as non-words if the subject is forming a phonological representation of the letter string. The phonological resemblance of homophonic non-words to real words makes it more difficult to recognize them as non-words. In Cohen and Freeman's experiment the homophones took longer to reject as non-words when presented to the left hemisphere, but not when presented to the right, indicating that the misleading phonological analysis occurred only in the left hemisphere.

Bradshaw (1974) showed that semantic information is extracted more readily from the right visual field. When a homographic word such as "palm" was displayed centrally, in between two peripherally located words (e.g. "tree" on the left and "hand" on the right), the subject's interpretation of the meaning of the homograph was more often influenced by the meaning of the flanking word in the right field. These results show that physical processing of language can be carried out by either hemisphere, but phonological and semantic processing are left hemisphere functions, and this conclusion is. in agreement with the results of the studies of split-brain patients.

Further support for a component stages approach comes from a letter recognition experiment (Cohen, 1976) which revealed asymmetries at the stage of iconic storage, and also at the stage of read-out from the icon into short-term memory. A letter display was presented in either the left or the right visual field and the number of letters correctly reported was compared in an unmasked condition, and with a delayed backward mask. The masked condition showed that read-out was faster in the right visual field; more letters had been read out from the icon before the mask terminated processing. However, the unmasked condition showed that the iconic representation of the letter display persisted slightly longer in the left visual field than in the right. Other experiments have shown that asymmetries shift when subjects change to a different encoding strategy. Wilkins and Stewart (1974) found that the left field advantage for physical identity matches of letter pairs presented successively dwindled if the interval between the two letters was increased, and disappeared when the second letter of the pair was presented more than 1 s after the first, indicating that subjects shifted from a visual matching strategy to a name match. Umilta et al. (1974) also found that asymmetries were related to encoding strategies. The right visual field was superior for discriminating the orientation of rectangles when the axes of orientation could be verbally labelled, but the left field was better when the axes could not easily be described.

These experimental findings are, of course, compatible with either the component stages approach, or with Kinsbourne's attentional theory. Strategy shifts may either serve to change the contribution of the different component stages, or to change the pattern of activation of the hemispheres. The two theories are not necessarily mutually exclusive, and both explanations could be correct.

D. The Mode of Processing Theory

This approach suggests that hemispheric asymmetries are determined by differences in the characteristic mode of processing of each hemisphere. Many tasks can be performed either by an analytic serial processing of discrete elements or features, or by an holistic, simultaneous or parallel processing of a configuration or set of features. Because of the sequential nature of language, verbally mediated processing tends to be serial. Parallel processing is commonly confined to non-verbal tasks, or to the physical analysis stage of verbal processing. Hence it is reasonable to assume that the left verbal hemisphere should operate as a serial processor, and the right, non-verbal hemisphere as a parallel processor. Experimental tests of this hypothesis have yielded mixed results. In one experiment (Cohen, 1973), left hemisphere processing times increased with the number of letters in the display, as would be predicted by a serial processing model, while right hemisphere processing times did not increase, and were consistent with a parallel process. When the display consisted of unnameable shapes, instead of letters, both hemispheres appeared to employ a parallel mode of processing, although Patterson and Bradshaw (1975) did find evidence for left hemisphere serial processing and right hemisphere parallel processing of non-verbal stimuli. Other results can be cited which run counter to the theory. Umilta *et al.* (1972) found reaction times increased with the number of letters in a display in both left and right hemispheres, and Klatzky and Atkinson (1971) also found increasing linear functions for reaction times plotted against set size, for both letter and picture stimuli, in both hemispheres. Some support for the theory comes from studies showing that complex visual configurations are handled by the right hemisphere in an integrative fashion, and by the left analytically (Levy–Agresti and Sperry, 1968). In the split-brain, the right hemisphere is better able to generate the concept of a whole figure from the perception of a part (Nebes, 1971), and lesion studies have shown that the right hemisphere is less sensitive to incompleteness or fragmentation of figures (Lansdell, 1961). Bever and Chiarello (1974) found a left ear advantage for musical sequences in musically unsophisticated listeners, while advanced music students showed a right ear advantage. They concluded that the non-musicians processed the music holistically, and the musicians processed analytically. Carmon and Nachshon (1971) have reported that the perception of temporal order is mediated by the left hemisphere, since it is impaired by unilateral left-sided lesions, and in normal subjects Halperin *et al.* (1973) similarly found a right ear, left hemisphere superiority for the perception of complex temporal patterns. Since it can be argued that temporal order must necessarily be processed serially, these findings reinforce the view that serial processing is the characteristic mode of the left hemisphere.

The theories and findings discussed so far have mainly been concerned to examine and explain the differences between the two hemispheres, and consequently have tended to consider each as a separate system. Other studies emphasize the interactive nature of hemispheric organization, and serve as a reminder that the two sides of the brain do not function in isolation from each other, but form a highly integrated system. It is possible to demonstrate both inter-hemispheric interference and inter-hemispheric co-operation. Several experiments have compared matching efficiency when two stimuli are presented either to the same hemisphere, or to different hemispheres. Bradshaw *et al.* (1973) presented pairs of outlines of facial profiles in mirror-reversed, or non-reversed, orientations to same or different hemispheres. Mirror-reversed pairs were harder to judge as same, but the decrement was much less when each member of the pair was presented to a different hemisphere instead of both being presented to the same hemisphere. Davis and Schmit (1971) and Dimond and Beaumont (1971) have also both reported superior performance when the two stimuli are projected to different hemispheres, so that the processing load is shared between them. Despite the fact that between-hemisphere matching must require transmission of information across the corpus callosum, co-operative processing can still be superior to the independent functioning of either hemisphere alone. The existence of inter-hemispheric interference effects was suggested by the data from an experiment by Cohen and Martin (1975). Subjects were asked to judge the pitch of a word sung on a high note or on a low note. In some cases the word and pitch were compatible (the word "high" sung on the high note, and the word "low" sung on the low note); in other examples the word and pitch were incompatible ("high" on the low note, and "low" on the high note). Subjects were asked to ignore the verbal information and respond only to the pitch. As predicted, the effect of word meaning on response times was greater when the stimuli were presented to the left hemisphere. Nevertheless, the right hemisphere response times were also affected, being faster when word and pitch were compatible, and slower when word and pitch were incompatible. Although it seems likely that word meaning could only be analysed in the left hemisphere, it still interacted with the pitch analysis going on in the right hemisphere. Presumably in everyday life, listening to speech or to singing requires an integration of the linguistic elements with the intonational or musical pattern, so it is not surprising if this kind of interaction is difficult to suppress.

V. NEW DEVELOPMENTS IN THE STUDY OF HEMISPHERE DIFFERENCES

New techniques for investigating hemisphere differences are being used to reinforce the behavioural measures with physiological ones. Evoked potentials, monitored during performance of various tasks, show asymmetries which correspond to the performance asymmetries. Wood *et al.* (1971) asked subjects to discriminate between the stop consonants *ba* and *da* (a linguistic discrimination) or between fundamental frequency of *ba* at 140 Hz and *ba* at 104 Hz (a non-linguistic discrimination). The evoked responses for the two tasks differed significantly in the left hemisphere, showing that there were different neural consequences depending on whether the type of processing required was linguistic or non-linguistic, even though the acoustic signals were identical. The evoked responses for the two kinds of judgement did not differ in the right hemisphere. Other experiments have shown a relationship between electroencephalogram (EEG) recordings and the functional organization of the brain (Shaw *et al.*, in press). The change from the synchronous activity pattern that characterizes rest, to the desynchronized pattern evident during processing activity, differs as a function of left or right handedness, and with the type of task. Difficulties in selecting the areas and the time epochs to be sampled have not yet been entirely resolved, so that these techniques are not very precise, but they offer a potentially useful method of confirming and extending the behavioural evidence of hemispheric asymmetry.

Conditioning paradigms have also been used to demonstrate hemisphere differences. Hellige (1975) found that eye-blink conditioning to a verbal conditioned stimulus was more effective when the stimulus was presented in the right visual field. Entus (1976) conditioned a sucking response in infants aged 3–20 weeks to dichotically presented pairs of stimuli which could be two speech sounds (*ba* and *da*) or two musical sounds. After the rate of sucking had habituated to a particular pair, the sound in one ear only was changed. Recovery from habituation was greater for speech sounds when the right ear stimulus was changed, and for musical sounds when the left ear stimulus was changed. The conditioning paradigm provides a valuable addition to the battery of research methods, since it enables lateralization to be studied in very young infants, and Entus's experiment suggests that some functional specialization is already established very soon after birth. In addition, further possibilities of new methods of research are opening up since the discovery that lateralization of function is not a unique feature of the human brain, but it also discernible in other species (Harnad *et al.*, 1976), including rabbits, cats and monkeys.

In humans, attempts have also been made to demonstrate that the cognitive abilities and intellectual biases of an individual reflect the lateralization pattern of his brain. Levy (1969) found that when left-handers were given verbal and visuo-spatial performance I.Q. tests, they were significantly worse at the visuo-spatial tests, and suggested that the bilateral representation of function sometimes associated with left-handedness is less efficient than a pure, well-lateralized representation. Buffery and Gray (1972) draw the opposite conclusion from their comparison of male and female abilities, arguing that males have less complete lateralization of visuo-spatial abilities, and that this produced superior performance, so while Levy concludes that a concentrated unilateral representation is more efficient, Buffery and Gray maintain that a diffuse bilateral representation is more advantageous. The discrepancy between these studies may be due to inaccurate assessment of the degree of lateralization in the individual subjects.

It is unfortunate that the serious study of hemisphere differences has succeeded in attracting a lunatic fringe of adherents who have been engaged in parcelling out attributes and functions between the hemispheres on grounds that are more mystical than scientific. In the popular literature on this subject, the right hemisphere is sometimes characterized as sensual, artistic, intuitive and as the predominant influence in oriental cultures; while the left is considered as rational, logical, intellectual and predominant in Western cultures. The following quotation is an example of this kind of myth-making drawn from an article on architecture.

> The monopoly of language by this left-sided unit sealed man's fate. Human progress, especially in the west, has been a monumental testimony to the biological rule that strong systems become stronger...Classicism is the outcome of left cerebral dominance...aesthetic canons are drawn into the left-sided system of values. They are 'reasonable' and always consistent with 'good taste', which is another way of saying that they observe the rules conceived within a rationally-intensive ethos (Smith, 1975).

It is hard to see how research on hemisphere differences, however imperfect it may be, could have generated this kind of nonsense. In spite of the methodological criticisms that can justifiably be made of experimental techniques, and in spite of the lack of a theoretical explanation that can satisfactorily account for all of the findings, the convergence of results from a wide variety of different sources has provided a solid empirical basis of evidence for functional specialization of the hemispheres, and it would be a pity if this should be tainted by the wilder speculations that have been advanced.

REFERENCES

Annett, M. (1970). A classification of hand preference. *British Journal of Psychology* 61, 303-322.

Bakker, D. J. (1970). Ear asymmetry with monaurual stimulation: relations to lateral dominance and lateral awareness. *Neuropsychologia* 8, 103-117.

Berlucchi, G., Brizzolara, D., Marzi, C. A., Rizzolatti, G. and Umilta, C. (1974). Can lateral asymmetries in attention explain inter-field differences in visual perception? *Cortex* X, 177-185.

Bever, T. G. and Chiarello, R. J. (1974). Cerebral dominance in musicians and nonmusicians, *Science, N.Y.* 185, 537-539.

Bonin, G., von. (1962). Anatomical asymmetries of the cerebral hemispheres. *In* "Interhemispheric Relations and Cerebral Dominance" (V. B. Mountcastle, ed.). The John Hopkins Press, Baltimore.

Bouma, H. (1976). Eye movements and functional visual field. Paper presented at "Attention and Performance VII". Academic Press, London and New York.

Bradshaw, J. L. (1974). Peripherally presented and unreported words may bias the perceived meaning of a centrally fixated homograph. *Journal of Experimental Psychology* 103, 1200-1202.

Bradshaw, J. L., Nettleton, N. C. and Patterson, K. (1973). Identification of mirror reversed and nonreversed facial profiles in same and opposite visual fields. *Journal of Experimental Psychology* 99, 42-48.

Broca, P. (1865). Sur la faculté du langage articulé. *Bulletin Société Anthropologie, Paris.* 6, 493-494.

Buffery, A. W. H. and Gray, J. A. (1972). Sex differences in spatial and linguistic skills. *In* "Gender differences—Their Ontogeny and Significance" 'C. Ounsted and D. C. Taylor, eds). Churchill Livingstone, London and Edinburgh.

Carmon, A. and Nachshon, I. (1971). Effects of unilateral brain damage on perception of temporal order. *Cortex* VII, 410-418.

Carmon, A., Nachshon, I., Isserof, A. and Kleiner, M. (1972). Visual field differences in reaction times to Hebrew letters. *Psychonomic Science* 28, 222-224.

Cohen, G. (1972). Hemisphere differences in a letter classification task. *Perception and Psychophysics* 11, 139-142.

Cohen, G. (1973). Hemisphere differences in serial versus parallel processing. *Journal of Experimental Psychology* 97, 349-356.

Cohen, G. (1975). Hemisphere differences in the effects of cueing. *Journal of Experimental Psychology*: Human Perception and Performance 1, 366-373.

Cohen, G. (1976). Components of the laterality effect in letter recognition: asymmetries in iconic storage. *Quarterly Journal of Experimental Psychology* 28, 105-114.

Cohen, G. and Freeman, R. H. (1976). Individual differences in reading strategies in relation to handedness and cerebral asymmetry. Paper presented at "Attention and Performance VII". Academic Press, London and New York.

Cohen, G. and Martin, M. (1975). Hemisphere differences in an auditory stroop task. *Perception and Psychophysics* 17, 79-83.

Davis, R. and Schmit, V. (1971). Timing the transfer of information between the hemispheres in man. *Acta Psychologica* 35, 333-346.

Dimond, S. and Beaumont, G. (1971). Hemisphere function and vigilance. *Quarterly Journal of Experimental Psychology* 23, 443-448.

Entus, A. K. (1976). Hemisphere asymmetry in processing dichotically presented speech and nonspeech stimuli by infants. *In* "Proceedings of the Conference on Language Development and Neurological Theory" (S. Segalowitz, ed.). Academic Press, New York and London.

Filbey, R. A. and Gazzaniga, M. S. (1969). Splitting the normal brain with reaction times. *Psychonomic Science* 12, 335-336.

Fleminger, J. J., Horne, D. J. de L., and Nott, P. N. (1970). Unilateral electro-convulsive therapy and cerebral dominance: the effect of right and left sided placement on verbal memory. *Journal of Neurology, Neurosurgery and Psychiatry* 33, 408-411.

Gazzaniga, M. S. (1970). "The Bisected Brain". Appleton Century Crofts, New York.

Gazzaniga, M. S., Bogen, J. E. and Sperry, R. W. (1962). Some functional effects of sectioning the cerebral commissures in man. *Proceedings of the National Academy of Science, U.S.A.* 48, 1765-1769.

Geffen, G., Bradshaw, J. L. and Wallace, G. (1971). Interhemispheric effects on reaction times to verbal and nonverbal stimuli. *Journal of Experimental Psychology* 87, 415-422.

Geffen, G., Bradshaw, J. L. and Nettleton, N. C. (1972). Hemispheric asymmetry: verbal and spatial encoding of visual stimuli. *Journal of Experimental Psychology* 95, 25-31

Geffen, G., Bradshaw, J. L. and Nettleton, N. C. (1973). Attention and hemispheric differences in reaction times during simultaneous audio-visual tests. *Quarterly Journal of Experimental Psychology* 25, 404-412.

Geschwind, N. (1972). Language and the Brain. *Scientific American* 226, 76-83.

Goodglass, H., Shai, A., Rosen, M. and Berman, M. O. (1971). New observations on right-left differences in tachistoscopic recognition of verbal and nonverbal stimuli. Paper presented at the International Conference of Neuropsychology, Washington, D.C.

Halperin, Y., Nachshon, I. and Carmon, A. (1973). Shift of ear superiority in dichotic listening to temporally patterned nonverbal stimuli. *Journal of the Acoustical Society of America* 53, 46-50.

Harnad, S. R., Doty, R., Goldstein, L., Jaynes, J. and Krauthamer, G. (eds). (1976). "Lateralization in the Nervous System". Academic Press, London and New York.

Hellige, J. B. (1975). Hemispheric processing differences revealed by differential conditioning and reaction time performance. *Journal of Experimental Psychology: General* 104, 309-326.

Hughlings Jackson, J. (1880). On aphasia with left hemiplegia. *Lancet* 1, 637-638.

Hyde, J. B., Akesson, E. J. and Bernstein, E. (1973). Asymmetrical growth of superior temporal gyri in man. *Experientia* **29**, 431.

Kallman, H. J. and Corballis, M. C. (1975). Ear asymmetry in reaction times to musical sounds. *Perception and Psychophysics* **17**, 368-370.

Kimura, D. (1961). Cerebral dominance and the perception of verbal stimuli. *Canadian Journal of Psychology* **15**, 166-171.

Kimura, D. (1966). Dual functional asymmetry of the brain in visual perception. *Neuropsychologia* **4**, 275-285.

Kimura, D. (1967). Functional asymmetry of the brain in dichotic listening. *Cortex* **3**, 163-178.

Kinsbourne, M. (1970). The cerebral basis of asymmetries in attention. *Acta Psychologica* **33**, 193-201.

Kinsbourne, M. (1971). The minor hemisphere as a source of aphasic speech. *Archives of Neurology* **25**, 302-306.

Klatzky, R. and Atkinson, R. C. (1971). Specialization of the cerebral hemispheres in scanning for information in short term memory. *Perception and Psychophysics* **10**, 335-338.

Lansdell, H. C. (1961). Two selective deficits found to be lateralized in temporal neurosurgery patients. Paper presented at the Eastern Psychological Association, Philadelphia.

Ledlow, A., Swanson, J. M. and Carter, B. (1972). Specialization of the hemispheres for physical and associational memory comparisons. Paper presented at the Convention of the Midwestern Psychological Association, Cleveland.

Lenneberg, E. H. (1967). Biological Foundations of Language. John Wiley and Sons, New York and London.

Levy, J. (1969). Possible basis for the evolution of lateral specialization of the human brain. *Nature, Lond.* **222**, 614-615.

Levy, J. and Trevarthen, C. (1977). Perceptual, semantic and phonetic aspects of elementary language processes in split-brain patients. *Brain* (in press).

Levy-Agresti, J. and Sperry, R. W. (1968). Differential perceptual capacities in major and minor hemispheres. *Proceedings of the National Academy of Sciences* **61**, 1151.

Miller, B. (1974). The effects of bilateral and unilateral ECT on nonverbal memory in depressed psychiatric patients. Unpublished Ph.D. Thesis, Department of Psychiatry, McGill University.

Milner, B. (1962). Laterality effects in audition. *In* "Interhemispheric Relations and Cerebral Dominance" (V. B. Mountcastle, ed.). John Hopkins Press, Baltimore.

Milner, B. (1971). Interhemispheric differences and psychological processes. *British Medical Bulletin* **27**, 272-277.

Milner, B. and Taylor, L. (1972). Right hemisphere superiority in tactile pattern recognition after cerebral commissurotomy: evidence for nonverbal memory. *Neuropsychologia* **10**, 1-15.

Moscovitch, M. and Catlin, J. (1970). Interhemispheric transmission of information: measurement in normal man. *Psychonomic Science* **18**, 211-213.

Myers, R. E. (1962). Transmission of visual information within and between the hemispheres: a behavioural study. *In* "Interhemispheric Relations and Cerebral Dominance" (V. B. Mountcastle, ed.). The John Hopkins Press, Baltimore.

Nebes, R. D. (1971). Perception of part-whole relations in commissurotomized man. *Cortex* **IV**, 333-349.

Newcombe, F. (1969). "Missile Wounds of the Brain". Oxford University Press, Oxford.

Newcombe, F. and Ratcliff, G. (1973). Two Brains: Independence or Interaction? Paper presented at the British Association for the Advancement of Science.

Oldfield, R. C. (1971). The Assessment of handedness: the Edinburgh inventory. *Neuropsychologia* 9, 97-111.

Patterson, K. and Bradshaw, J. L. (1975). Differential hemispheric mediation of non-verbal stimuli. *Journal of Experimental Psychology*: Human Perception and Performance 1, 246-252.

Penfield, W. and Perot, P. (1963). The brain's record of auditory and visual experience: a final summary and discussion. *Brain* 86, 595-702.

Posner, M. I. and Mitchell, R. F. (1967). Chronometric analysis of classification. *Psychological Review* 74, 392-409.

Renzi, E. de, Faglioni, P. and Spinnler, H. (1968). The performance of patients with unilateral brain damage on face recognition tasks. *Cortex* IV, 17.

Rossi, G. E. and Rosadini, G. (1965). *In* "Brain Mechanisms Underlying Speech and Language" (F. L. Darley and Millikan, eds). Grune and Stratton, New York and London.

Shaw, J. C., O'Connor, K. and Ongley, C. (in press). EEG coherence as a measure of cerebral functional organization. IBRO monograph series, Vol. 3. Raven Press, New York.

Smith, P. F. (1975). The conservation syndrome. *Built Environment Quarterly*, September, 162-165.

Spellacy, F. and Blumstein, S. (1970). The influence of language set on ear preference in phoneme recognition. *Cortex* 6, 430-439.

Studdert-Kennedy, M. and Shankweiler, D. (1970). Hemispheric specialization for speech perception. *Journal of the Acoustical Society of America* 48, 579-594.

Teuber, H-L. (1962). Effects of brain wounds implicating right and left hemispheres. *In* "Interhemispheric Relations and Cerebral Dominance" (V. B. Mountcastle, ed.). The John Hopkins Press, Baltimore.

Umilta, C., Frost, N. and Hyman, R. (1972). Interhemispheric effects of choice reaction times to one, two and three letter displays. *Journal of Experimental Psychology* 93, 198-204.

Umilta, C., Rizzolatti, G., Marzi, C. A., Zamboni, G., Franzini, C., Camarda, R. and Berlucchi, G. (1974). Hemisphere differences in the discrimination of line orientation. *Neuropsychologia* 12, 165-174.

Warrington, E. K. and Rabin, P. (1970). Perceptual matching in patients with cerebral lesions. *Neuropsychologia* 8, 475.

White, M. J. (1969). Laterality differences in perception: a review. *Psychological Bulletin* 72, 387-405.

White, M. J. (1972). Hemisphere asymmetries in tachistoscopic information processing. *British Journal of Psychology* 63, 497-508.

Wilkins, A. and Stewart, A. (1974). The time course of lateral asymmetries in visual perception of letters. *Journal of Experimental Psychology* 102, 905-908.

Wood, C. C., Goff, W. R. and Day, R. S. (1971). Auditory evoked potentials during speech perception. *Science, N.Y.* 173, 1248-1251.

Zangwill, O. L. (1947). Psychological aspects of rehabilitation in cases of brain injury. *British Journal of Psychology* 37, 60-69.

Zangwill, O. L. (1960). "Cerebral Dominance and the Relation to Psychological Function". Oliver and Boyde, Edinburgh.

9

The State of Cognitive Psychology: Problems and Panaceas

Since about 1973 a number of psychologists have expressed dissatisfaction and disappointment with the aims and achievements of psychology, especially in the field of cognition. Both the validity of the aims, and the efficiency of various methods of research have been called into question. In spite of technological progress, and the enormous amount of experimental work which has been carried out, the actual advance in knowledge of the subject has been, it is argued, distressingly slight both empirically and theoretically. The empirical findings which emerge from experiments are constantly challenged or qualified by further experiments, and theoretical models discarded or revised with a rapidity that leaves many psychologists despairingly questing for firm ground on which to stand. Listening to the critics it is easy to form the impression that each step forward is succeeded by two half-steps back. There are many signs that confidence among psychologists is at a low ebb, and the belief that psychological research would eventually provide definitive answers to questions about the functioning of the human brain appears to be losing ground.

How far is this failure of nerve justified? This chapter will review, and attempt to assess some of the soul-searching and self-criticism which is currently being voiced, and will consider the diagnoses and the suggested cures. Ideally, this task should be undertaken from both a philosophical and a psychological standpoint, but most psychologists are not philosophers of science, and few philosophers of science have a detailed knowledge of psychology. A closer liaison between the two would undoubtedly enable us to formulate a much more powerful and sophisticated analysis of the problems of psychological research. Meanwhile, it is salutary for psychologists themselves to engage in some house-cleaning, to air their doubts and confusions, and to try positively to chart the most promising course for the future.

I. EXPERIMENTAL PROBLEMS IN PSYCHOLOGICAL RESEARCH

One of the first to give public expression to the current pessimism was Newell (1973) in a paper entitled *You can't play twenty questions with nature and win*. He asked whether psychology would have made any significant advance by some date in the future, given that the prevailing experimental approach and rate of productivity were maintained. Assessing past progress, and extrapolating forwards, he reached a very discouraging estimate. Newell makes a number of specific criticisms in an effort to analyse the causes of this lack of progress. Firstly, he points out that research is what he calls "phenomena-driven". By this he means that the discovery of a new phenomenon (and he lists many examples) generates an explosion of related experiments. "We explore what it is a function of, and the combinatorial variations flow from our experimental laboratories". His second criticism is that the exploration of these phenomena, the explosion of follow-up experiments, is guided by a conceptual framework of binary opposition. We ask of each phenomenon "Is it A or is it B?". Is it serial or parallel processing? Is it innate or is it learned? Is forgetting due to interference or to decay? Newell concludes that in 30 years' time we may have discovered another hundred or so phenomena, and formulated another dozen or so binary oppositions, but that instead of a cumulative and orderly growth of knowledge, this method will produce an ever-increasing number of unresolved issues, many of which are finally abandoned only because of the confusion and boredom of the researchers. "It seems to me," Newell complains, "that clarity is never achieved. Matters simply become muddier and muddier". Although Newell's diagnosis of the ills of psychology is based mainly on these two short-comings—the inbreeding of experimental paradigms, and the dichotomous nature of the hypotheses that are formulated—he also makes some further, more specific criticisms. He notes that researchers may fail to identify the exact strategies employed by individual subjects in cognitive tasks, and points out that averaging over the results of subjects who are using a variety of different strategies, or even a single subject who is using a mixture of strategies, conceals, rather than reveals, what is actually going on. As he says "You get garbage, or, even worse, spurious regularity". Newell argues that unless we can specify all the possible strategies in a given task, and separate them out by the experimental design and analysis, we are not going to characterize performance correctly, and we are not going to arrive at correct explanations for· the phenomenon under investigation. Furthermore, even when we have identified all the possible operations in a task, we still need to specify the control structure which governs which particular operations, and which order of operations is selected on any one occasion. In short, to explain performance in a cognitive task satisfactorily, we have to know what different strategies are employed, and what governs the choice of strategy. Unless we can define the control structure, we cannot formulate any theoretical explanation for the welter of discrepant results which builds up, as more and more versions of the original experiment are explored. Finally, Newell deplores the looseness of the linkage between related experiments. Instead of an orderly sequence whereby possible interpretations are systematically tested, and critical variables isolated, researchers pick and choose arbitrarily which aspects of the original experiment to explore in their follow-up studies. What commonly happens is that when secondary experiments are designed to test the validity of a particular interpretation of the "parent" experiment, so many features of the original design are changed that it is impossible to draw any conclusions about the relationship between the different experiments. An example is to be found in the modality specific interference experiments described in Chapter 2. Designed to test the hypothesis that visual memory and verbal memory are specifically more vulnerable to interference from concurrent tasks employing the same modality than tasks employing the other modality, these experiments have varied the amount and nature of the memory load, the nature and difficulty of the concurrent tasks, the timing of the operations, and the response requirements, to the extent that inconsistencies in the results resist interpretation. When many of the potentially critical factors are varied simultaneously, it is impossible to isolate the necessary and sufficient conditions for the phenomenon under investigation.

Newell advocates several possible remedies. He argues that we need to construct more complete processing models for cognitive tasks, including control structures, taking into account all possible strategies for performing the task. Another suggestion is that we should focus large numbers of closely integrated experimental studies—entire programmes of research—on a single complex task, and mount co-operative endeavours to achieve a more thorough understanding of a few areas of cognitive performance. In his view, computer simulation provides the best example at present available of cumulative progress and genuine advance.

How far are Newell's criticisms valid, and how helpful are his suggestions? With respect to Newell's first major objection, the complaint that psychology is phenomena-driven, and that discovery of new phenomena generates large numbers of experiments "to verify their reality and confirm their nature", it is difficult to conceive of an alternative. Many experiments are *necessary* to define a psychological phenomenon, and to identify the boundary conditions for its existence. The root of the trouble seems to be not that research is phenomena-driven, but that it is driven too erratically. That is to say, that the follow-up experiments which are carried out are often not selected according to an orderly guiding principle. Newell's objection that experiments are too loosely linked, and fail to form a cumulative sequence, comes closer to the real source of confusion and lack of progress. But the problem of achieving this orderly sequence, of selecting the most important and most informative variables to test out of the immense number of possibilities, is not one that can readily be solved. Even with the wisest research policies, we cannot always hope to discern the right track, we cannot recognize the ideal sequence of experimentation, until we have already proceeded far along the paths that get, as Newell says, muddier and muddier. It is not the fault of the psychologist that behaviour is so complex. As Fodor (1975) remarks "Perhaps there are bounds to the options that organisms enjoy ... but if there are no one knows where to set them. Psychology is very hard". The fact that what initially appears to be a simple phenomenon comes to look increasingly complicated as we learn more about it, is a fact of life in psychology, and not necessarily due to the ineptitude of the researchers.

In some instances it is possible to find short cuts whereby we can verify the reality of a phenomenon without exhaustive exploration within a single paradigm. This occurs when evidence from different sources converges, and can be combined. One such example is provided by the work on hemispheric specialization reviewed in Chapter 8, where clinical, developmental and animal studies complement and qualify the results of experimental research on normal human cognitive performance. Studies of the role of language in thinking described in Chapters 4 and 5, have similarly benefited from a multi-faceted approach. We gain far more insight into the importance of language in thinking by studying the cognitive abilities of the deaf, the pre-linguistic child, the a-linguistic primates and clinical cases of language disorder, than by confining ourselves to the study of normal adult performance on verbal and non-verbal tasks. Essentially this is an argument against "paradigm-bound" psychology: it is an argument against increasingly narrow specialization within the subject without exchange and cross-fertilization between the different splinter groups. Hebb (1974) put this case forcefully:

> Psychology is not clinical psychology; it is not physiological psychology; it is not social or comparative or developmental or human experimental psychology. It is something more, comprising all those lines of approach to the central mystery. ... it may be disastrous when the specialist digging his own path deeper and deeper loses sight of what others are doing in other fields, and so loses an invaluable perspective.

Such a view does not imply that digging deeply, and pursuing a narrowly focused sequence of experiments is a futile and misguided endeavour, but it does claim that a broader perspective is supplied by trying to relate evidence across the rather arbitrary divisions into specialist fields that have grown up in psychology, and that this broader perspective may help us to assess the importance, generality and nature of a given phenomenon.

What of Newell's other main objection—that the hypotheses we test are too often formulated in terms of binary oppositions? Newell himself lists enough examples of these oppositions to demonstrate convincingly that this kind of conceptualization is indeed very prevalent. How far it is harmful, and whether better alternatives are available is more debatable. Formulating an experimental hypothesis in terms of a dichotomous question such as "Is X caused by A or B?" can be misleading in several ways. It is misconceived if in fact there are other possible causes (C, D etc.) which are excluded from consideration or overlooked. (These are the cases where not-A does not entail B.) It is also misconceived in the cases where A and B are not mutually exclusive, and X may be caused by an interactive combination of A and B (and possibly C, D etc., also). A belated recognition of this latter misconception has been a common outcome of much psychological research. Thus we may come to realize that both nature and nurture play a part, or that both interference and decay are implicated in forgetting. Sometimes we realize that the terms of the opposition need to be broken down into sub-divisions, as in the heredity *vs.* environment I.Q. debate, where it is of obvious practical importance to partition "environment" into social, educational, nutritional and other factors. Often we need to revise the original question "A or B?", and ask instead "How much A and how much B?" or "In what circumstances A and in what circumstances B?". Sometimes we find, as in the case of the serial and parallel processing opposition, that although the terms are conceptually distinct, it is not always possible to distinguish between them experimentally. As research proceeds, further possibilities besides the original A or B opposition become evident. An example occurs in the research on selective attention where, after extensive testing of perception *vs.* response models (that is, models in which irrelevant information is filtered out at the stage of perception, as opposed to models in which irrelevant information is filtered out at the stage of response), a new version such as Broadbent's (1973) model is proposed which includes three filters operating at successive stages of processing. All these cases conform to Newell's claim that the binary opposition form of hypothesis leads to an ever increasing pile of issues, but he does not tell us how this is to be avoided. If an issue is genuinely complex, its complexity will have to be confronted. Perhaps we should start out with more complex multi-factor hypotheses instead of the oversimplified binary ones. But in many cases it is only hindsight that enables us to discern the relevance of additional factors; the complexities do not become apparent until some experimental progress has been made. To maintain that our initial conceptual framework should explicitly include the possibility of an interactive relationship between the terms of the opposition is a more feasible proposal. However, the omission is not necessarily fatal if the experimental data can be subsequently examined for interactive effects. While it is indisputably true that psychological issues which seem simple at the outset tend to become increasingly complex as research proceeds, it is not so much that we move from clarity to confusion, but that we come to recognize the delusive simplicity of the earlier formulations.

    Neither of the two major faults which Newell detects in current methods of psychological research, the obsessive exploration of phenomena and the prevalence of dichotomous hypotheses, is wholly without justification when analysed in more detail. Although it is clear that these methods are not always optimal, there are some cases when they are inevitable, and some cases when they are not culpable.

Newell's attack on the state of cognitive psychology has been endorsed and amplified by Allport (1975). Taking up the task of diagnosing the ills of psychology, Allport finds himself "essentially but reluctantly in agreement with the verdict". He elaborates and emphasizes some of the points made by Newell, and goes on to add some strictures of his own. The main force of Allport's onslaught is directed against the loose linkage of experiments, and the habit of picking and choosing particular aspects of the data from a given experiment, and selectively citing results of other related experiments which happen to lend confirmation to a preferred interpretation. Counter-examples and anomalies are conveniently ignored so that a spuriously convincing case can be made out, and the evidence is tailored and distorted to fit tenaciously held preconceptions. Indeed, negative results and failed replications are rarely published, and are usually consigned to the oblivion of the researcher's desk drawers. This custom is particularly odd since so many scientists pay lip-service to the view of Popper (1959) that science advances by falsification of hypotheses, and it has the consequence of making theories appear to be better supported than they actually are. This failure to assess results in the wide context of all the available pertinent evidence, and this biased selectivity, are seen by Allport as an important cause of "the nagging failure of our discipline to converge, to integrate, and hence to cumulate". In some examples cited by Allport, cognitive psychologists ignore the work of other cognitive psychologists which is potentially damaging to their entrenched positions. In other examples, such as studies of the effects of context on comprehensions, human experimental research proceeds without reference to parallel research in computer simulation. Whether or not these views are exaggerated, Allport is not alone in expressing them. The same concern has been voiced by Bruner (1975) who, reflecting on this habit of building "little hillocks of disconnected data", suspects that:

> they have faded away for lack of a connexion to the main bodies of knowledge out of which they emerged, or perhaps the main bodies of knowledge were insufficiently structured to support such massive but narrow structures.

While most psychologists would agree in deploring this state of affairs, it is by no means easy to see how it should be remedied. Newell (1973) proposed greater co-operation so that experimental efforts could be more closely co-ordinated and focused. But who is to master-mind a large scale co-operative endeavour of this kind?

Hudson (1976) shows a greater awareness of the practical difficulties attending such a scheme:

> It may be that a degree of seignorial bullying and autocracy is necessary if any set of ideas is to be formulated and systematically explored . . . the snag is that schools of thought . . . characteristically address different issues in different ways, the consequence being a political free-for-all . . . When we are in the grip of a strongly held belief, we may find that we have shuffled numbers into places where they look appropriate; not because we are rogues, but because human intelligence and human recollection are deeply fallible mechanisms.

It could be more dangerous to rely on the impartiality of a mastermind, than to continue the present system of independent free-for-all research. Hudson's view of the schismatic nature of psychological research may be too pessimistic. During recent years there have been signs that psychologists are becoming more aware of the shortcomings of splinter-group research. There has been a marked increase in the number of inter-disciplinary meetings and conferences where clinicians, cognitive psychologists, computer scientists, linguists and philosophers have tried to exchange ideas and to integrate their approaches on an informal basis. Differences in view-points, in goals, in training and in background knowledge make these attempts difficult, and the bridges that are built are frail and precarious, but the need has been recognized, and some efforts are being made. Informal co-operation of this kind can provide a wider perspective without the disadvantages of formal co-ordination which might stifle dissent.

Allport also discusses Newell's recommendation that models of cognitive processing should aim for greater completeness, and, for more precise specification of alternative strategies and of control structures. As Allport quite rightly points out, one of the most intractable and crucial problems in psychology is that of identifying what aspects of cognitive performance are structurally determined, and so fixed and invariant, and what aspects are determined by strategies which are optional and variable. Unless this distinction can be clearly made we cannot say how far results are generalizable, and how far they are situation-specific. Tentative answers emerge only after extensive comparisons across task variations and individual subjects. Computer simulation of a given task is not necessarily as Newell implies, a panacea for this problem. Although simulation guarantees that processes are specified precisely, it does not guarantee that the simulated processes represent the only way to perform the task, or the optimal way to perform the task, or even the most frequently adopted strategy. The assumptions made in designing a computer simulation are just as likely to be arbitrary and selective as the assumptions made in constructing a psychological model. In essence, the problem of separating out structure from strategy, the basic control structure from the optional operations, is very similar to the problem of distinguishing between competence and performance which has recurred continually throughout this book.

In a trenchant summary of the major faults of psychological research, Allport lists:

> an uncritical or selective, or frankly cavalier attitude to experimental data; a pervasive atmosphere of special pleading; a curious parochialism in acknowledging even the existence of other workers, and other approaches to the phenomena under discussion; interpretations of data relying on multiple arbitrary choice-points; and underlying all else, the near vacuum of theoretical structure within which to inter-relate different sets of experimental results, or to direct the search for significant new phenomena.

The remainder of this chapter now focuses on Allport's last point, and is concerned with the current theoretical state of cognitive psychology.

II. THEORETICAL PROBLEMS IN PSYCHOLOGY: THE DEBATE ON REDUCTIONISM

The lack of any general theoretical framework in many areas of psychology is glaringly obvious at the moment. It is a state of affairs which is baffling to the student, and leaves the researcher disoriented in a pathless wilderness. It is worth trying to see why it has come about, and what can or should be done to rectify it.

Psychologists seem currently to be much more reluctant to formulate or adopt the broad general theories, the global explanations of behaviour, that characterized psychology in the past. Since the heydays of Gestalt psychology, S-R theory, or information theory, there has been a tendency to forsake such high levels of generality, and to concentrate on specific areas of human behaviour. Theories which do have considerable generality, such as the TOTE model of Miller *et al.* (1960) described in Chapter 3, or the Hypothesis-testing theory of Levine (1962, 1966) outlined in Chapter 6, have not commanded such strong allegiances, or spear-headed major trends in psychological inquiry. One of the reasons why psychologists have turned away from theorizing on the grand scale is perhaps the realization that in psychology a high level of generality is only achieved at the expense of loss of explanatory power and of predictive power in specific situations. An S-R theory or a TOTE model may offer us a common mechanism for diverse tasks from problem solving to learning motor skills, but will not tell us how people process negative information, or perceive speech in noisy conditions. It is not difficult to see why this is so. The explanation lies in the importance of strategies as determining factors in human performance, which has already been stressed in the previous section. In the 1971 William James lectures, Broadbent said:

> I want to emphasize the importance of optional rather than obligatory strategies in mental performance. There is an unfortunate habit of mind amongst most researchers; they look for a constant rule of behaviour which will apply to all people, and to the same person on all occasions. Much recent work however shows that quite different strategies of performance can be adopted regularly by different people, or from time to time by the same person.

As we become more aware of the range and variability of human strategies, we necessarily become less concerned with the constant rules, the common mechanisms. In determining the performance of a given individual in a particular task, the influence of fixed and law-like processes is outweighed by the effect of the variable optional strategies, so that the fixed laws would neither predict nor explain the outcome, even if we knew what they were. It is also true that when research priorities favour studies that have some practical application, and put a premium on utility, this has the effect of shifting the focus of psychology from the general to the specific, from high-level theories and competence models to actual performance, from laws to strategies. But this change of focus has also been at least partly responsible for the splintering of psychology into small separate areas, islands of intensive research which are no longer linked by any unifying thread. Without high-level general theories some disintegration is inevitable. Freed from the constraints of a unifying theory, many psychologists feel isolated and unsure where they are heading. Of course, all this should not be taken to imply that psychology has become completely a-theoretical. Specific theories and models for specific aspects of human performance such as semantic memory, attention and pattern recognition continue to be constructed and tested, but these have limited scope and the overall linkage is lacking.

One possible solution to this problem is a move towards some form of reductionism, and the merits of reductionist approaches have been the subject of considerable controversy. Some psychologists see the answer in a closer relationship between psychology and biology or physiology, seeking explanations of man's behaviour in his biological nature, or in physiological mechanisms. Ideally, such explanations would have a high level of generality and provide a unifying base for psychological research, close the dualist gap between mind and matter, and have a concreteness and precision often lacking in purely psychological theories. Hebb (1974) advocates the biological approach as a corrective to misconceptions in psychology. The study of man as a biosocial animal gives, he argues, a wider perspective. The determinants of behaviour are more easily discerned in the less complex social groups and environments of animals, and throw light on the social behaviour of man, on motivation and on the aetiology of mental disorders. Hebb's point of view is a partisan one, stressing the advantages of the biological approach without attempting an objective assessment of the relative advantages and disadvantages of different methodologies. The difficulties of extrapolating from one species to another species are not discussed, although they must constitute a serious limitation for biological reductionism. Nor is it the case that self-evident and indisputable truths necessarily emerge from ethological studies of animal societies. Mistaken interpretations can, and have, been made. That the ethologist, as well as the psychologist, is liable to error is apparent from a quotation by Wilson (1975), in his book *Sociobiology: The New Synthesis*:

> The evidence of murder and cannibalism in mammals and other vertebrates has now accumulated to the point where we must completely revise the conclusion advanced by Konrad Lorenz . . . murder is far more common and hence normal in many vertebrate species than in man . . . I have been impressed by how often such behaviour becomes apparent only when the observation time devoted to a species passes the thousand hour mark.

Evidently biological reductionism, whether or not it can provide a useful corrective to the state of psychology, is not without its own problems.

Physiological reductionism, the attempt to explain psychological behaviour in terms of neurophysiological mechanisms, exerts a powerful attraction for many psychologists, and induces an equally powerful repugnance in others. Regrettably, there are signs of a methodological schism developing between pro and anti reductionists as divisive as any of the theoretical controversies of the past. Indeed it may well prove even more divisive, since moral and ideological convictions are imported into the debate, obscuring the scientific issues and turning rational discussion into an exchange of dogmas.

Arguments against reductionism tend to be arguments against an extreme form of reductionism. Putnam (1973) claims that "reductionism asserts that psychology is deducible from the functional organization of the brain". Many of the opponents of reductionism are concerned to point out that physiological mechanisms do not provide a *complete* explanation of *all* aspects of human behaviour. In fact it is doubtful whether there are many physiologically oriented psychologists who would make so extreme a claim. Many would be content with the more modest claim that a knowledge of the underlying physiological mechanisms provides an explanation of *some* aspects of behaviour, that our understanding in areas such as perception and memory, the effects of stress, and the nature of schizophrenia, has been illuminated by neurophysiological and biochemical research.

The central issues of the reductionist debate are not confined to physiological reductionism, but are also relevant to biological reductionism, to machine reductionism, which seeks to explain behaviour in terms of the logic of computer simulation, and to experimental reductionism which reduces behaviour to models of the component structures and processing stages. Behaviourist reductionism is, of course, a form of experimental reductionism, but the arguments which are specifically directed against behaviourism have been sufficiently rehearsed elsewhere (e.g. Taylor, 1964), and the points raised here apply to experimental reductionism in general. There are two main objections commonly levelled at reductionist approaches. First, that low-level sciences like neurophysiology, biology or cybernetics cannot "explain" the phenomena of high-level sciences like psychology, but only redescribe them in other terms. The second, less radical objection claims that those aspects of behaviour which are amenable to reductionist explanations are not the most important or significant aspects of man's behaviour.

The first objection is expressed most clearly by Putnam (1973). He argues that facts derived from low-level sciences are largely irrelevant to the explanation of high-level behavioural phenomena, and as an analogy he considers the case of a board with two holes, and a peg which will fit into one of the holes and not into the other. This phenomenon, in Putnam's view, is adequately explained by the relative sizes of the peg and the holes; the microstructure of the board, in terms of its elementary particles, is irrelevant to the explanation. What is critical here is not so much the truth of this claim, but whether this example is representative of psychological phenomena and their explanation. Arguably, the relationships of pegs to holes is not analogous to human behaviour, and there are good reasons why same-level explanations are unsatisfactory to the psychologist, and lower-level explanations are relevant. Human behaviour, unlike Putnam's pegs, is multiply determined and variable. The psychologist cannot hope for single causal explanations, but must seek multiple causes and try to assess the contribution of various causal factors, and identify the various conditions in which they exert varying degrees of influence on behaviour. If we take an example from cognitive behaviour, instead of pegs and holes, we can see that this is so. Suppose our problem is "Why do people make errors in recalling items from memory?". A same-level explanation like "Because they forget", or "Because they become confused", is not adequate. We want to know why they remember some items and not others; why some people make more errors than others; why some kinds of instructions, or degrees of practice, or lengths of list produce more or fewer errors; why old people make more errors than young ones; and why people who have had blows on the head make more errors than people who have not had blows on the head. Once we are confronted with a variety of different causal explanations, we have to seek further explanations of the causes themselves. The psychologist is driven inexorably to keep on asking "Why?", and the recurring why leads down inexorably from higher-level to lower-level explanations. Processing models, and anatomical and biochemical facts, are relevant to errors of recall because we are not concerned with a unitary and invariant phenomenon. It is also misleading to suppose that the psychologist is seeking only to identify causes. In fact he is not only asking why. He is also asking how. How does the causal relationship work? Is it invariant or does it hold only when some other conditions are fulfilled? How does it get damaged, and how can it be improved? Same-level explanations cannot supply answers to these questions, and lower-level explanations are required. It should also be pointed out that the reductionist approaches exemplified in information processing models and computer simulations are not necessarily intended to provide causal explanations, but are often best viewed as analogies or metaphors that help us to understand more clearly what problems we are confronting, and what questions we need to ask. Reductionist explanations are not complete, and the chain of relationship between the different levels is sometimes obscure, but to admit this is only to say that the work is unfinished, and not that the method is fundamentally wrong.

Next, let us consider the second objection to reductionism—that it is too limited in scope, and leaves out too much that is relevant to the understanding of behaviour. Physiological research, it is argued, typically concentrates on only a few aspects of a phenomenon, and omits others. Rose and Rose (1973) note, for example, that the physiological reductionist considers the problems of alcoholism and schizophrenia in terms of biochemical reactions, and ignores the sociological aspects of social and family environment, and personal history. Bruner (1976) implies that the reductionist standpoint is to blame for narrowly mechanistic studies of cognitive processes such as the use of language or playing chess, which fail to relate these activities to a wider context which includes the stored knowledge of the individual, social and cultural norms, and the mentalistic concepts of intentions, purposes and expectations, which he considers vital for the explanation of behaviour. By concentrating on the molecular level, exploring small isolated segments of behaviour, Bruner believes that psychologists throw away their chance to contribute effectively to policy-making, to make practical recommendations in the spheres of education, sociology and economics. His attack includes not only physiological, biological and machine reductionism, but experimental reductionism as well, since those who employ experimental techniques are also guilty of focusing on restricted segments of performance, and failing to adopt the panoramic view that Bruner advocates instead.

Fortunately, there is no need for reductionists to be too dismayed by this onslaught, for defence and counter-attack are both possible. Some of the accusations can be rebutted, and the alternatives to reductionism, as we shall see, are not necessarily superior. Although the vagueness of anti-reductionist programmes makes them difficult to assess, their feasibility is doubtful. Proposals of so grand a scope may sound very well, but be impossible to implement in practice.

It is not accurate, for example, to say that reductionists have failed to include expectations, the will, purposes and intentions in their accounts of behaviour, although these concepts appear under other names, and are operationally defined. In the cognitive psychology of problem solving reviewed in Chapter 3, intentions and purposes can be identified with goals, and the operations programmed to achieve these goals. Expectations are incorporated in the definition of "set", and perceptual, cognitive, attentional and response sets have been intensively investigated in many different experimental paradigms. On the physiological side, the study of expectations in the guise of mechanisms of arousal, facilitation and inhibition has gone far to reveal the relation between mental states and neural functioning. It is not clear that concepts like intention and purpose lose anything except mystique by this kind of reductionist treatment.

The claim that the worm's eye view of the reductionist is too narrowly focused, and too small scale to yield insights into the psychology of behaviour, is harder to counter. Chapter 7 illustrated the way in which machine simulations may fail to replicate, or even approximate to, human performance because the situational context and background knowledge they incorporate is too sharply limited. Putnam (1973) believes "that psychology is as under-determined by biology as it is by elementary particle physics, and that people's psychology is partly a reflection of deeply entrenched societal beliefs". In other words, behaviour is causally determined by social and cultural factors and by personal history to a much greater extent than it is determined by processing mechanisms. The validity of this argument depends very largely on the kind of behaviour under consideration. Experimental techniques can tell us a good deal about how we remember telephone numbers, or what are the optimal conditions for maintaining vigilance while monitoring signals for long periods, or how contrast illusions are produced. They may be less successful at answering larger and more complex questions about how we understand language, form opinions or choose careers. If the problem is a specific one, the worm's eye view may be better than the bird's. Whether processing mechanisms or sociological ˉinfluences are more powerful determinants of behaviour also depends on whether we are concerned with identifying the norms or habits of behaviour, or the limits of capacity. How somebody drives a car along an empty road may well be primarily determined by the rules and conventions of his society, and his personal habits; but how he manages to avoid a collision when another driver pulls out of a side road in front of him depends much more on the speed of his reactions, his visual acuity, and his level of arousal.

Whether cognitive psychology is able to exercise any influence on practical affairs and public concerns also depends very much on the kind of problems we are talking about. Psychologists are continually engaged in research which is applied to a wide range of concrete problems such as underwater perception, traffic control, the optimal lay-out of buildings, techniques of storing and disseminating information, methods of teaching reading, and the task requirements of industrial operations. To complain, as Bruner does, that psychology has failed to influence economic policy is a criticism of its scope, and not of its practical value. (Indeed it is more probably a reflection on the nature of economics than on the state of psychology.)

What alternatives do the anti-reductionists offer? One approach is what Rose and Rose (1975) call autonomism, exemplified in the past, when philosophy and psychology were indistinguishable, by the speculative introspectionist tradition, by Freudian theory, and more recently by the humanist approach of Laing. Autonomism offers same-level explanations instead of lower-level explanations, and behaviour is described and analysed in terms of specifically human mentalist properties such as choice, experience, emotion and sensation. An autonomist explanation which ignores the biological character and physiological state of the organism is surely as open to the criticism of incompleteness as the most extreme form of reductionism. Another alternative to narrow forms of reductionism is presented by what might be called the "slice of life" school, advocating that psychologists should study naturally occurring behaviour in large slices of "real life". It is a plea for the wide-angle lens, the bird's eye view, which will take in the whole context in which behaviour patterns occur. This approach necessarily entails the abandonment of much experimental control, and a move toward an observational, descriptive methodology since strict control procedures are incompatible with natural behaviour. This reaction against the artificiality of rigorous laboratory experiments can be a valuable corrective. Many experimental paradigms involve requirements so remote from everyday life versions of the task that there may be little overlap between the processes employed in the laboratory and in the outside world. This point was stressed in the review of concept-learning experiments in Chapter 6, but it represents an argument for re-thinking our experimental designs rather than discarding an experimental approach altogether. Moreover, the "slice of life" approach, however seductive it may seem, is certainly not without problems—problems of feasibility, and problems of selection and de-limitation. Since no study can encompass the whole of the social setting and the life of the individuals within it, some limits must be imposed. Where are these limits to be set? How much of the personal history of the individual and his socio-cultural background is relevant to the phenomenon we are trying to explicate? How much can a single study, or a set of studies, include without being strangled by its own complexity? If we advocate research on this ambitious scale is it going to be feasible? If it would require teams of co-operating researchers to achieve the desired breadth, is it practicable to organize co-ordination on this scale? These questions are not just rhetorical; they are real and difficult problems for the researcher who wishes to operate in this way. We have already remarked that co-operative endeavours might be dangerously dependent on the intellectual biases of whoever directed the scheme. Once we move psychology out of the laboratory, and into the real world, the number of variables that influence behaviour escalates, and once we abandon the attempt to limit and manipulate them, it becomes correspondingly more difficult to determine their relative importance and how they operate.

The best and sanest alternative to pure reductionism is surely what Rose and Rose (1973) call interactionism—a methodology which recognizes the relevance and complementarity of many different approaches; which takes into consideration biological and physiological factors as well as social and personal factors; which is willing to admit experimental and observational evidence, clinical results and machine analogies. It is easy to see many advantages in an interactionist, polymorphous approach to the study of psychology. In this book, the chapters on language and thought, and on hemisphere differences, have tried to illustrate the convergence of evidence from different sources, and to show how conclusions can be strengthened, and misconceptions corrected, when a synthesis of the results of different research methodologies is attempted. Every kind of psychological research, whether reductionist or not, is liable to error. The results may be artefactual, or unrepresentative, or wrongly interpreted. However, it is *a priori* very unlikely that widely different methods of investigation would produce the same errors. Therefore, when the findings of these different methods concur, and the different pieces of the jigsaw fit together to form a coherent pattern, we can be much more confident that our conclusions are valid, and that the pattern is a genuine reflection of the truth, than if we had relied on one method alone. Even if it is not feasible to set up large scale programmes co-ordinating the different methodologies, it is still possible to draw upon the results of ongoing research emerging from the various approaches.

To advocate this kind of combinatorial, interactionist methodology is not necessarily to reject the possibility that reductionism will ultimately prove capable of providing complete explanations for psychological phenomena, but only to urge that, given the present fragmentary state of our knowledge, we should not neglect any source of evidence, nor put all our eggs into a single methodological basket.

Psychologists have never been noted for a spirit of compromise, and the subject has had rather a faction-ridden history. But in a science as complex and many-faceted as psychology the assumption that any one methodology has an exclusive monopoly of the way to the truth cannot be justifiable. Although this review of what Bruner has called "the winter of discontent" in psychology does not succeed in identifying any easy solutions to the many difficulties that beset psychological research, it does suggest that future progress will be best ensured by the cultivation of greater methodological eclecticism.

REFERENCES

Allport, D. A. (1975). The state of cognitive psychology. *Quarterly Journal of Experimental Psychology* 27, 141-152.
Broadbent, D. E. (1973). "In Defence of Empirical Psychology". Methuen, London.
Bruner, J. S. (1975). The objectives of development psychology. Paper delivered to the American Psychological Association, September, 1975.
Bruner, J. S. (1976). Psychology and the image of man. Herbert Spencer Lecture delivered at the University of Oxford, 1976, and reprinted in the *Times Literary Supplement*, December 17th, 1976.
Fodor, J. A. (1975). "The Language of Thought". Thomas Y. Crowell, New York.
Hebb, D. O. (1974). What psychology is about. *The American Psychologist* 29, 71-87.
Hudson, L. (1976). Psychological warfare: evidence and objectivity. *Encounter* 80-84.
Levine, M. (1962). Cue neutralization: the effects of random reinforcements upon discrimination learning. *Journal of Experimental Psychology* 63, 438-443.
Levine, M. (1966). Hypothesis behaviour by humans during discrimination learning. *Journal of Experimental Psychology* 71, 331-338.
Miller, G. A., Galanter, E. and Pribram, K. H. (1960). "Plans and the Structure of Behaviour". Holt, New York.
Newell, A. (1973). You can't play twenty questions with nature and win. *In* "Visual Information Processing" (W. G. Chase, ed.). Academic Press, London and New York.
Popper, K. R. (1959). "The Logic of Scientific Discovery". Hutchinson, London.
Putnam, H. (1973). Reductionism and the nature of psychology. *Cognition* 2, 131-146.
Rose, S. E. R. and Rose, H. (1973). Do not adjust your mind, there is a fault in reality—ideology in neurobiology. *Cognition* 2, 479-502.
Taylor, C. (1964). "The Explanation of Behaviour". Routledge and Kegan Paul, London.
Wilson, E. O. (1975). "Sociobiology: the New Synthesis". University of Chicago Press, Illinois.

Author Index

Subject Index